Patterns

Patterns

Theory of the Digital Society

Armin Nassehi

Translated by Mirko Wittwar

polity

Originally published in German as *Muster. Theorie der digitalen Gesellschaft* © Verlag C. H. Beck oHG, München 2021

The translation of this book was made possible through funding from the Fritz Thyssen Foundation, Cologne.

Polity Press
65 Bridge Street
Cambridge CB2 1UR, UK

Polity Press
111 River Street
Hoboken, NJ 07030, USA

ISBN-13: 978-1-5095-5821-6 (hardback)
ISBN-13: 978-1-5095-5822-3 (paperback)

A catalogue record for this book is available from the British Library.

Library of Congress Control Number: 2023936983

Typeset in 10.5 on 12 pt Times New Roman MT
by Fakenham Prepress Solutions, Fakenham, Norfolk NR21 8NL
Printed and bound in Great Britain by TJ Books Ltd, Padstow, Cornwall

For further information on Polity, visit our website:
politybooks.com

Contents

Preface to the German edition

I wrote this book in the winter of 2018/19. The manuscript was completed in April 2019. It makes the somewhat presumptuous attempt to fill in a gap, namely to think beyond the consequences of digitalization in general and beyond the consequences of concrete technologies or practices introduced by them. A great deal of work is being done on these topics, and although quite a few scholars predict disruptions, transformations, and even catastrophic shifts, the reactions of the academic community to these diagnoses are fairly bland. Initially they accepted digitalization as a reality, then harnessed all the fireworks – the concepts normally available to cultural studies and the social sciences – but disruptions and transformations were muted and routine forms of thinking took their place, along with the discovery of a new field of criticism, accompanied by the typically uncritical adoption of terms such as 'artificial intelligence', 'data self-determination', or 'protection of privacy'.

The approach I take here is different. This book does not presuppose digitality and digitalization but asks why such a phenomenon could come into being, why it is obviously plausible for our society, in other words why it is not perceived as a disruption, and why it persists. Had it not suited this society, digitality would have never come into being or would have disappeared long ago. But, since it – whatever 'it' is – shows no tendency to vanish, it is worth asking, in a systematic manner, what problem is solved by digitalization. Hence I have not attempted to cram between these covers everything that I, or anyone, know or could hope to know about digitalization. The book should contain instead everything one needs to know in order to answer this question: what problem does digitalization solve?

The text is framed by two pictures by Vera Molnar, a Hungarian-born French artist who created art with the help of the computer as early as the late 1950s. This pioneer of computer art, now a nonagenerian, experimented early with digitalizing her hand drawings, for example of squares, and with calculating other shapes from them or expanding them via computer-controlled random generators. Her entire art is marked by the depiction of her fascination with patterns and by constant reference to patterns through their alienation or change, their variation and refraction. Two of her pictures are used here: at the beginning of the book, *Hypertransformation*, a plotter drawing from 1974; at the end, *Aleatory Division of 4 Elements*, from 1959, almost a parable of how patterns can emerge from very simple elements, strictly matched, as it were, through loosely matched recombinations. This will be one of the theses of the present book: how simple media generate complex forms. I thank Vera Molnar for granting me permission to use these images, which are about the same thing as the book itself: patterns and their variation range.

The book follows up on works from recent years. Although these hardly deal with matters of digitalization, they are in many respects preliminary research for this book. My thanks go to many participants in lectures and congresses where I had numerous opportunities to test the arguments presented here. Some critical questions helped in refining things. The same applies to those who attended my various lectures and seminars.

I have particularly benefitted, as always, from the very lively discussions at my chair in Munich. Most of all, the readings and critical comments from Gina Atzeni, Niklas Barth, Magdalena Göbl, and Julian Müller have been very helpful. I express my thanks to Till Ernstsohn and Christina Behler for help with my research. Christina Behler also contributed to proofreading and to compiling the index.

Irmhild Saake constantly shared with me her thoughts on the topic, and our long years of cooperation have left on this project more traces than can be seen. I cannot thank her enough.

I thank the C. H. Beck publishing house for their assistance with the publication of the German edition, in particular Matthias Hansl for editing.

Munich, Easter Monday, 2019
Armin Nassehi

Preface to the English edition

I am very pleased that my theory of digital society, published in German by C. H. Beck Verlag, Munich, in 2019, is now being published in an English-language version.

My ambition was to fill a void, namely not only to make a sociological observation and analysis of digital technology, but to answer the question why digital technology is related fundamentally to the structure of modern society.

I am very grateful to Mirko Wittwar for translating the German text into English, to Polity Press for including the book in its programme, and especially to Manuela Tecusan for her thorough review of the English text. I would also like to thank my students Katharina Berger and Lukas Müller, who compiled the English-language material (translations and original versions) for the German-language quotations used in the German edition.

Without the generous support of the Fritz Thyssen Foundation, Cologne, this English-language edition would not have been possible.

Munich, November 2023
Armin Nassehi

Introduction

This book presents a sociological theory of the digital society. If I were to see a book of this title, I would probably be sceptical – had I not written it myself. There is a long tradition of pinning societal diagnoses on *one* aspect only. Yet we know that in a *risk society* there is more than risk, that in an *experience society* action takes place too (if we pay heed to the distinction between action and experience), that even in an *automobile society* people sometimes fly or take the underground, that even in an *accelerated society* one must sometimes wait, and that even in a *multi-option society* there is often no choice. It has never really helped to define society by just one feature. In most cases this is only a makeshift solution or an attention grabber. In any event, tuning the diagnosis to a true feature makes things easier only at first sight; often it is not the authors themselves who invent such striking names, but those who understand a thing or two about how the economics of attention works in the book market.

This is now different. Of course, the society we live in is no digital society in the sense that everything happening within it can be explained by the digital nature of a kind of technology labelled 'digital'. Nevertheless, in the course of the book I am going to claim that modern society is, in a way, *digital* even without digital technology, or that it can be understood only by applying digital means. I am going to go even further: I am going to claim that social modernity has always been digital, and hence that the digital technology is, after all, just the logical consequence of a society that is *digital* by its fundamental structure.

The first time I tested this idea was during the Hegel Lecture of 7 December 2017, at the Free University of Berlin.[1] To understand digitalization – that cultural phenomenon that can be compared perhaps only with two other great inventions: the letterpress and the steam engine – we must not simply presuppose digitalization. Most discourses on digitalization always know already what it is about. In this book I would like to start by excluding this knowledge in order to answer the following crucial question:

What problem does digitalization solve?

The wording of this question is methodologically precise. It is a question about the function of digitalization. It does not define what digitality and digitalization are, but approaches the phenomenon by asking about the problem that digitalization is a *societal* solution for. So we are dealing with its *societal* function. Once this question has been answered, we are also going to unlock the technological dimensions of digitalization. If we do not want to talk about something that, after all, we know only through its user interface, we must begin with a methodically controlled question like this one.

How to think about digitalization

If we look at discourses on the digital, it is conspicuous that they already presuppose the digital in a quite knowledgeable way. Either these are technological discourses that explain what the digital world can do – and then they clarify notions like search engine optimization, big data, augmented reality, or Internet of things as technological phenomena – or they slave away on the consequences of digitalization for labour markets, product markets, and attention markets; they diagnose shifts in the capitalist (re)production of value and of the concentration of economic power; and they venture prognoses of stronger or weaker disruption.[2] Or else they focus on the practical everyday consequences of how digitalization affects its users.

Apart from a general thematic of anti-capitalist critique directed at the digitalized economy, scholars in social sciences, and especially in cultural studies, seem to be interested in a mixture of critical attitudes and descriptions of everyday life – which is, anyway, one of the most connectable forms of development and stabilization of topics, especially for sociology. It is not as if one could claim that the same thematic, let alone topical consensus, prevails everywhere, but obviously a sociological approach to digitalization is taking place under the keywords 'subjectivation', 'self-techniques', 'optimization', and 'self-control'. The starting point, then, is that practices of self-tracking, for example, or of visual and textual presentation of one's own self or control of it obey the rule of staging oneself. These approaches are thoroughly linked to the data processing of those traces that we leave behind through individual practices and that make us stage ourselves according to numerical practices, mostly metrical and comparative. It is particularly attractive to identify a neoliberal regime of technologies of the self that are designed to optimize the interface between self and world and to transform public control into self-control while concomitantly you become visible to public, official actors as well as to private market-based ones.

I would like to avail myself of some examples to explain these popular reflections on digitalization, based as they are on the social sciences – or rather cultural studies. More than twenty years ago Sherry Turkle had already raised the identity question, in light of the new ways of communicating on the Internet.[3] Today Deborah Lupton's *Digital Sociology* explores the significance of digitalization for sociology and takes up the challenge for sociology of a completely new way of accessing the data; but in the end she stumbles again upon its consequences for our way of life and our security.[4] *Data Revolution*, by Rob Kitchin, focuses mostly on data infrastructure and its political, organizational, and technological constitution.[5] Shoshana Zuboff's *The Age of Surveillance Capitalism: The Fight for a Human Future at the New Frontier*, a study rich in material, reflects above all on the control surplus that comes along with digital media.[6] And *Digital Societies*, too, a volume edited by Jessie Daniels, Karen Gregory, and Tressie McMillan Cottom, focuses on the consequences of digitalization on specific aspects of the narrative.[7] German counterparts such as Steffen Mau's *The Metric Society*, with its wealth of informative material, take a similar line.[8] There digitalization is presented as an aspect of behaviour that, after all, also works at the surplus of control. This holds even for technologically outstandingly informed works such as those by Dirk Helbing.[9] Not even media theory works such as *There Is No Software*, by Friedrich Kittler,[10] which has become almost a classic, or Sybille Krämer's study *Symbolische Maschinen*[11] perceive any of the social–structural radicality of the digital, according to which the place where we should look for a reference point for such culture-changing practices is the complexity of society; and neither do cultural studies' dissociations from the technological infrastructure and its practices as ways of modelling, of collecting, imaging, and quantifying.[12] To this series belongs also the very readable *The Digital Condition*, by Felix Stalder, which takes a media theory perspective.[13]

Such perspectives will not be denied at all – at least not yet, at this stage of elaboration, and not in principle. However, these are perspectives that ultimately take no interest in digitalization as such, but presuppose it as a technological, social, and cultural infrastructure. We should recall here, if only in passing, that in the pre-digital world western middle-class lifestyles were already characterized by various kinds of self-tracking, self-controlling behaviours, and disciplining. It looks as if many social sciences perspectives on digitalization do not let themselves be disturbed by digitalization itself. Rather they identify all other social aspects also as digitalization phenomena – from gender issues[14] through inequality issues[15] to the critique (already mentioned) of strategies of self-optimization.

Things are different with science and technology studies (STS). The French sociologist Dominique Cardon describes as simple-minded the disapproval of the power of algorithms that comes from interest-driven, especially economy-led critiques; and he does so on the grounds that ultimately they fail to see how the production of algorithms creates a new way of thinking. By referring to Gilbert Simondon, Cardon emphasizes that technology must be taken seriously on its own, if we want to be able to understand the algorithmization of social processes. Then the most criticized practices turn out to be secondary consequences rather than the starting point of the problem.[16] This is the view I follow – but without restricting the enquiry to practices, as is commonly done in most STS works, mainly for ethnographic reasons. My motivation is shaped by the question of the social function of what is meant by digitalization.

A technological–sociological intuition

Here it must be stated from the start that it is possible to ponder over issues of digitalization without considering digitalization itself, that is, without asking what it is that we are talking about when we speak of digitalization. Here I should point out that something similar occurs also in a different area: we think about society without asking what it is that we are talking about when we speak of society. I assume that these two conditions are systematically connected. *Forgetting about society when talking about society runs parallel with forgetting about digitalization when talking about digitalization.*

It is precisely this connection that I would like to unfold here, in systematic fashion, by which I mean explicitly sociologically; and this is no surprise, since making society our standard already introduces a sociological perspective. At any rate, I would like to emphasize, for starters, that I do not intend to ask the sociological question about digitalization just by way of presupposing 'digitalization' as an independent variable, only to answer, then, which other variables are affected by it.

This is not yet another contribution to the debate on the disruptions caused by digitalization and the practices supported by the digital infrastructure. Rather I would like to conceptualize the reference problem – the problem of the social reference of the digital. What I am interested in is why a technology that, quite obviously, was not designed for what it is currently doing was able to become so successful so extremely fast and ultimately to penetrate almost all parts of society. It will turn out that one of the success factors of this technology is indeed its technicity.

Structuring the problem around how digitalization affects, has affected, and will affect society would really make digitalization into an independent variable. I let myself be guided instead by a techno-sociological intuition: an idea that technology and society are not different entities, but that technologies and techniques can be successful only if they are compatible with the structure of a society. In other words, the fact that digitalization could be so successful – just like printing, the railway, the car, the radio, the nuclear bomb, or the technologization of medicine in earlier periods – is to be explained only by the structure of expectations – or rather the processing power – of the society in which it happens. To give just one example: the establishment of radio and of broadcasting technology already presupposes societies with potential listeners; it presupposes the idea of accessibility, as well as the appropriate centralist power structures of modern statehood. Radio and broadcasting technology requires a reservoir of what can be said; and it deals with the heterogeneity of a pluralist audience by assuming the homogeneity of addresses or addressees. It expects that what is spread via the radio will make a difference that attracts enough attention and – not least – motivates millions of people to buy a radio receiver. Mind you, the audience is not there yet, but there must be an amalgam of situations whose inner complexity makes something like an accessible audience not completely improbable. So the steam engine was not implemented only when its industrial conditions had come to exist: some accommodative conditions were already there. And the role the railway played in opening up North America gives a telling indication that technology can meet a demand that it itself creates, but that has requirements of its own.

It should be possible to provide evidence for something of this kind in the case of digitalization, too. Then the question will be: *Which dispositions of modernity sensitize it to a technology such as digitalization (if anything like digitalization can be considered a reliable concept at all)? What is it about modernity, about social*

modernity, that was perhaps already 'digital', even before digitali-
zation, to allow digital technology to start this triumphal procession,
which actually is not in line with the intentions of its creators – just
as the triumph of earlier technologies can never be explained as an
intentional outcome either? The causal chain from idea to realization
is too short-sighted, even if long causal chains are established.

This is not the place to lecture on the history and shallows of
functionalism.[17] Let me say just this: I am not dealing here with a
set of clearly defined problems, to which we need to find solutions.
The point is rather to understand better and determine both *the
problem* and *the solution.* Concretely, I can define the problem that
digitalization is a solution for only if I am aware of both solutions
and problems – and, most of all, of how these two aspects relate to
each other.

To repeat, one must extend considerably the functionalist frame
of mind if one is to answer the question I have already indicated:
What problem is digitalization meant to solve? And the question
must be asked in such a way as to presuppose neither the problem
nor the solution – so that there may be neither an existing list of
problems nor an all-too-clear list of solutions for comparing the
items to each other. A proper functionalist method must take both
sides to be contingent; they must be of interest for the configuration
itself. From a formal point of view, functionalism tells us that, if y
is a function of x ($y=f(x)$), then both y and x must be taken to be
contingent; and this rules out the possibility of taking one of them
as an absolute value. This is exactly the problem that the critique of
functionalism wrestles with.

For our topic, this means that, if the reference problem – that is,
the problem–solution configuration of the digital – is to be determined, one must really start on both sides. If my initial intuition that
technologies get implemented only if they are compatible with their
social contexts is correct, this means that they solve a problem. So
then, we should take both sides to be undetermined: *what* problem
and *what* solution? By the way, solution means only that the process
may go on, that compatibility has been created; hence it is not about
what digitalization is, but about what it does and how it relates
problem and solution.

This is exactly the beginning of the first chapter, which presents
perhaps the most important thesis of the book: *that digitalization is
immediately related to the social structure.* For this makes digitalization into a strange sort of disturbance – strange because it refers
to the familiar with a radicalism that was not known previously.
I am even going to claim that digitalization is not only a social
phenomenon but *a sociological project.* Much of what digitalization

does embodies a really sociological kind of thought: it makes use of social structures, it renders social dynamics visible, and out of these ways of recognizing patterns it creates added value. Of course, its actors are no sociological actors – they are enterprises and states, prosecuting authorities and media providers, communication agencies and the military, urban and social planning as well as the sciences. Yet what makes it sociological is that it recognizes or generates latent patterns and does something with them.

Early technology pushes

I am going to demonstrate that modern society was provided with a digital structure even before the use of digital computer technologies. What this means I am going to explain at a later stage. But the unmediated use of digital technology is a rather recent phenomenon. This piece of information probably makes a very modest contribution to knowledge, but, born as I was in 1960, I probably belong to one of the last promotions to have completed a university degree without any digital instruction. I passed my *Abiturprüfung* – my high school or baccalaureate exam – in Gelsenkirchen in 1979, to then study at the University of Münster, where I read educational sciences in parallel with philosophy, both with sociology as the secondary subject. I had to write a lot during my studies, as was (and still is) appropriate for university studies. Initially I had a mechanical typewriter from my parents, and working on it was pretty laborious. I think it was in my third semester, I don't remember exactly when, that my studies received a first technological push. I bought a used Robotron 202, an electric typewriter made in East Germany by VEB Robotron Buchungsmaschinenwerk in Karl-Marx-Stadt. Calling this machine robust would be a blatant understatement. It was very heavy, the chassis extravagantly made of metal that was at least two millimetres thick. The engine of this machine had certainly not been developed for typewriters; you could command with it even more solid cultural goods than philosophical, educational, psychological, and sociological seminar papers. It was a very loud machine, which certainly shouldn't come as a surprise. This held for both the engine and the typebars, which hit the paper and the platen roller with enormous power. I remember very well how the carriage return made the side table next to my desk sway. And I remember even more vividly how any keyboard mistake immediately affected what was written, corrections being almost impossible. This is what we call analogous technology – that is, a kind of technology designed for something like a one-on-one transfer of cause and effect, signal

and reaction, control and implementation. Even corrections of
mistakes with Tipp-Ex were always visible. The written text on the
paper had healed, but the scars could be seen by everyone.

In 1985 I passed my examinations in educational sciences. For
this purpose I had to write a thesis on sociology. It had about 350
pages – in those days we were still given that much time for our first
qualification paper – handwritten to begin with, then copied out on
my Robotron machine. Copying out meant giving it a form that was
good enough for a professional office to make it into a paper that
could be submitted. The master I had produced was not really bad
but, in true analogous fashion, it contained all those irregularities,
mistakes, and corrections that I had made during typing – indeed
scars that bore testimony to the laborious process of tinkering with
thoughts to make them into a text that could be read in a linear way.
What was interesting was the office whose service I had employed:
it advertised that, before the final printing, the client would be
given a preliminary copy so that any remaining mistakes may be
corrected, provided that the corrections did not alter the pagination.
Technologically, this correction process was carried out on a very
modern typewriter, which was very expensive – I could afford it only
because my parents made a financial contribution. All of a sudden a
printed text – that is, an analogous record of a one-on-one relation
of production and product – not only became repeatable but could
even be changed. And this change remained invisible! No scars! This
had an effect on the reality status of the text, which suddenly was
something else. What remained analogous was just the result, no
longer the process of producing it.

After having completed my studies, I made efforts to be granted
a PhD scholarship and imagined that in the future I would do
precisely what I have been doing for three decades now: work as
a sociologist and turn the results of this activity in particular into
texts. All my studies (at least on the technological side of the means
of production) could be conducted exclusively with analogous
technology. Even the search for literature was still done without
databases, with the help of a catalogue system whose materiality was
similar to that of my Robotron machine. I still remember the sound
at the university library in Münster when the box with the index
cards was pushed back into the register – a veritable bang. By the
way, taking the train to Bielefeld, which was about 100 kilometres
away, was worth the effort in spite of the bad connection: Bielefeld
had not only a much better stocked social science library but even
a microfiche system that made research much easier. But even
this feature was radically analogous – though at least it remained
invisible without a device that consumed electricity.

Immediately after having completed my studies, my desired profession in mind, I started looking for an affordable computer that, unlike the very successful C64 Commodore computers, would not be for recreational use but would be a proper work tool. What I needed, then, was what even in those days was called 'the industry standard', namely a device compatible with the Microsoft Disc Operating System (MS-DOS), which was roughly equivalent in technology with the classic IBM PC. At the time, however, there was only one IBM branch in Münster; and a real IBM PC, as it was on the market since 1981, would have been completely unaffordable. For this reason one also had to go to Bielefeld, where some computer wizards were running a shop that offered reasonably priced components for an IBM-compatible computer like the first IBM PC – with an 8088 processor and 4.77 megacycles. My first device had no hard disc but just two floppy disk drives, one of which had always to be used with floppy disks for the operating system and the application programs. While the first disk was uploading the DOS, you inserted a floppy disk with a text-processing system; I was using Word Perfect then. When you wanted to use for the first time a special feature, for example italics, you had to insert another floppy disk, which supplied this tool. And when the text was finished you used another floppy disk, on which the finished document had to be stored.

This device had a dot matrix printer whose noise was in no way inferior to that of the Robotron machine. The whole device was expensive, although still cheaper than an IBM ball-head typewriter, which was the world-class standard at the time; hence it was something of a Cadillac by comparison with the Wartburg car represented by my Robotron. These ball-head typewriters were no longer the industrial standard but could be found in every university institute office, where they served a generation of professors who used to write almost everything by hand, because their text-processing program sat in front of the IBM typewriter and was not compatible with any kind of software, but with the idiosyncratic handwritings of the gentlemen professors (for once this is not a generic masculine!).

One year later I bought a hard disk – you could do this even in Münster those days – and faced the difficult choice between one with a capacity of 1 MB and one with a capacity of 5 MB. I opted for 1 MB because one could hardly imagine filling 5 MB of storage capacity in the course of a human life. From then on my digital biography was like everybody else's: Windows appeared, then computers with greater capacity, more efficient peripheral devices, the Internet; my data became permanently accessible, no matter where I was. The transition from the download Internet to the upload Internet was very significant, then the transition from the stationary to the mobile Internet. With the Internet research possibilities emerged that made the Bielefeld microfiche period look antediluvial. And so on and so on. I wrote and completed this book (and earlier ones, too) in the form of files that were stored by the commercial cloud of a text-processing provider and that I was able to consult and edit to their current state on all my devices as well as on other people's – from stationary computers to smartphones.

During my first semesters of studying, that is, between 1979 and 1981, when the first IBM PC appeared on the market – I made much money by repairing cars: the Volkswagen Beetle and the VW minibus, the Citroen 2CV and GX, the Renault 4 and 5, the Opel Kadett, the VW Polo and Golf I, and even the old Stroke 8 Mercedes diesel. That was as illegal as could be (though time-barred by now), because in those days cars were indeed analogous machines that could be tinkered together. For a little while cars were still devices that converted fossil into kinetic energy; but the processes were increasingly controlled, first through electric circuits and then through computer technology. Today I could at most change the tyres and the windscreen wipers on my automobile (a rather digitalized successor of the old Stroke 8). Consequently in 2001 the profession of car mechanic – probably the most desired apprenticeship, at least among boys – was renamed 'mechatronics engineer'; the training profile had been changed even earlier.

Original and copy

What I'm getting at is probably clear by now: I, along with those born in the 1960s, can perhaps be described as the first digital gener-ation.[18] Indeed, the first PC was more than just some improved kind of typewriter. It was a medium that in fact changed the reality status of work results. In his famous 1936 essay 'The Work of Art in the Age of Mechanical Reproduction', Walter Benjamin supported the thesis that the experience of art had radically changed because it was possible to reproduce artistic exhibits: now the work of art had to prove its worth to a quite different kind of audience – and also to an audience no longer embedded in the bourgeois practices of enjoying art.[19] The result was a sort of enjoyment of art *en passant* – which of course can be deplored only if the only thing one appreciates in art is its function of creating distinctiveness. But what mattered to

Benjamin was what he called the 'loss of aura', that is, the loss of that cairological uniqueness that could extend into the chronological precisely through the repeatability of experience. Whoever quotes Benjamin certainly has in mind Adorno's vitriolic accusation that Benjamin made the work of art into a fetish. But in my view this is a typical reaction to new kinds of media – be it Socrates's praise of conversation in contrast to the distancing effect of writing, or the criticism of television as levelling things by comparison with real-world experience: an attempt to ennoble older forms with the help of semantics, in order to cope with the enormity of modern technology and its consequences.

The everyday use of digital technology has created something very similar – and, expressly, I am not talking here about the great cultural changes of the digital age, but about minor changes in the text production of a young scientist – or rather a youth who wanted to become a scientist. As a writing tool, the computer has not simply dematerialized writing. Before a text is brought to paper in the analogous way, it exists virtually. Its virtuality consists in remaining permanently open to change without having to change as a whole. Insertions, reformulations, revisions do not leave traces any longer; one would probably say, with Benjamin, that the text has lost its *aura*. Everything remains open to revision until the very end, and at the same time even preliminary versions seem aesthetically ready. Thanks to the functions of a text-processing software, absolutely incomplete texts could be presented all at once as if the text were indeed a text. One would not have done this in the past, on a Robotron 202, because that would have involved the considerable additional effort of rewriting everything all the time. Now, my concern in the present book is not to tell one of those popular stories about the impact of digitalization on everyday practices that make up the bulk of sociological literature on the topic. The example is intended only to show how digital technology is diffused into society – how small-scale it is and how suitable for daily use, how almost invisible yet effective, how unspectacular yet radical – and how swiftly the shift from an analog to a digital society has happened.

Productively wrong and predetermined breaking point

By itself, this book is not an immune reaction to digitalization, even if digitalization undoubtedly leads to disruptions of social routines that need our attention. I have already indicated what makes it interesting to social science scholars. Perhaps the most important discourse is the one about the future of work. It is highly likely that the digitalization of both production and products will have an impact on employment and on the continuity of professional biographies. But there is blatant disagreement on how digitalization will affect these issues. A lot is simply unknown. Also, there is little doubt that the accessibility of voluminous data sets will affect scientific insights. Fear of a theory-free science, which only looks for traces in data sets, looms everywhere;[20] and there is the conundrum of whom to attribute knowledge to when intelligent algorithms conduct epistemic processes.[21] It is definitely to be expected that there will be problems with adapting individual lifestyles to the mechanisms of control, by oneself or others, that will arise from the availability of growing masses of data. Likewise, there is little doubt that the pricing structure in many sectors will change as a result of completely new transparency and comparison models. Equally undisputed is a tendency towards the concentration of capital that runs parallel to the concentration of data.[22] This is due to both economic and genuinely technological reasons. It is also certain that the debate on artificial intelligence will influence the self-understanding of human intelligence, which we label 'natural'.[23] And nobody will be able to ignore that new constellations and concentrations of power will appear along with digitalization.[24] All this has been discussed for a long time: this is how society adjusts to such (self-imposed) disturbances. In this respect, digitalization is not really an exciting theme.

Although many of the topics mentioned here occur quite explicitly in the present book, they do not constitute the core of its content. To put it another way, they are not the starting point of my reflections, but feature *only* as epiphenomena of the actual object of investigation. For all these discussions about the disruption of social routines by an encroaching digital technology ultimately get by without any grounded theory of digitalization – they just presuppose digitalization as a phenomenon. This book will attempt to close this gap.

It may not be an exaggeration to claim that a gap is being filled here. The plan is no less than to present the first social theory of the digital society. This is a scholarly endeavour and not a superficially diagnostic one, let alone one that generates instructions for action. It is an attempt to understand digitalization as a social–cultural phenomenon.

Here digitalization is not simply applied to modern society as one topic among others. The theoretical claim is far more ambitious. For, according to my techno-sociological intuition, an appropriate theory of digitalization would not have to present a colonial or disruptive history of digitalization, but would have to be capable of identifying the reference problem of digitalization within society and its structure. In this respect, the subtitle has been chosen with great precision. We are dealing not with a *theory of digitalization*, but with *a theory of digital society*.

1
The Reference Problem of Digitalization

What problem does digitalization solve? If I am right, this question about the reference problem of digitalization has not yet been asked; and how you ask makes a difference. I do not ask, 'What is digitalization?' Nor do I ask, 'What is the problem with digitalization?', or 'What problems does digitalization cause?'. Particularly about this last one, we sometimes know more than we do about my main question, on the reference problem. We know for example that digitalization is a threat to privacy, that it destroys jobs through its efficiency, especially in repetitive activities, that it can also be an economic opportunity, that it opens up possibilities of control that did not exist before, and so on. In a way, such statements presuppose digitalization as an independent variable, in order to enquire about its consequences. My question starts at a completely different point. *What problem does it solve?*

My answer is going to be as follows: *the reference problem of digitalization is the complexity and, above all, the regularity of society itself.* The argument is that modern society, especially through its digital kind of self-observation, encounters only those regularities, that stubbornness and resistance that make up social relations. True, society is a fluid, fast-moving, accelerated object, yet it is enormously stable, regular, and indeed predictable in many respects. This object contains patterns that are not recognizable at first sight. The second glance, which of course reveals them, is increasingly a digital one.

Should this thesis prove to be sustainable, it has considerable consequences for a sociological theory of digitalization that does not simply examine the consequences of digitalization and the manner of disruption attached to a certain kind of technology and technique but rather starts with the foundations of modern society itself. And this means that we do not see digitalization, but crucial parts of society are already seeing in digital fashion. Digitality is one of society's crucial self-references. To be on the safe side, I should say right away that here I don't take the digital as a *metaphor*. But more on this later.

This much is already clear: in the elaboration of a theory of digital society, methodological questions arise first, that is, questions of theory construction. If these are not answered, the few statements made so far remain simple assertions. The question about the reference problem is a functionalist one. Functionalist questions are not causal; they are about the relation between problem and solution.

Functionalist questions

Perhaps the most important foundation of functionalist thought comes from Ernst Cassirer. In his early book *Substance and Function* he postulated a transition from concepts of substance to concepts of function, thus presenting a critique not only of the ontological understanding of the world but also of the retrospective ontologization of the epistemic process. For Cassirer, epistemic objects are constituted in and by the cognitive process itself, which thereby becomes an undetermined point (or one to be determined) within a network of relations: 'Thus we do not know "objects" as if they were already independently determined and given *as objects* – but we know *objectively*, by producing certain limitations and by fixating certain permanent elements and connections within the uniform flow of experience.'[1]

Cassirer calls the fact that cognition identifies 'objects' a 'formula of confirmation'; and the identified objects are thus not so much '"signs of something objective" as rather objective signs',[2] whose objectivity is due to the fact that they prove their worth empirically.[3]

Then, from a mathematical perspective, the observation of something is always a function of this observation – and this conception of functionalism breaks with the idea that the indeterminacy of the world could be resolved or dissolved through unambiguous determinacy. This manner of relating is a feature not only of scientific insight but of practice in general. It makes visible how concrete decisions relate to something and how something appears the way it does as a result of a particular practice. Thus *functionalism* always has to do with indeterminacy, or, better still, with the practical production of determinacy – both on the side of cognition and on the side of the object.

Now this is not about epistemological questions around functionalism but actually about the question of the problem–solution constellation of what we call digitality or digitalization. So the thesis could be that we do not see the digital but that we see digitally, so that something like the digital may successfully become visible or emerge. One of the pioneers who do not just describe the digital but demonstrate how we *should see digitally* to describe the modern world is Dirk Helbing. This trained physicist describes for example the automatization of areas of society not as a mere disturbance that comes from the outside to a certain extent, but, on the contrary, as a part of the social structure that makes possible in the first place the description of disturbances such as the cascade effects in complex systems (e.g. energy supply).[4] Consequently Helbing describes the digital revolution as a revolution of the complexity of society itself.

Connecting data: offline

If a functionalist way of thinking is characterized by the need to keep both the cognition side and the object side contingent, it is worth starting with a phenomenological description of digital technologies. In other words, we must adopt an offline view to begin with and completely dispense with the description of the thing itself – that is, of digital technology – so as to get the fundamental structure of society into perspective. If there is anything that the entire digital shares, it is the capability of connecting data with data, that is, the capability of apparatuses to connect data points to one another. The raw material consists of data that exist in counted or countable form and whose form has such a low threshold that they can actually combine and recombine among themselves.

One of the earliest forms of digital – that is, countable – data processing was certainly government social statistics, which developed together with the establishment of the modern state. Thus the 'social physicist' Adolphe Quetelet (1796–1874) was one of the first to apply statistical methods to society and social planning. He wondered how much regularity is to be found in human behaviour, for example in marriage. Marital behaviour is in each case an individual kind of behaviour. Concretely, you are dealing with two people who decide to get married. But, numerically, what you are dealing with is slightly different. The piece of information 'marriage' recombines with other features, to then make visible what was not really visible before. Now, we must concede that even our everyday understanding works with probability assumptions concerning which marriage is to be expected and which is not. The idea of stratification in society, of cultural or denominational matching, of age distribution within couples, of economic and biographic preconditions, and so on is already rooted in our perceptual schemes and stereotypes, so that we recognize the regularity assumptions of our perceptions only in cases of deviation. But social statistics is able to conceptualize such regularities and ultimately to make them manageable; and through its quantitative capacity it is able to identify rather invisible regularities, which to everyday reasoning look like coincidences or like the contingent result of individual decision-makings.[5]

The prerequisite for all this is the form of data, a form that has become countable through the recoding of typical features, and a form of digital data, which can be recombined among themselves. Thus the material of data processing or digitality is items that in principle can be recombined among themselves and whose informational value consists precisely in the limited nature of possible combinations. More specifically, if any possible element were linked to any other possible element, the data could not provide any information at all, and so they could not make any difference. By the way, Quetelet regarded deviations from the normal distribution as a disturbance and ended up being fascinated by the idea of an *homme moyen*, an average person who can be calculated accordingly and who at the same time constitutes the foundation of all those practices through which humans are shaped as self-responsible individuals.

Thus the raw material of the digital consists in lists of coded numerical values, and the *solution* consists of information about everything that is possible on the basis of data. More specifically, these are probability statements about combinatorics, about how individual items are related – or, even more precisely, about the limits of combinatorics, because only data in which not everything combines with everything else can contain or generate information. This can be information of an entirely different nature:

- the intelligent steering of a machine that is able to adjust itself to changing environmental conditions and to process data in such a way as to react to them through its own specifications;
- the intelligent self-monitoring of mechanical machines through sensory data that indicate irregularities;
- predictive possibilities of retrieving information on sales opportunities, narrowing down the suspects, or finding out about the recurrence of topics in a specific space, all from historical data on buying decisions, from deviant behaviour, or through search engine queries;
- the optimization of logistic processing rules;
- weather forecasts and climate models;
- market monitoring and market development;

- intelligent traffic control;
- influencing voting behaviour in certain definable groups, or identifying uncertain decision-making situations in voting behaviour – for special promotional measures are worth using only there;
- object recognition as a feature of self-driving vehicles;
- diagnostic programs in medical imaging diagnostics;
- assessments of electrocardiographic, electroencephalographic, and similar sets of data;
- the forensic and literary analysis of textual authorship;
- even the production of editorial texts through the processing of agency reports;
- translation and speech recognition programs;
- voice recognition;
- the assessment of emotional states;
- the detection of movement profiles of all kinds.

What all these examples have in common is that the interaction of different parameters is observed in terms of how the relation between different influencing variables changes as a result of the change in such relations, how high the probability is for certain desired or undesired states, or which influencing variables can change probabilities in a certain direction. If you want somehow to get to the heart of the digital, in the last resort it is nothing but a *duplication* of the world in the form of data, with the technological possibility of relating the data to one another, in order to retranslate this arrangement into specific questions. Comparability results from the fact that these signals are retranslated into a uniform medium, which makes the incommensurable at least relatable.

After all, this is already a precise definition of what a computer does. A computer is a computing machine capable of connecting the data through its own data management – that is, through meta-data – and of processing very large amounts of data thanks to its discrete – that is, binary – form of representing the 'world'. Not only does this exceed the quantitative capacity of natural, consciousness-based intelligence, but a qualitative reversal also takes place, because the results of computations may again become prerequisites for new computations.

The connection between quantity and quality is indeed complex in this context, because it is precisely the quantitative nature of the feedback that lends the computer its particular quality. At any rate, digitality should be seen as a combination between simplification and enhanced complexity. One brings analog forms into digital shape, recombines this digital shape in terms of structures, and then applies these structures to the analog world whence the data come

– or, better, whence the world has been duplicated in data form. I will come back to this doubling function in more detail. Anyway, the use of computers does not rely simply on the internal processing of data but on their being retranslated into analog forms. This is why computers always have at least two interfaces: on the one hand, the input of material in the form of data (of any kind); on the other hand, the output of material in the form of data that are (re)translated into meaningful information. Such interfaces may be screens, 2D or 3D printers, plotters, machine control signals, computational results, statistic charges, or indeed text. There follows at this point a retranslation of the data forms into other media.

The first thing I should say is that even this short and succinct definition of the digital indicates the kind of solution that this technology can offer. For this is precisely the *solution*: uncovering probability relations in data sets of any kind. That this is a socially relevant solution is immediately obvious from the fact that no special area for the digital can be found in society. The digital can be used, rather indifferently, for almost anything. It controls toasters as well as the entire energy supply of a country; smart electric toothbrushes as well as the self-monitoring of stock exchanges; children's toys or the model railway of the former Bavarian prime minister as well as space stations, programmable weapons or the ventilators of anaesthetists; it assesses an electrocardiogram just as it controls video games. *What makes this technology specific is its unspecific character.* It is a really ubiquitous form – until now reserved exclusively to the presence of God and the use of writing.

What is the problem?

But what is the *problem*? What reference problem does digitalization provide a *solution* for? What I have emphasized earlier about methodology shall be taken really seriously here: the relation between problem and solution should look at both sides and determine how they stand to each other. It should then be possible to infer the reference problem of digitalization from the structure of the solutions offered. Elsewhere I explained in detail that the functionalist method is an interpretative one.[6] The method must understand why something like processing data by digital means has such a problem-solving capacity. So this is not just about what data processing is, or digitality, but about what they do and what problem is solved in the process. Even the act of seeing what they *do* can be understood only interpretatively. What they do is indeed a recombination of discrete forms that offer the representation of something else and, through radical simplification, allow for comparisons between things that are much too different in their full analog form.

The solution, then, concerns the limited recombinability of items in data sets, and consequently the problem can only be the demand for such recombinatorics. The problem must be found in the features, needs, or functional requirements of the society in which this kind of technology can be established. Also, the problem must be explored through interpretation, because it is not positively present and in the last analysis it must be extremely abstract, if it is able to identify properly the manifold uses of this technology.

As I announced earlier, the diagnosis I propose is as follows: *the reference problem of digital technology is the complexity of society itself*. Like any other social system, society is of course characterized by the fact that it cannot link all its elements to all others at the same time. This is why societies, like all systems, are marked by internal stopping rules, interruptions of interdependencies, and limitations of the capability to connect. Systems can have a structure only because they are provided with internal processing rules that rule out more than they allow for. Thus the higher the number of elements and the more far-reaching the action and interconnection chains, the more complex these processing rules.

After all, this is a basic sociological law. Order is possible only if the possibilities of behaviour are limited. Structures are, in the last resort, nothing but a limitation of expectations in certain situations. To put it trivially, if I go to the bakery I should not ask for beetroots. This is, in itself, quite an effective internal rule for processing complexity, as it enables some connections by excluding others. Now, not all structures are as simple, and especially not as plainly visible, as this pastries–beetroots relation. But the form of the world's comprehensibility and the possibility of gaining information in the light of other possibilities presuppose that the ability to connect one's own elements is limited. Since not everything can be connected with everything at the same time, the structure of a society consists precisely in this self-limitation, so that it may keep itself in a connectable state. The emphasis is now on the form of limiting, and thus on the internal rules, regularities, habits, traditions, decisions, and so on according to which such forms can be established; on how they change and how they might perhaps be changed even intentionally, hence systematically; or on the points where they are so stubborn as to remain unimpressed even by intentions of change.

To be able to understand societies (and other social systems), one must thus take a close look at the regularity of connections between individual elements. One will find out that, as complexity grows, these regularities tend increasingly towards invisibility, or at least towards not being clearly and positively identifiable. It is one of the fundamental experiences of social modernity that we no longer believe in the perpetuation of traditions and long lines. In a nutshell, *one's own experience that society no longer seems to be of one piece indicates that different forces that are simultaneously at work affect the present and are faced with the fact that one and the same thing can be described in very different ways.* This sounds very abstract but reflects precisely what may be described as a fundamental experience of social modernity: an interplay of transparency and non-transparency.

Society is starting to know more and more about itself – economically, scientifically, culturally, technologically, and so on – and is more and more dependent on separating these spheres from one another and establishing mutual kinds of non-transparency. If it is true that what is politically advisable will have uncontrollable consequences for the economy (or the other way round), if it is true that the scientific formulation of problems is different from their technological, social, or cultural implementation, if it is true that an increasing number of decisions in these different realms of society – along with biographic decisions, consumption decisions, matters of faith – are made individually rather than collectively, this indicates very complex patterns of creating order, in which it is less and less possible to infer from one concrete feature to all others. To use a formula again, while in the old world it was possible to deduce almost every parameter of a person's life from very little information – place of birth, family, place among siblings, gender – this is not so easy in modern society. What appears to us as freedom and a liberalization of decision-making is most of all a messy effect of the driving forces whose interplay creates structures and order.

Many believe that modernity and modernization processes are a loss of order. However, this is a clear misunderstanding. Modernization is not at all a loss of order, but an explicit indication of order or the formation of order: order becomes now an explicit topic.[7] Political and legal institutions in national states, the switch to money transfers, the establishment of ordinary life courses, the nationalization of the tax system, the establishment of standard CVs, the institution of gender roles and lifestyles related to the environment – all this (and I mentioned just a few parameters) indicates not loss of order but the forming of order, that is, how contingent and internally diverse orders appear these days. We may underestimate earlier orders if we pretend that they had nothing to do with order forming. If we consider for example the very complex hierarchical relations between individuals and estates in earlier societies or other very complicated indications of inequality, they are very clearly differentiated from modern social forms, namely in that they represented a rather transparent kind of order, which looked the same from any position in society. Niklas Luhmann gave a very apt summary when he said that, in premodern societies with stratified social differentiations, 'overall world selectivity' looks the same from any position within the social system.[8] Or, more simply, if everything is coded 'up' and 'down', the overall structure of the world will look the same for everybody: up is up and down is down, no matter whether we look from above or from below. At the time, the problems to do with order were mainly how to enforce it and how to maintain loyalties, but there were no problems around describing and understanding this order; those appear only when other kinds of order begin to assert themselves, for example the independence of economic calculations or scientific knowledge, or the emancipation of the secular from ecclesiastical rule. Then order itself becomes a problem, because observing it is no longer trivial. This is the structural antecedent condition for the development of the digital.

This has to do mainly with visibilities. Again, to exaggerate in line with an ideal typology, another person's position in society and social status, for example, were already transparent all the time in earlier societies. There even existed more or less refined signs, especially signs of rank and function such as dress codes, so that the social structure could be made visible in a fairly simple way, by analogy. 'By analogy' means observable in full and concrete empirical fashion, by ordinary means. One derived relevant knowledge [*Wissen*] about society from the plain grasp [*Kenntnis*] of what could be seen, combined with the forms of evaluation expressed by the corresponding cultural signs. This world was not simple and sometimes it was quite complicated, but it was never really complex, because most of it could be described pretty clearly.

This is exactly what modernity has lost. Today, for example, if I am to understand who my competitor is in the labour, marriage, housing, or supply markets, I can rely less and less on visible signs; I must instead combine different features to narrow down the potential competitors. In the premodern case, social groups are visible in the truest sense of the word, whereas these days such competitive relationships can be made visible, strictly speaking, only as statistical groups. Even class theory, which has been popular since the nineteenth century in the depiction of social inequality, had to wrestle with this problem. With the help of methods from social science and political economy, it was possible to determine situations of risk, exploitation, and inequality, but the problem was that in the end no subjective class situation arose from the objective class situation. The class in itself and the class for itself remained almost systematically separated from each other, because the former *was* or *is* a statistical group and the latter *was supposed* to be a social group.

More radically, although in premodern times the categorization of people and their social positions really seemed to be without any alternative, for purposes of social interaction they were quite transparent: positions within classes, families, regions, professions, functions, ranks, and the like were in principle comprehensible and were accessible in any social contact. In any social communication, the person's ranking was a more important coding than the content of the communication. Those of lower rank were not entitled to anything like a better argument, more far-reaching information, or special access to resources. Social exclusion prevented it.

Generally speaking, the stratified world of premodernity was anything but simple. But the basic principle of differentiation was very simple indeed. The up–down scheme can hardly be surpassed in simplicity; perhaps we may even call it digital, because it showed a binary mediacy coupled with finely chiselled concrete forms. Of course, these forms were also the reason for a strict limitation of the observations and forms that could evade the clear pattern.

However, the frequency of validity claims that run across the differentiation scheme increases with the emancipation of new forms of observation.[9] In the course of social modernization, this generates a lot of confusion. Questions of truth carefully started disentangling themselves from questions of rank, political power and religious salvation became at least distinguishable, and the printing press together with the literacy of the population made it possible to differentiate between various truths. This has led to the development of a modern society in which the primary scheme of differentiation can no longer order everything into a simple up–down pattern, but is oriented towards social functions. The basic distinctions at the level of the whole society are no longer hierarchically ordered layers but matter-of-fact functions such as politics, economy, law, science, media, medicine, education, and more. This not only makes society as a whole less transparent; the placement of individuals no longer follows any clear principle, even if relatively stable structures of class and inequality develop.

In spite of these rather confusing conditions in which the individual lifestyle is reevaluated, throughout the life course decisions are enforced almost non-stop. In other words, what makes modernity stressful is the compulsion to lead one's life, partial freedom in a world that is as it is, the necessity to find points of accountability for decisions taken under risky and uncertain conditions. What is demanded is to make individual desires and motivations transparent while the consequences are unpredictable. Perhaps one of the strangest contradictions is that members of staff in modern societies are accustomed more than ever before to giving information about themselves, and in this way they can distinguish themselves from others.

The discomfort with digital culture

The relationship with the self is the relationship with the world – but in no other society do we know so little about ourselves as in this one. The digital way of processing information knows more about us than we do ourselves – and that was so even before the existence of the electronic mediatization of information as we know it today. Social statistics, which started in the nineteenth century, already enabled what Michel Foucault was to call, later, the 'biopolitics of the population':[10] in a sense, this was a professionalization of observing individuals who ostensibly were able to provide extensive information about themselves but on whom one could gain more knowledge than they had themselves – medically, psychologically, forensically, and in terms of social statistics and consumer habits. The social sciences themselves developed in the context of this experience. They were interested in those regularities and predictabilities that the actors, from their own perspective, believed to be the result of their own decisions, their own characters, and, at a pinch, their own quirks. This is why, in modernity, they want so much to be subjects: it is a theoretical and moral imposition that arose at the very moment when it became impossible.

The discomfort with digital culture feeds on the visibility of this modern experience. It is now becoming even more obvious that the digital possibilities of extensive observation, the recombination of data, and the possibilities of calculation make actors aware of what they were able earlier to keep latent: *how regular and predictable their behaviour is*. The discomfort with the digital culture is perhaps the mirror that this technology holds up to society: it overtaxes society and its structures so much that what was previously protected by latency is made visible.

Once more, the theoretical thesis of this book is as follows: digital practices and routines, detector functions and fields of application are discussed as disruptive and practically liquefying phenomena, but they point to the exact opposite: to the strange stability of the social subject, its patternicity, and its structure.

Is the digitalized society still a modern society at all? In recent years, the sociologist and cultural theorist Dirk Baecker argued for the view that the triumph of digital technology will not force upon society a catastrophe of the same kind as the advent of the printing press did. Baecker meant 'catastrophe' in the literal sense, as a change in the fundamental structure, namely as reversal. The 'next society',[11] he says, will be a society where, given the challenges imposed by the computer, the fundamental structures of classical modernity are no longer valid. The project of modernity was total inclusion of the population into its functional systems. This project was followed by the 'project of the digital society, by the transformation of analog processes into processes that can be discretely counted, binarily coded, statistically evaluated, and automatically calculated'.[12] This wording is more careful than it looks at first sight. At first Baecker leaves it open whether modernity, the functionally differentiated society, comes to its end in this way or not; but the tone already moves towards affirming a project [*Projekthafte*] that goes hand in hand with the mechanisms of digitalization.

Perhaps the project is too strongly oriented to society's self-descriptions. This is true: through its programmes of subjectivity and individualization, of juridification of access to key authorities in society, through its abstract promise of equality in the face of concrete consequences of inequality, and, not least, by establishing reading audiences through compulsory schooling and the differentiation of a system of mass media, modernity had described itself as a project of including everyone in all the functional spheres of society, and it is from this that it has drawn its normative power. The 'project of modernity', as Habermas had classically described it the 1980s,[13] was indeed a great equality generator, as it attempted by the same move to establish individuality both as a social programme and as an individual asset. The project of modernity produced a surplus of criticism: criticism was expected almost everywhere in order to enable improvement, allow for growth, include alternatives into the system, make variation possible, and, not least, make individuals look like people who build a critical relationship with themselves.

The project of digitalization, on the other hand, is a project of control: a surplus of control[14] that society must now come to terms with – and here I agree with Baecker. As a matter of fact control becomes the decisive productive force, both technologically and socially. This is why the social sciences have set their heart so much on criticizing this control and especially its transformation into self-control. Above all, the countability of behaviour enables outside control and transforms this outside steering into the disciplining practices of self-tracking.[15] But most of all it is the process of making visible the invisibility of the antecedent social conditions of individual life that generates discomfort.

The metaphor of the user interface and the machine behind it can operate here – it is definitely a suitable metaphor. The self-descriptions, the semanticizations, the deliberate performings of life, the lifestyle programs, even the attitudes and convictions – all these make a user surface with which we create something like the ecologic environments in which we move. Indeed, the social sciences have known for quite some time that behind this user surface a 'machine' is at work that can hardly be transparent to the actors themselves. They have recalculated people's individual, decision-based behaviour in relation to their class situations, their cultural backgrounds, their social–structural interests, their social positions, their lifeworld limitations, their traditions and the afferent conventions and have thus discovered background structures that, on the user surface, can be recognized only as expectable behaviour.

The digital discovery of 'society'

Digitalization makes these regularities visible without having invented them. All digital technology is ultimately based on the pattern-like regularity of stable structures or on a deviation from them. Where the object of digital recording is social practices and regularities, which include of course the materiality of social processes, digital technology uncovers regularities or is able to identify deviation probabilities only because it can count on relatively stable structures.

This can be statistically reconstructed. If all points in a data set were connected to all points in the same way, nothing could be explained with this data set. One would not be able to unlock from it any information at all, because statistical analysis – any kind of it – depends on the existence of a selective, that is, limited and structured, relation between elements, which can then be calculated at different levels and by different means, each according to its correlations. Only an object of some regularity lends itself to digital observation. This sounds counterintuitive, because the semantic field of 'digitalization' is close to the semantic extension of 'fluid structures' or 'dissolution of what may be expected'; but this is just prejudice. Digital technology, even the digital technology of official economic and scientific statistics that developed in the nineteenth century, indicates a structurality of the object that remains hidden to natural awareness and to the naked eye. Otherwise digital modes of cognition would be useless.

I would like to sharpen this idea still further: digitalization is actually the *third*, perhaps even the final discovery of society. Naturally, it was preceded by two others.

It was in the eighteenth and nineteenth centuries that society became aware of itself qua society *for the first time*: that was when the process of shaping the world was not just taken up with perpetuating the tradition but some of it went into shaping the new. This was true for instance of the emergence of national states in the decades after the French Revolution, which had to establish a new array of institutions and new laws for all, then face up to the clash between the promises of legal and political equality and the effects of economic and environmental inequality and actively deal with them. The revolutionary framers of society were oriented to creating rather than discovering society, because they wanted to dissolve with all their might what already existed. Hence it was probably the reactionaries who perceived and uncovered society in the most radical way. In the historiography of social science, one begins all too soon with self-portrayals of figures who celebrate the new – such as the inventor of the label 'sociology', Auguste Comte, who saw the dawn of a 'scientific' age – an age in which, by the way, the quantitative calculation of social dynamics with seemingly transparent forms already played a special role.[16] But perhaps the counter-revolution is much more revealing.

Let us think for example of the French counter-Enlightenment espoused by someone like Joseph de Maistre, who attempted to defend the persistence and stability of an evolved society against the Enlightenment's and the Revolution's demands for equality: he set the resistance of a social structure against the revolutionaries' will to change.[17] And history agrees not only with the revolutionaries, who actually established new institutions, new forms of rule, and new institutional arrangements; the considerable persistence of the 'natural' differences, classifications, routines, and experiences of a stagnant social structure rather played into the hands of the reactionaries as well, and more than the revolutionaries and the egalitarians could have expected. This tension is still alive today.

Since the French Revolution, 'society' was the symbol of the experience of a contradiction between the desire to create and structural inertia. Even those who wanted to impose equality and novelty came up against the inertia of traditions and of the world. How can freedom be established in a world that already is the way it is? How can we break the resistance of the structures contained within the structures? How much change can the structures take, and how much change can the people take? These questions accompanied the entire nineteenth century and gave the notion of society a meaning that was simultaneously progressive (design, reform, revolution) and conservative (established structures, traditions) – which is why revolution and restauration, or revolution and order, frequently came into conflict with each other. For the modern world's self-understanding, which is so effective as publicity, the establishment of an already counting – that is, digital – self-observation of society remained rather unnoticed, by the way. Society supplied itself with observations about itself, with statistics and quantitative surveys, with assessments of needs – and, not least, in the form of money. Money always comes in a countable format. It is a digital medium per se, simply because you can transfer money only in counted form. It is not possible just to give money to somebody. Money always takes discrete forms. I may give someone twenty euros, but not just money – and especially the economic description of society, in its regularities, comes up against a view that observes processes numerically, in the emergent creation of patterns.

The *second* discovery followed in the mid-twentieth century at the latest, from its liberalizations and pluralizations, when the concept of society started to have a special semantic career too. This discovery of society ran parallel with flare-ups of inclusivity and social climbing opportunities, as one discovered the contradiction between on the one hand the political will to include groups hardly considered before – such as workers and the lower social classes to begin with, then women and sexual minorities, and finally ethnic strangers – and, on the other, the possibilities of implementing an egalitarian society. This period of awakening after the Second World War, commonly referred to as the experience of the '68 generation, was the result of radical increases in the complexity of industrial society, which was characterized by great optimism about planning, progress, and growth.[18] The West's self-confidence was then at its peak, and this was reflected in economic, scientific, and technological innovations, but most of all in the liberalization and pluralization of lifestyles. At that time, discovering society meant in the first place combining the cultural elements of the existing world in a new way, namely through more pluralistic forms of life and more occasions to communicate – in partnerships, in sexuality, in art and culture, in the democratic public life, and (last but not least) in private consumption.

But even this second discovery of 'society' had the same double experience as the first. Notwithstanding all the euphoric mood of renewal brought by the revolution, all the semantic surpluses of configurability, and all the optimism around the reformability of existing structures and routines, one had to experience how resistant the social structure was. One of the distinctive media of change those days was the belief in the egalitarian effects of education – it was the age of educational expansion, of founding new universities and colleges, of the academization of professions, and of enabling social advancement through the promotion of education. But, for all the euphoria of reform, one had to realize that social structures were not as easy to change as one had expected.

In this context, the sociological studies of education by Pierre Bourdieu and Claude Passeron in France achieved almost the status of classics. Their thesis of the 'illusion of equal opportunity' of 1970 demonstrated firmly that the promise of equality of access to educational institutions not only was unable to override the power of one's origins but in the end made it even more visible.[19] The thesis was that, no matter how much energy is invested in overcoming social inequalities, for example through educational efforts, the structural inertia of social masses is greater. In the language of the metaphor proposed earlier, the user surface suggests possibilities of causal influence that can be primarily represented politically and culturally, but the social machinery in the background is not so easily changed. Thus the discovery of society is, simultaneously, the discovery of its changeability and the discovery of its inertia, which is downright resistant to change. Thus the title and the content of 'Illusion der Chancengleichheit' ('Illusion of Equal Opportunity')[20] had an almost defining influence on these two sides of the discovery of society; where sociology, as it is perceived by the public, is not satisfied with promoting the user surface (which it sometimes does, unfortunately all too often), it encounters the constraints of regularities that do not fit in at all with the self-portrayal of a fluid, dissolving, accelerated, and malleable modernity.

This was already known in classical class theory of the Marxian variety, which never achieved the transition from theory to 'praxis', mainly because of the difference between 'class in itself' and 'class for itself'. It never succeeded in aligning the *subjective class situation* (user surface) with the *objective class situation* (machinery).[21] Class theory always suffered from the fact that people were not ready to understand themselves as 'social' subjects, but were corrupted by the 'bourgeois' user surface.

I give this simple example to demonstrate what sort of means are required if we want to be able to understand society. I am not interested in class theory, which I consider to be, in its theoretical structure, rather unsuitable for explaining social and especially economic inequality. But the example may be helpful when it comes to describing the question of the self-description and self-visibility of modern societies. It makes obvious that, given its complexity, modern society will hardly be able to be aware of itself by analog means; only digital means will do. Abstractions must be generated, namely abstractions from analog visibility. These are then transformed into data, so that mutual relations may be related to each other in order to finally identify statistical groups, statistical clusters, and patterns of data that are not themselves visible in the everyday lives of the actors.

My example is just one among many. In all functional systems of society issues of self-observation arise that can no longer be dealt with simply by relying on visible structures and features. Market observation and currency changes in the economy, voting behaviour, chances of approval and interests in politics, capacities of control in the administration – all these issues are increasingly dependent on non-analog observation.

Consequently, the *third* discovery of society is its *digital discovery*. The triumph of the digital – that is, the countable self-observation of regularities, patterns, and clusters invisible at first sight – is perhaps the strongest empirical proof that *there is* such a thing as society: a social order that comes before the behaviour of individuals. Data that individuals leave behind via payments, via the movement profiles of their mobile devices, via purchase behaviour, via search routines on the Internet, via connections to social networks, via car number plates on record, and so on are of interest to companies, law enforcement agencies, market observation, behaviour control, traffic control, and so on only because the accumulation of individual behaviour can be rounded to 'social' patterns with which we can see in digital format what remains hidden in analog format.

If I break this down to my own behaviour and observe only what is visible about me in analog format, my thoroughly individual behaviour is more predictable than is good for one's self-image: my lifestyle, my daily aesthetic choices, my personal taste in furniture and music, my consumer habits, the brands of my clothes, my writing tools, my electronic devices, my use of media, my political beliefs, even the car I drive – none of this is really surprising. There would have been alternatives for all this, but even these would have fallen within the bounds of what fits a given pattern. Digital market observation is interested precisely in these probabilities of variation in order to extend its markets, just as the digital observation of traffic flows or spatial behaviour can control the dynamics of processes exactly like this, through the probability of variance of structures.[22]

My great passion is music. It is at once wonderful and humiliating that the music streaming services and digital music portals I use know exactly, from my previous purchases (and who knows what other consumer information), what I would have bought next, had I found it myself: wonderful insofar as it has extended my horizon, humiliating insofar as it demonstrates how limited and predictable my horizon is. The patterns in which we live are ultimately the very social structure, which becomes visible to us only in the regularity of our behaviour or in the regularity of social processes. Together with Peter Felixberger I have once reconstructed this as a 'screenplay': if you look at public debates, you can see relatively quickly how predictable and typical the behaviour of participants is.[23] Of course this screenplay does not exist in explicit form, and what happens is not rehearsed or staged by anyone. However, it follows invisible scripts and regularities that become visible in the end as a structure in event-like processes. The patterns of this kind of behaviour – and also of abstract processes such as market dynamics, political semantic conjectures, or medical infection rates – are much more effective than the actors involved realize.

In our everyday lives we are indeed used to deciphering at least patterns of behaviour. For example, the members of a given society always have a sensorium for distinguishing similarities from dissimilarities, for disentangling certain symbols and indications with respect to their closeness to the lifeworld, or for making evaluations – in most cases implicitly rather than explicitly. But the patterns of behaviour go even further. They make use of discrete data to calculate analogous behaviour. In the old language of class theory, they need not rely on the subjective social situation, that is, on what I actually know about myself; they know even the objective social situation, that is, what I ultimately do not know too well about myself.

This makes us realize how sluggish, how stable, how shaped and structured, how predictable and calculable the social substrate of our sociality is. It is perhaps an unexpected diagnosis, given that we are dealing with diagnoses of acceleration and disruptive change. Particularly plausible are diagnoses that claim that hardly one stone will be left standing. According to them, social change has increased its speed and ambivalences have multiplied. We would have to bear a lot more contingency and put up with constantly renewed versions of solutions and strategies. In a sense, it looks as if we are confronted with permanent updates, just as in the use of software, and nothing seems stable.

It is precisely the social and cultural sciences that increase this impression. One imagines oneself in a postmodernity that dissolves all meanings – and students at universities are taught the art of dissolving meanings by an academic staff engaged in relatively stable middle-class relationships. The deconstruction of identity impositions is booming. The term 'woman' is too narrow for what is given empirically in females of the species. Cultures are nothing but contingent constructions; true, they show some historical impact, but 'in reality' have no legitimate use as criteria of demarcation. Allegedly environmental and constitutional inequalities are differentiated, but at the same time they are branded as overly academic systems and practices of classification. Sexual styles and forms of desire fall under the suspicion of carrying too much identity with them as soon as they have a name – and so on. For parts of the social science academia, acknowledging the *potency* of social and cultural constructions has become completely implausible.

Often the meaning of the deconstruction of meanings is misunderstood. These theorists, who came from textual studies for the most part – think of Jacques Derrida,[24] Gilles Deleuze,[25] or Jean-François Lyotard[26] – did not aim at the dissolution of meanings into the arbitrary. So, what is discussed under the all-too-sweeping label of postmodernity is often summarized with naïvety, although some academic practices indeed support this prejudice. Fluidization and liquefaction (or dissolution) do not indicate that meanings are arbitrary but that practically, operatively, it is contingently and *in actu* that they are created, stabilized, and made to persist. Strictly speaking, theories of difference[27] of this kind explain not the arbitrariness of any practice, but the patterned nature of any practice. They wonder about the stability of practices that have to be, again and again, newly confirmed by practice. They look at a fundamentally fluid practice and recognize stable patterns one can hardly escape.

This is precisely what is significant for the compatibility of digitality with modern society: the links, networks, structures, and developing patterns are neither clearly determined nor arbitrary and must be detected precisely for this reason. The third discovery of society, through digitalization, is thus the result of the experience that there is a mutual relationship of increase between order and possibilities of variation, between definiteness and indeterminacy, between determinations and possibilities to recombine. Modernity does not mark the end of an order, it generates orders in ways that have never existed before and thereby discovers the problem of the self-control of a social practice that was previously structured in much simpler forms – more hierarchical, more direct, and more sanctionable. In modernity, classifications are much more subtle than they were before.

If there is one piece of theory that I am currently least able to make plausible to students, that is the mechanism of typecasting. We can hardly move around in our everyday lives without stereotyping ideas of order. To infer role expectations from partial aspects of people's behaviour, we must bear in mind typologies and taxonomies that make us capable of acting at all. We can assess what the other will do and what we might expect from that person only if we are in a position to draw on social structures in the form of types. This is, ultimately, the fundamental business condition of social sciences: our actions are, first and foremost, an expression of social positions and possibilities. Now, students find this highly implausible; I have often been asked, in a first reaction to this fundamental insight, how such typologies, stereotypes, and preordained categorizations can be avoided or overcome. It is not my intention to justify prejudices or to cast doubt on the individuality of the person. Nevertheless, perhaps the sociality of society becomes most obvious at the very moment when one no longer reckons with the *social* – not even if it is explicitly the topic of one's own discipline.

Empirical social research as pattern recognition

Empirical social research is itself a part of the history of the digitalization of modern society. If it is true that 'society' is a cipher for regularities, especially regularities and patterns not immediately visible to the naked eye, the emergence of empirical social research is itself a reaction to this experience of pattern-like structuration of society. In his textbook on empirical social research, Andreas Diekmann describes how the methods of social research have developed precisely from the experience of identifying patterns of social practice. It was above all 'political arithmetic' – in the form of obituary columns, statistics on generative behaviour, and the like – that enabled social planners to control the observation of society methodically. This is what Diekmann writes about the demographer John Gaunt, one of the founders of political arithmetic in the seventeenth century:

> Gaunt's innovations in his classic demographical *Observations* were manifold: he was interested in the measurement and quantitative analysis of social processes. Consequently he used statistical data that had been collected for other purposes; so, in modern terminology, he made *secondary analyses*. When this was not possible he conducted his own *primary surveys*, in order to estimate the size of London's population. In doing so, he was probably the first demographer to apply a method of *representative sampling*, whose results were extrapolated to estimate the size of the population. Finally, he paid attention to the *regularities* of population dynamics – in other words not only to the description of individual cases.[28]

This is precisely the reference problem of digitalization as I have presented it: the complex regularity of society itself and the non-randomness of individual behaviour. It is the somewhat counterintuitive experience that, although the self-descriptions of individual behaviour correspond to more or less abstract patterns and regularities of a social nature, this need not be transparent to the actors themselves. For example, the discovery of the normal distribution in statistics, or the interest in averages such as Quetelet's *homme moyen* (already mentioned) should be considered a breakthrough from the perspective of the digital observation of society through empirical social research.[29]

Empirical social research reveals patterns that may be latent and remain invisible without this kind of research, but can be made visible in a methodically controlled way. The digitality of modern society actually requires a social science perspective on itself, and this is why it was in the end involved in all three discoveries of society: in the first one, in the form of discovery of regularities; in the second, in the form of a scientific description of society's resistance, but also malleability; and, in the third, insofar as it itself uses digitalized methods, deals with data sets, and can discover by itself that somehow science-like forms get established that nevertheless do not pursue scientific but rather economic, political, forensic, or technical goals.

Already in the early phase of recognition of patterns in society in the broadest social science sense, disputes occurred about having social research more of the quantitative or the qualitative variety. Diekmann describes this as a conflict between quantitative political arithmetic and a 'university statistics' that did not work statistically but idiographically and downgraded political arithmetic to the rank of a technique of 'table servants' and a 'number people'. Diekmann writes:

> 'Qualitative' university statistics and 'quantitative' political arithmetic are a pair of opposites that have emerged repeatedly in different forms throughout the history of social research. In view of the sometimes heated debate on quantitative and qualitative research methods, one should be aware that the core of this controversy is not at all new.[30]

The latent controversy is between social research that operates with quantitative data sources and gets its results through quantitative data assessment procedures and social research where the data consist either of natural language, in texts or from interview material, or of the observation of practices, which are then evaluated in a methodically controlled way.

Of course, it would be a misunderstanding – and this is the only reason why I bring this up here – to associate the digitality of society only with quantitative social research. For both kinds feed on the reference problem of digitalization, namely the complex regularity of the social world. Even if qualitative data are seldom metric data, and even if they apply understanding and hermeneutic methods, qua social research their interest is not in individual cases but in discovering patterns, in recombining meaningful utterances, and in finding in them regularities, repetitions, types, path dependencies, and so on.[31] Strictly speaking, qualitative social research is also a method of pattern recognition that concerns itself with the development of order, that is, with a reconstructible process of ruling out other possibilities.[32] Those who believe that qualitative social research is research that makes the subject speak or that gets closer to reality because the data for research are 'natural' and close to everyday life are simply doing bad sociology, as this kind of research is also about supraindividual patterns and about the methodically controllable recombination of meaning. And, in quantitative social research, those who practise a simple sociology of variables in which these are statistically matched with one another in an arbitrary manner, without any question behind the process, also do bad sociology. For both fail to see that the reference problem is not the complicated nature of society but its complexity, that is, the patterned nature of how features are related to one another. For this reason alone, the relationship between quantitative data and qualitative research cannot be represented through the distinction between 'facts' and 'interpretations', as is sometimes done, in gross oversimplification and ignorance of the epistemological foundations.[33]

Incidentally, the cross-method understanding of empirical social research as pattern recognition presided over the beginnings of sociology in German-speaking universities. Max Weber's famous definition of sociology as a discipline that is supposed to *understand* social behaviour *interpretatively* and *explain* it *causally* already combined the two basic forms of pattern recognition. Causal explanation refers to the quantitative–statistical observation of regularities and causal relations; interpretative understanding refers to the possibility of understanding the assumed subjective meaning of actors by recognizing certain cultural patterns or their derivatives in those actors. In both cases, we are not talking about arbitrary individual correlations but rather about identifying patterns that make it possible to determine concrete actions only sociologically. In my own parlance, sociology starts out from the digitality of society, from the reference problem of complex regularities – and a

sociology of digitalization can therefore discover the latter not only
in its subject area but also in itself.

'Society' as digitalization material

On the other hand, the digital age, or rather the triumph of digitalization, absorbs precisely the sociality of society. In other words,
the sociality of society provides the material for digitalization.
Digital technology calculates with those exact regularities and
exact internal differentiations and deviations that constitute what
has turned out to be the concept of society and the social since
the eighteenth–nineteenth centuries. The digital observation of the
world is primarily interested not in the concrete individual, but in
certain types, namely in mining typologies for customer tracking
and for statistical groups and clusters dedicated to measuring
behavioural dispositions in road traffic, in energy consumption, in
partner choices or in political preferences, in law enforcement or
in marketing. The electronic, digital, and hence countable way of
observing collective activities relies on a relatively stable society, and
hence on regularities that are quite obviously more stable and calculable than those provided by the analog self-descriptions of actors
and their society.

To avoid misunderstanding, the digital, statistical *discovery of
society* does not simply come across the quantifiable form of
society; first it must render these quantifications countable through
categories. Just as society, through the printing press, which I am
going to discuss later, provided itself with categories of observation such that something of a discourse on forms of observation
and systems of classification has emerged, the digital discovery of
society cannot simply perceive regularities by itself. It is dependent
on developing its own systems of classification, without which it
would not be possible to capture any digital information. As demonstrated in a study by Rebecca Jean Emigh, Dylan Riley and Patricia
Ahmed, in the United States it was not only state authorities that
provided countable classification systems but also public discourses,
which reacted to changing social practices and thus redefined the
pattern of society.[34]

From an epistemological angle, patterns cannot simply be
depicted; one needs categories to make them visible, which sounds
contradictory. Such categories develop from the self-observation of
society in its own discourses; and indeed it was not just the state
authorities themselves but also private statistical associations that,
in the nineteenth century, dedicated themselves to the question of

how social developments could be represented statistically. Thus something almost like a new literacy emerged in relation to digital forms of pattern recognition; structurally, this phenomenon is definitely comparable to those literary salons where the bourgeois elite practised testing discursive patterns in order to develop figures of argument. Now it was digitalized categories that promoted social self-description – demographic and economic categories, for example. The digital view of society emerged from this interplay of scientific, state, but also private efforts towards categorization.[35] This view was directed especially at patterns, abstract regularities, and the possibilities of structural comparison. Since then the digital self-observation of society has become a permanently accompanying routine. Society discovers itself with the help of a digital gaze.

As a matter of fact, it is the technologies of digital pattern recognition in the realm of the social that provide what I call the *third* discovery of society. *Perhaps this is the most radical discovery of society at the moment of its disappearance.* It looks as if thought steeped in sociology has long passed its prime. *However, it is precisely the techniques of pattern recognition that really follow through with the social sciences' old basic conviction that behind the backs of actors lie structures and regularities that they are not aware of and that are not reflected in self-descriptions.*

I pointed out earlier that in modern society the difference between social and statistical groups begins to be noticed even before the ubiquitous use of computers. As soon as one starts working with intelligent ways of combining and recombining features and discovers statistical correlations beyond coincidental accumulations, one encounters connections that are analogously invisible but may well be inferred from the discrete, in other words numerical material. For example, one may find that groups in society that are culturally, socio-ethically, or even economically very different and belong to different social categories are similar in one or more features and thus form a statistical category. These are regularities of the social that do not really stand out in society's own self-descriptions – but this is precisely the sort of material to which it's worth applying discrete methods of observation, if we want to encounter regularities that may then be exploited economically, politically, for policing purposes, scientifically, for medical purposes, or even in the media. All these techniques, which I'm just hinting at here for the time being, count on society. They constitute this *third* discovery of society, which of course emerges with a rather non-sociological vocabulary. Semantically, then, this is no longer a matter of what the concept of society was used for, but functionally it is a matter of what this concept had previously concealed about itself.

To put it more precisely, again, the discovery of society in its first two variants discovered the malleability of the world, and ultimately also the politicization of society as a result of experiencing the world's variability. But then, in its scientific incarnation as sociology and social science, it found an expression for the disappointment that society cannot be changed as easily as political programmes suggest. This strange term, 'social policy', which is used most of all by those who consider society to be a rather political event, draws our attention to this fact, whereas sociological, methodologically controlled observation, whether it likes or not, gives expression precisely to this disappointment, that the regularities are stronger than politically formulated expectations.

No doubt the heyday of sociology's pervasive influence on ordinary language was in the 1970s, when social science concepts migrated into the everyday discourse: that we are socialized by our environment; that traditions are only conventions; that we must transcend the certainties in our lifeworld; that everybody is just playing a role; that we must learn about our class status; that criticism is possible; that interests are expressions of social conditions; and that rule requires legitimation – all this accompanied social debates and self-descriptions. This resulted in the optimistic basic attitude that things can be changed if we only want to.[36] But at the same time the experience of a disappointment set in – that society, through the persistence of its structures, the stability of its traditions, and its imperviousness to political interventions, followed only conditionally the liquefaction attempts of the semantics of the time. Even if there was indeed a great deal of change in the 1970s and the expansion of education, the social advancement of previously underprivileged groups, and – not least – consumer and pop cultures left significant traces on the self-consciousness of public discourse, the social stratification of society, for instance, has remained more stable than intended.[37]

But the third, digital discovery of society turns out to be anything but disappointed with such regularities and stabilities. Rather they are its material. They are the fabric out of which capital can be created – both economically and politically, both medically and forensically. If in the cultural self-descriptions of the observed actors classification and the stereotypical way of processing information are rather implausible, or even frowned upon, this is precisely the antecedent condition for society's digital information processing to pay off. It may well be that the whole potential of digitalization comes on the scene only at the moment of the disappearance of discourse as *social* discourse. Today this disappearance of the social is frequently compensated in the social sciences with discourses of identity and culture. Then it all comes down to the symmetrizing criticism of patterns, which one would rather like to get rid of through the moral impetus of their deconstruction. In this way the treatment of society is left to other authorities, for instance digital technology, which, for all its non-scientific interests, is now possibly doing a better kind of sociology than some professional sociologists who are rather interested in the fluidity of their subject. But I am not going to pursue this line here.

To summarize the first step of my thought, in this first chapter I am looking for the reference problem of the digital or, more precisely, for the condition under which the digital could establish itself as a technology. The answer must be determined offline, as it were, to avoid a *petitio principii* – begging the question. Offline does not mean using digital technology itself as an explanation, but rather the form of the solution. It is already clear: if the kind of solution provided by digital technology consists in linking the data among themselves, and if the structures of order can be made visible only in this way, then the answer to the question about the reference problem is not digital technology, but the digitality of society itself. Modern societies can be understood only digitally, which is why digital technologies bind to them. At first digital technology does not change society, but the digitality of society really requires that at least some of its primarily planning and administrating authorities deal with the processing of its digital patterns.

If we look at the historical starting conditions for the development of the digital, it was really a form of social self-discovery that, in the control and management of processes, increasingly different kinds of information and active forces had to be processed at the same time. Incidentally, the origin of this way of digitalizing problems goes back a whole century before the invention of the computer. It was not the computer that brought about data processing, but the centralization of rule in national states, urban planning and the running of cities, the need for a rapid provision of goods to an abstract number of companies, consumers, and cities or regions. I have already mentioned the symbolic figure of Adolphe Quetelet – a pioneer of the digitalization of real problems. If you want to know, for example, how much wheat a city of a given size needs, what transport routes from the surrounding countryside are needed to secure supplies, how this infrastructure is financed through loans or public spending, what the capacity of an underground sewer system in a city must be, or even for what professions you should secure available training places, the premodern way of looking at concrete problems from a restricted local angle is no longer sufficient. Rather an understanding of the simultaneity of a wide variety of forces is required if you want to place solutions on the horizon of problems. Hence I locate the beginning of the digitalization of society in early modernity – an argument also supported by the cultural studies scholar Felix Stalder. But, unlike Stalder, I see the reference problem for the emergence of the digital–technological processing of information less in the *quantitative* aspect of a growing demand for computation;[38] I see this growing demand rather in the *qualitative* change of socially complex situations.

It is no coincidence that idea and practice of data processing by digital means coincide exactly with the historical period in which societies began to describe themselves as societies, but at the same time became increasingly invisible because they were more obscure to themselves. From a sociological point of view, ancient society was a society too, as were the advanced civilizations of South America, or ancient Egypt. But it had never occurred to them to describe themselves as societies. Societies have described themselves as societies only when they encountered completely new problems, which had to do with supra-individual solutions pertaining to structural changes. One could say, then, that *the reference problem of digitalization is the sociality of society itself, and (modern) society is itself a digital phenomenon.* Shouldn't this actually herald the finest hour of the social sciences, of sociology?

The cyborg as a means of overcoming society?

Perhaps one of the most interesting texts about the third discovery of society through digitalization is 'A Cyborg Manifesto: Science, Technology, and Socialist Feminism in the Late Twentieth Century' by the feminist philosopher and science historian Donna Haraway.[39] Being a feminist, Haraway starts from the question of the predictability of women and comes across the concurrent contingency and stability of what she calls 'women's experience'.[40] She explains that, in line with emancipation, one must both acknowledge and construe this experience, but at the same time one should try to get rid of it. Her utopia is a 'world without gender',[41] that is, a world where in the end this category has no effect and can be unmade as a topic. This is the old question from that paradox – through emphasis on the irrelevance of a distinction, what is distinguished is necessarily made all the more visible; undoing gender must reckon with gender. There seems to be no escape from this.[42]

The gender issue is of interest particularly insofar as poststructuralist and postmodern kinds of theory have set out to deconstruct any discourse about 'the' woman, only to discover how powerful the gender attribution is. Donna Haraway starts here with her ironic proposal; she pleads for a cyborg that, precisely by recombining the elements, creates an entity that evades classic categorization. 'The cyborg is resolutely committed to partiality, irony, intimacy, and perversity.'[43] She (*sic!*) comes out as a result of the fact that the borders between categorizations are now broken, and thus new points of attribution develop through recombination.

Haraway digitalizes reality by recombining individual entities in different ways. On distinctions of gender and race, for example, she writes: 'ideologies about human diversity have to be formulated in terms of frequencies of parameters, like blood groups or intelligence scores. It is "irrational" to invoke concepts like primitive and civilized.'[44]

Haraway recombines afresh, though in the spirit of those programmable machines that are the cyborgs, whose programming is contingent – it is not predetermined but reveals degrees of freedom. It is no coincidence that, of all things, she anchors her criticism of the category of gender to a programmable, digitalized machine: a cyborg whose femininity is an ironic element, because this attribution is at once cancelled – like the figure of the 'liberal ironist' in Richard Rorty.[45] This discourse is 30 years old; in today's culture wars of identity politics, the liberals have long ceased being ironists.[46]

With her technological deconstruction of gender – and here gender can be taken as a placeholder for quite different human categories and groups of features – Haraway very precisely points out the double meaning of the digital discovery of society. On the one hand, she sketches the high potential for dissolution in a society in which the image of the world changes when individual parameters are rearranged, recombined, and linked in unusual ways; on the other hand, she describes this against the background of an experience that situations and practices are more stable than one could even imagine from an ironic deconstructivist point of view. She writes: 'Late twentieth-century (programmable, AN) machines have made thoroughly ambiguous the difference between natural and artificial, mind and body, self-developing and externally designed, and many other distinctions that used to apply to organisms and machines. Our machines are disturbingly lively, and we ourselves fighteningly inert.'[47] She encounters the sluggishness of society, its patterns and its persistence, its structures and its practices – and she does so with a digitalized gaze that is capable only of perceiving the powerfulness of these patterns *as patterns*. Her irony is an irony of the gaze. The cyborg is a half-real, half-fictitious figure, which points out that the structure of society itself seems to be surmountable from a logical perspective – but from a sociological perspective it is much more sluggish and persistent than it appears to the actors themselves. Haraway's cyborgs are those figures whose digitality can see only what is possible and what is not. And the desire to overcome society, for example the category of 'gender', comes up against the very limits of what, as a structure, is more stable than recombinability of categories would suggest. This is exactly how digitalization discovers society as an inert structure – but also as the material for shaping it.

2

The Idiosyncrasy of the Digital

Thus, if we wish to understand digitalization as well as its afferent technology, we must indeed start from the structures of society itself. In practice, one can translate this statement into one that says: digitalization must be considered a *sociological* phenomenon, and not just a *social* phenomenon – that is, one that is looked at in relation to its social preconditions and consequences. The switch from analogous to digital questions for society – or the acknowledgement of society's digitality – is itself a genuinely sociological topic. Strictly speaking, then, a sociology of digitalization is almost a sociology of sociology, for the questions that arise as digital questions are immediately related to sociological questions.

Thus the functional explanation of the victory of digital technology lies in the structure of society itself, which creates and finds a demand for the use of forms of processing information that are not immediately visible in the sense that they are data-like, and therefore countable. To this extent, any attempt to write a sociology of digitalization is a challenging enterprise, because here the subject and the mode of thinking cannot really be separated from each other. If one ventures a first glance at the *praxis* of the digital, it quickly becomes obvious that these practices are very similar to the sociological. The digital solution, as I have worked it out, makes structures visible through data sets that are invisible at first sight – and this is also the solution offered by sociological practices. The special surprise value of sociology lies in its wresting the surprise element from the obvious and in offering counter-intuitive points.

Let us take a look at the practices themselves. Anyone who uses data sets to profit from his or her customer base, for example through targeted marketing, or who processes data material related to criminal or terrorist threats is indeed doing something very similar to the practices of a social scientist. He or she will first take care to be provided with data, then will organize and assess them according to certain criteria, work out specific questions, think methodically about how to achieve valid results, and so on. Working with data is not scientific work in the narrower sense, because in most cases it is only very indirectly concerned with questions of scientific truth – for example when new customer relationships are established, when a circle of suspects is to be determined, or when the traffic flows in a big city are to be controlled. But, even if the non-scientific forms of processing digitalized information are not a scientific form of hypothesis testing, the practices involved do not differ significantly. Those who want to sell something do not want to test hypotheses, and those who want to monitor something do not necessarily want it either. All this is simply a matter of cultivating the form of pattern recognition made possible by the large amount of data in order to do something with it.

These practices are science-like, scientoid. They analyse the world with the help of self-created data that are not the world itself. Of course, here we should stick not to the official manner in which science describes itself, but rather to its self-referential practices. In his sociology of science, Niklas Luhmann writes that even science itself is only science-like. He says, tersely: 'In a way, this method is like toying with coincidence, and then, through a mixture of skilfulness and good luck, research will produce results that may stimulate or discourage further research. The complexity of the world appears in the surprise value of self-generated data.'[1] This surprise value of self-generated data is what represents the information status of science, and one should imagine in a similar way the handing of digitalized information, which, by recombining elements, produces surprises that may then be helpful. Luhmann writes further about science: 'Thus the appropriate method teaches you first to compensate for the system's inferior complexity through self-generated complexity, and then to search for results in the world of self-generated data by eliminating countless possible combinations.'[2]

Dominique Cardon has very aptly conceptualized the scientoid nature of these practices by systematizing the practices of data analyses in social networks and search engines and by differentiating the various observer positions, as well as the principle with which users are targeted through the results. He demonstrates, for example, that different kinds of calculation – such as classifications, benchmarks, or machine-learning forms of prediction – are subject to different principles and, not least, rely on different types of data. No epistemological issues lurk here in the background, but only the kind mediated via the practices of the providers themselves.[3] The technique – in line with what Luhmann describes for science

– consists in using self-generated recombination possibilities in order to arrive at selective statements.

This is not defeatism in science but the insight that the world's representation in data through methodically controlled procedures lends the data an intrinsic value, and this produces a kind of surprise that would not exist without them. We shall understand the social significance of digitalization only when we also get to understand with greater precision what is actually science-like about it. And, again, this will happen only when we determine with greater precision what distinguishes a scientific approach to the world from other approaches. The first chapter produced the conclusion that the reference problem of digitalization is the social structure itself and that a third 'discovery of society' has taken place as a result. Now, it would be a blatant underestimation of digitalization to consider this an already exhaustive analysis, for so far I have not even touched on the question of what is special about the digitalization of society through data. Therefore my next step will be to take up the thread of the science-like nature of digital practices in order to connect it to a social theory argument that finds the form of digitality to be already present in the structure of modern society and, again, in order to be able from there to formulate in greater detail my thesis about the reference problem of the digital.

The inexact exactness of the world

One key text for understanding the digital revolution is certainly Edmund Husserl's crisis paper of 1935–6. To give a very simplifying summary, in *The Crisis of European Sciences and Transcendental Phenomenology* Husserl criticized modern science by saying that on the one hand it shows an amazing degree of exactness and precision, but on the other hand this exactness is due to a kind of self-created idealization. He writes: '*What constitutes "exactness"?* Obviously, nothing other than what we exposed above: empirical measuring with increasing precision, but under the guidance of a world of idealities, or rather a world of certain particular ideal structures that can be correlated with given scales of measurement – such a world having been objectified in advance through idealization and construction.'[4] This is not just a critique of quantitative data, quantifiable measures, and their mathematization but most of all a critique of the modern sciences' having lost contact with the 'lifeworld', that is, up to a point, with the pre-scientific basis of meaning.

This is definitely a phenotypical critique of the independence of the sciences, whose success has something to do with allegedly having lost all sense of being grounded in the pre-scientific world. To quote Husserl again, '[t]his arithmetization of geometry leads almost automatically, in a certain way, to the emptying of its meaning. The actually spatiotemporal idealities, as they are presented first hand [*originär*] in geometrical thinking under the common rubric of "pure intuitions," are transformed, so to speak, into pure numerical configurations, into algebraic structures.'[5] Here Husserl describes the translation of 'original' [*originär*] entities, which are given by phenomenal intuition, not just into a more abstract, more general, or simply more comprehensible form but into a completely different medium, which no longer has the configuration of perception itself. In more concrete terms, a geometric shape becomes a coded shape of numbers and quantities. As we would say today, it is *digitalized*.

Then the crucial statement follows elsewhere. 'In algebraic calculation, one lets the geometric signification recede into the background as a matter of course, indeed drops it altogether; one calculates, remembering only at the end that the numbers signify magnitudes.'[6] Once again, Husserl does not formulate here an anti-scientist critique of the sciences or a philosophy of cultural or social originality. Rather he points out how the idiosyncrasy of modern science is really an idiosyncrasy that has moved away from the originality of sense perception. So, given the 'objectivism' of scientific claims to truth, his concern is not to stop here but to 'radical[ly] inquir[e] back into subjectivity – and specifically the subjectivity which *ultimately* brings about all world-validity, with its content and in all its prescientific and scientific modes'.[7] This does not refer to the subjective authenticity of the individual, and hence to a critique of science in terms of its relevance to the life of the individual tied to the lifeworld; that would be cultural criticism of a simplistic and bad sort. What subjectivity points to is the question of how the objective truths of science generate themselves from a constitutive and a logical point of view. 'Subjectively' means via phenomenologically proven acts of insight or recognition. Less philosophically put, Husserl is concerned here with the question of how those objectivities, those truths that seem to be so disjointed, are *created* after all. He does not ask *what is*, but *how* something is *created*. This is what he means by having a foundation in the lifeworld.

Let us for a moment move to another terrain and jump back to the 1980s, to David Cope's EMI project. EMI stands for Experiments in Musical Intelligence. Cope, musician and composer, is now a retired university professor of musicology in California, Santa Cruz, and he has algorithmized music to the point where the computer itself can produce Bach-like compositions that were not distinguishable from the original, at least to regular listeners.[8] The audio samples are astonishing, for example when you listen to pieces on CDs like *Bach by Design* or *Virtual Bach*,[9] which actually produce Bach music that is not by Bach but goes back to a computer program endowed with the capacity to isolate – or *objectivize*, understood in Husserl's sense – the patterns of Bach's music in such a way that by the end the data set has nothing to do with the music itself. This data set is of a different kind of reality. It only consists of discrete states and can, then, be technologically translated into music that is audible by analog means. What is interesting about this is not only the technological possibility. We are dealing with it every day, since data carriers for music have been available in digital form for a long time, after the disappearance of the analog record. What makes things different is the fact that, although the common CD or the data set downloaded from the Internet as a stream is indeed the result of electronic processing, it has a thoroughly analog source, namely music – played or sung. So listening to music is ultimately a kind of back translation of an analog signal from a data set of discrete states. In the case of *Bach by Design* it is not a back translation from analogous signals but an analogy, so far as discrete and therefore computable states are concerned. In this context, Bruce L. Jacob even speaks of an algorithmic model of creativity.[10]

Bach's harpsichord concertos, which were composed between 1713 and 1715, are much influenced by Antonio Vivaldi. On the one hand, this can be gathered from the music itself; on the other, one could also reconstruct analogously that at the time Bach must have had a printed version of Vivaldi's *L'estro armonico* [*Harmonic Inspiration*] to hand. This is something that Husserl would have understood as a phenomenological, constitutive–logical reconstruction: someone listens to music they process subjectively, and that music locks into their own stream of consciousness in such a way as to influence their own style of composing. One should not think only of music here. The way in which we learn language or speech, how our visual habits develop certain structures, how the world appears to us, what we believe to be relevant or not, how we assess and classify, what we overlook and where we have a distorted view – all this is the result of patterns. This is very vividly reflected in the fact that we ourselves adopt patterns from our environment, in our forms of speaking and acting. Our way of speaking is as specific to context and class as our actions; but our worldview may also depend on the profession we practise or have been trained in. There are family-specific speech patterns, let alone culture-dependent spaces of association, which are more likely to be found in some, less likely in others, as in a probabilistic pattern. Interesting are, for example, the speech patterns of people whose mother tongue is different. A native speaker of an Arabic language shows a tendency to reverse the order between subject and predicate in German, or to differentiate vowels in a different way. Native speakers of French, even those with a barely perceptible accent, can often be identified by their placing the stress on the last syllable in German too. And native speakers of British or American English have difficulty with the German article even when their German is perfect.[11] All these are rather simple indications that the perception of the world and the processing of information are most of all kinds of a pattern processing in which the patterns are not so much in the subject as in the objectivity created by perception.

Finally, with our sense perception we test hypotheses about the world – and this is what Husserl's concept of lifeworld refers to. We interpret the world in what is always an already self-interpreted world. And our consciousness must somewhat know beforehand what it is able to see, otherwise it would not be able to identify things. Phenomenology deals with these constitutive–logical issues of opening the world through one's own individual acts in an already open world. This is what it means for all knowledge to be grounded in the lifeworld; and it is even a perceptually and physiologically conditioned grounding, in a world that has always been already known and sets the benchmark for the processing of deviations.

The data set of *Bach by Design* does not recognize this pre-understanding of the world in the constitutive–logical acts of a consciousness but only as regularity, as pattern, as structure of a data set. When Bach broods over a Vivaldi score, or when I set up something with my own pre-understanding, which exists in my mind, these forms are somehow processed and translated in an analog modality. The composition algorithm, on the other hand, does not compare music but the digital traces of music. It does not recognize any Bach style. It recognizes patterns, which are not music to it, but signs that stand for something else without being treated as such. Strictly speaking, the algorithm processes just the ways in which signs are related, and in this context it doesn't matter what the signs stand for. The algorithm can learn and can make decisions, in other words it can compose in Bach's style within the limits of possible probabilities. It is even capable of making use of certain deviations that are also to be found in Bach's music, especially since Bach's music is not a monolithic block but a certain probability space for cultivated indeterminacies. This means that the data set with the information for the algorithm is a data set that is searched by a computer program for typical probabilities of connection and is tested for patterns. It is, then, through these patterns that variations and selections can be created: it is to a certain extent a revolutionary model, capable of making further calculations out of earlier ones. Then the computer will be programmed in such a way as to create a certain kind of similarity with the original material, which is not even identical: in reality the machine only scans probabilities against probabilities.

To make it in even clearer, this material is not Bach music but the inner structure of a data set from which signs can be generated that allow someone familiar with the music of Bach to recognize the music of Bach again. That person should not be too familiar with Bach, though, lest it be known that the piece in question has not been on record so far; but, even if one is reasonably acquainted with this kind of music, the quality of the music seems to offer the listening consciousness sufficient probability to classify the listening experience accordingly.

It is in this probability space that the algorithm works – like an algorithm that knows the probability of word sequences on a smartphone or in a word-processing program, or the probability of what should replace a misspelled word. Accordingly, for a long time the algorithm of my iPhone correction program suggested replacing 'PEGIDA'[12] with 'Pepita'. This would have been a nice solution to an ugly problem; however, the algorithm has no idea of the meaning of the suggested word. All it can do is decide, on the basis of empirical data, whether to follow the proposal or not. Via a language structure it recognizes and the user's rejection or acceptance practices, it may refine its decisions about increasing the probability of acceptance for suggested words. By the way, this means that the algorithm can get used to PEGIDA too, if it is taught long enough that this is a desired sequence of signs.

The fact that the digits, and hence the representing signs, are supposed to mean magnitudes is not only parenthetical to the algorithm but even absurd, because the algorithm cannot ask about the structure of meaning but only about the structure of distribution, fed in this case from a permanently expanding dictionary that does not come from the algorithm itself but constitutes its material. Everything processed by the algorithm is in the final analysis external to it; it originates in the structure of meaning of society – the society that constitutes the algorithm's environment. The algorithm only calculates a pattern, regardless of sense, regardless of meaning, regardless of what is represented. This is what Husserl criticizes in the modern sciences – and in the mid-1930s algorithms such as those used for EMI were not even available. But he had a sense that science actually creates a world of self-made data and that its material is not the materiality of its object but the data in which the world is supposed to materialize.

Of course, Husserl would have been interested in the rematerialization of digital data. In his *Phenomenology of Internal Time Consciousness* Husserl gives a phenomenological description of listening to a tune:

> The matter seems very simple at first; we hear a melody, i.e., we perceive it, for hearing is indeed perception. While the first tone is sounding, the second comes, then the third, and so on. Must we not say that when the second tone sounds I hear *it*, but I no longer hear the first, and so on? In truth, therefore, I do not hear the melody but only the particular tone which is actually present. That the expired part of the melody is objective to me is due – one is inclined to say – to memory, and it is due to expectation which looks ahead that, on encountering the tone actually sounding, I do not assume that that is all. We cannot rest satisfied with this explanation, however, for everything said until now depends on the individual tone. Every tone itself has a temporal extension: with the actual sounding I hear it as now. With its continued sounding, however, it has an ever new now, and the tone actually preceding is changing into something past. Therefore, I hear at any instant only the actual phase of the tone, and the Objectivity of the whole enduring tone is constituted in an act-continuum which in part is memory, in the smallest punctual part is perception, and in a more extensive part expectation.[13]

What Husserl describes in this way is the fact that the notes themselves, that is, each individual note in its concrete material or physical shape, is neither tone nor melody and ultimately has no meaning. It receives meaning only from the perceiving, recognizing, and hearing consciousness – and this *originally* in the sense that the melody is not perceived qua melody but is constituted by the time-specific capabilities of the consciousness, which, likewise, always operates only within concrete presences. This holds both for melodies and for sentences, but also for the perception of objects, which generates a shape out of single primordial perceptions; and in a special way this shape is both in the world and created by the recognizing consciousness. In this sense, the worldliness of the world is an 'act correlate' produced by the consciousness.

At first sight this looks complicated, but it is indispensable for understanding the world of data and digitalization. Husserl's example of the melody shows that even sensual perception and the processing of the outside world function with the help of self-generated data, if we take the term literally: it is about how the world is *given*, for this is what *data* means: *datum* means 'the given' – and their givenness always depends on their being processed. Thus what Husserl shows for science and its self-created objectivity is also true of the perception of the world in general. In the end, the brain processes no analog information, no depictions of an outside, but only self-created internal states of excitation, which produce that image in their internally self-organized interrelation, and the central organ of perception can then process that image as an analog form.

The distance, which Husserl diagnosed in his crisis paper, between the quantifiable form of scientific knowledge and its subjective genesis – or, to put it in more modern language, the representation of data in a way that no longer relates it as an analog to what is represented – has somehow turned into the image of nature and into the form of representing itself.

The particular idiosyncrasy of data

What is this supposed to mean? The example of biology perhaps conveys it best. The subject of the science of biology is no longer the observation and classification of firm, analog shapes and taxonomies whose systematization is oriented at the immediate appearance of the subjects of research. One of the most important methods of biological classification was drawing, that is, an analog mode of representation. As a discipline of molecular biology and genetics, biology lost this gestaltness. Since then, the nature of what is alive has been presented in completely new images – in the form of numerical codes, molecular models, or measurements. We have Husserl to thank for the insight that science has no immediate access to nature – a claim of that sort could not be seriously upheld since Descartes and Kant, at any rate, and has become impossible with Husserl. After all, his diagnosis of a crisis of the sciences in Europe is still characterized by the idea of a clearer relationship between the signifier and the signified, the sign and what it stands for, the form researched and the material accessible to research. In consequence, Husserl describes an experience of loss, but one in which he also recognizes the power of the scientific. He is concerned to show that science should at least reflect that its representations are only representations and not the things themselves.

Husserl's thesis about the distancing of the objectivizing data from the subjective practice of objectivizing is so relevant because it points to something that has become particularly effective and significant with the rapid success of the sciences in the twentieth century, namely the relationship between model and reality, between concept and fact, between representation and the represented. This relation was to become the fundamental topic of twentieth-century epistemology; and it is also key to understanding digital modernity and digital technology.

I am going to return to this relationship between represen-tation and the represented, because this is where what I call the duplication of the world through data manifests itself. But a first, preparatory approach to data as the basic material of digitalization already allows one to say that the data form of the processed material develops an idiosyncrasy (or stubbornness) that must always go beyond the threshold between the simply internal relations of elements, in probabilistic models and meaningful processing. Concretely, the question is whether one can make something with these relations, whether they can be translated into meaningful refer-ences, if they are of any benefit to users, indeed whether it is possible to generate meanings out of them. The task is basically similar to that of describing the ways of working of the brain. The brain has no 'knowledge' of what is perceived, it has no clear representations of meanings, it switches its states according to internal rules, and it is operationally closed, that is, it cannot react to the outside world – the world outside itself – directly, but only in the form of states of its own. And yet it is the basis for meaningful references, at least mentally represented ones, and for the fact that the corresponding patterns become meanings. The same is true of data processing. It, too, works according to internal rules, according to internal refer-ences. Data sets, combinations of data sets, the internal statistical description, both static and dynamic, of regularities and patterns must then be translated, in a second step, into a form that can be processed – and I mean meaningfully processed. From a perceptual–phenomenological angle, this would be something akin to Husserl's melody example, in which the melody is created only through an effort of consciousness, which makes a shape out of a relation between notes. This is also true of the processing of data, whose strong point is that it allows for providing internal relations with a structure that must then be made into meaningful references.

I have linked the science-like, scientoid nature of data processing to practices like the handling of data and the visualization of the patterns that lie 'behind' them and are not visible to the naked eye.[14] Of course data processing, with its orientation to applicability, is not a science but rather an application to the respective fields. Dirk Baecker expresses this in a succinct formula: 'Where mathematics is calculating to provide evidence, information science is programming for the sake of production.'[15] Thus we are actually dealing here only with a science-like practice, but one that encounters questions similar to those of the scientific handling of digital 'data', which are not simply 'given' but must be created. Concerning the sciences, Klaus Mainzer has worked out that the accuracy of research results does not necessarily increase with large amounts of data, especially in the social and economic sciences. 'What is striking in physics is the natural constants on which the mathematical laws of nature are based: Einstein's speed of light c, Planck's constant h, the gravitational constant G, to name just a few.'[16] The social sciences lack such constants (sometimes even complex biological systems lack them), and this, according to Mainzer, makes the significance of theories even stronger. His argument is this: in the field of natural constants one can count on reasonably precise correlations, but in sciences without such constants, in sciences that deal with a temporal–dynamic subject matter under conditions of complexity, one depends all the more on theories, that is, on dealing with data sets in an intelligent way. Not every statistical connection is significant, and not every connection is important. The concept of theory, too, changes in this respect, approaching the product orientation described by Baecker. Proving something becomes more improbable under complex conditions, which is why the concept of theory changes. Mainzer writes: 'With the growing complexity of fields of application, differential equations have become highly non-linear and stochastic (e.g. in climate models or in financial mathematics). Then, at best, only approximations under simplified conditions and numerical solutions are imaginable.'[17]

Essentially, in the wake of Big Data, the social world – that is, the ubiquitous data sets produced by the constant sensorization of the social environment, by the collection of all kinds of data, by the recording of traces of economic, political, scientific, and technological practices – exists in a form that allows for the discovery of unknown, potentially useful and usable patterns, which could produce something. What renders all this 'scientoid' is that the same data can be used by scientific actors, like those in social sciences, but also by non-scientific actors – and, in their case, primarily not even for matters related to truth.[18] In fact, all this is not about 'proving' anything but about 'producing' something. Danah Boyd and Kate Crawford express it in a simple formula: 'Big Data is notable not because of its size, but because of its relationality to other data. Due to efforts to mine and aggregate data, Big Data is fundamentally networked.'[19] This is exactly what I have already emphasized several times: the internal structural formation and reconstruction of this rather closed structure of data sets, whose genesis happens either explicitly or at any rate through social practices of data recording, be they in sensory or some other form. Thus the material *duplicates* the world in data form [*datenförmig*] – just as, since the printing press, the crucial aggregations and interconnections have unfolded in written form [*schriftförmig*].

But here is what needs to be said in the first place. Clearly the world of data, the informatization of the world, is not really in scientific form or science-like [*wissenschaftförmig*]; conversely, the new data situation rather affects science itself. Klaus Mainzer aptly encapsulates this in one concept by saying that he sees in Big Data the danger of an 'end of theory' – that is, a theoryless 'muddling through' in the sense of simply generating something from existing data because it can be generated. This may well be useless for scientific purposes, if there are no questions grounded in hypotheses or if no theory appropriate to the complexity of the subject is available. For all other applications, however, this *muddling through* may be the method of choice. Accordingly, it is on very rare occasions that Big Data strategies are research strategies.[20] In most cases they are simply a *technique* – that is, a simplified version of the ends–means relation. The (tautological) function of technology is that it functions, not that it produces conviction (scientifically). This is why the dataformness [*Datenförmigkeit*] of the world enables other functions besides the scientific ones. One may compare this to the fact that the spread of writing has brought into the world not only the proclamation of God's word, or the written form of arguing and convincing larger circles of readers, but also other forms, which have nothing to do with these functions. Like writing, the dataformness of the relationship with the world *duplicates* the world in a way that makes new forms of processing possible. I will discuss the matter of duplication in detail, because it has a social–theoretical potential to determine the function of data technology and digitalization with greater precision. I will begin by taking up again the thread of Husserl's criticism of science.

Cybernetics and the feedback of information

Strictly speaking, data technology creates a double independence of scientoid forms, just as Husserl described it in his crisis piece. On the one hand, there is this process of distancing of the database from the concrete acts of understanding, grasp, and perception – a process that, in a digital world, concerns the structure of the data themselves. So what Husserl says for example about physics gets radicalized here – namely that the mathematized form of data loses any sense of what it originally referred to. On the other hand, however, the data do not only become independent of the original formations they represent, but they become the actual material to be dealt with. We are no longer dealing with representing something in data form – the data themselves are the material with which something is created: insights and, beyond that, products, services, political control, persecution, espionage, technological control, and so on.

What Husserl criticized about scientific practice was to become shortly afterwards the very principle of scientific theorizing: the difference between digital data and the analog world – which is no longer perceived simply as a disturbance or as a kind of rash existential oblivion [*Seinsvergessenheit*] of theory but should lend it a helping hand in the future.

In his critique of technology, Martin Heidegger radicalized the idea of Husserl's crisis paper once again, then turned it into a general critique of culture and modernity. But Heidegger understood better than anyone the significance of cybernetics as a philosophical challenge, insofar as everything is reduced to homogeneous information. In his Athens lecture of 1967, 'The Provenance of Art and the Destination of Thought', he writes: ' The world of science becomes a cybernetic world. The cybernetic blueprint of the world presupposes that steering or regulating is the most fundamental characteristic of all calculable world-events. The regulation of one event by another is mediated by the transmission of a message, that is, by information. To the extent that the regulated event transmits messages to the one that regulated it and so informs it, the regulation has the character of a positive feedback-loop of information.'[21] Feedback and control are possible only because everything is translated into information and loses its firm shape. Heidegger does not simply describe how data technology increases but how references change: data are matched with data, information is sharpened against information. So the reference point is not the represented world itself, but the interplay of pieces of information that give one another feedback.

It is no coincidence that Heidegger contrasts cybernetics or modern technology to τέχνη (*technē*), that is, art, whose original name in ancient Greek is this very word. Art – 'that which reveals the form and gives the measure', in Heidegger's idiom[22] – refers to analog form, indeed to shape, something that itself is what it is. In this sense, technological information is indeed *existentially* oblivious or oblivious of being [*seinsvergessen*]. There is no need to adopt Heidegger's vocabulary to recognize here a thoroughly eloquent, forceful, and appropriate description of what this is all about: information is stripped of its shape, and only because of this can it inform or enable feedbacks, that is, refer to different things at the same time.

In that lecture, Heidegger goes on to say: 'The world as represented in cybernetic terms abolishes the difference between automatic machines and living beings. It is neutralized in this indiscriminate processing of information.'[23] One underestimates this diagnosis when reading it only as the radical critique of science and technology that it undoubtedly also is. But at the same time it is a precise analysis of the precondition of all digitalization, namely that 'uniformity' in which '[h]umanity also has its place assigned to it'.[24] If, for example, one takes a look at the molecular–biological and genetic analysis of nature (even of human beings), it does indeed solidify into information processing. Genetics identifies encodings that are able, say, to describe quantitatively the fact that *Homo sapiens sapiens* shares more than 90 per cent of genetic codes with *Pan troglodytes*, the common chimpanzee. We could not say the same about the difference in shape between ape and human, although there are many similarities precisely in the difference between ape and human. But in this case it is even possible to specify a calculable percentage of informational identity, which in 90 per cent of genetic sequences really is and means identity. Even the human, even the brain, even the physiology of perception, and even the state of consciousness of humans (and related anthropoids) can be represented as information. The radicality of Heidegger's diagnosis is that he takes the cybernetic form really seriously; it is not just an add-on but becomes a prominent means of representation. Shape, that which he calls 'art', is digitalized, as we would say today.

The precondition for the kind of technology that is constitutive for modernity depends precisely on the possibility of making the incommensurable commensurable. What is different – different shapes, different analog forms – acquires the shape of information, as I described in the example of the computer-aided composition of Bach music. Perhaps now it becomes clear why I chose this example: it is an artistic phenomenon, a phenomenon that lives on the distinction of shape [*Gestalt-Unterscheidung*], and, to be a melody, it must first be constituted subjectively, in concrete, alive acts of a consciousness, in Husserl's sense. And even this shape is to be translated into information; it can not only be stored but even generated digitally – and the concrete, material shape of the columns of numbers that bring potential music into digital shape is formally no different from that of data sets that can express something else, too.

Perhaps it makes sense to pause here. So far the argument oscillates between description of a phenomenon – namely digitalization – and a question about the categories under which this description should unfold. Husserl's and Heidegger's critique of science and technology make it clear that the objectivity of the phenomenon is reflected even in the description of the thing itself. Julian Müller speaks pointedly of 'cybernetic orders of meaning'.[25] Of course, we have not learned much about digitalization itself so far. But the thesis developed in the first chapter ties the describability of digitalization to the basic structure of modern society itself; thus the thesis depends on developing in the first place the categories with which digitalization can be described – and doing so with the help of an appropriate description of society. This comes close to a *petitio principii* – a circular argument – because the reference problem of the digital is grounded in the claimed digitality of society. However, the reference problem does not exist in a positive sense but is absolutely consistent with the matter itself.

The same goes for the question of the objectivity of science as put by Husserl and for the question of informatization in Heidegger's conceptualization. Husserl's thesis in the crisis paper is, pointedly, that the diagnosis of a decoupling of the objectivity claims of modern science from any reflection of the phenomenal constituting acts of the observing subject, and thus also from the observer's lifeworld, must establish a theory of observation that reaches 'the things themselves' (as the slogan of phenomenology runs) only via the detour of phenomenal representation. And Heidegger exacerbates the situation by assuming that modern technology, with its cybernetic feedback, has an active power that lies not just in the effectiveness of such technological methods but in a completely new form of referring to the world [*Weltbezug*]. With the help of the term Gestell, Heidegger describes with a fair amount of precision how this new kind of technology was not simply chosen, but itself placed the observer where she finds herself.

In an almost materialist manner, Heidegger points out that humans have no choice but to be drawn into the categories of exploitation of the technological age. In his famous 1949 lecture 'Das Ge-Stell', almost twenty years before the Athens lecture, Heidegger is not yet able to speak about cybernetics but must content himself with the 'machinery' of classical industry. But he states, with great sociological precision:

> The human of this age, however, is positioned into positionality even when he does not stand immediately before machines or in the industry of a machinery. The forester, for example, who surveys the felled wood in the forest and who to all appearances still goes along the same paths in the same way as his grandfather is today positioned by the lumber industry. Whether he knows it or not, he is in his own way a piece of inventory in the cellulose

stock and its orderability for the paper that is delivered to the newspapers and tabloids that impose themselves upon the public sphere so as to be devoured by it.[26]

If, as an experiment, we cancel Heidegger's critical attitude to culture and modernity and emancipate ourselves from the knowledge of his deplorable entanglement with the political denials of modernity, this still has the resonance of a highly modern diagnosis. At least it does not differ fundamentally from, say, Bruno Latour's early diagnosis that we have never been modern – in the sense that our access to nature, to technology, to the human, and to modern society does not conform to that all-too-simplistic idea that the sphere of culture and society is the realm of freedom and the sphere of nature is the realm of necessity, which since time immemorial had to be both understood and controlled.[27] The relationships are not just reversed but restructured, and we are *positioned* [*gestellt*] in them, in the sense that the meanings of things are a result of their configurations.

The example of the 'forester' shows that what happens there in the analog mode, shapewise, cannot evade the processing of information just by itself. Although in this early text Heidegger does not (and cannot) even mention the processing of information, the example is striking: not only is the felled wood subjected to the measuring logic of the wood industry and wood market, but this also makes possible the information technology of the newspaper. Maybe it's just a literary surplus, but it illustrates the intertwining of reflection and subject that Heidegger wants to bring to the concept of *Ge-Stell*.

Consequently, theoretical forms of description and subject matter fall into one. With the description, means of describing also develop – for the description. Heidegger conceptualized this connection very clearly: not only did he claim, at the phenomenal level, that technology was currently turning into information technology; he even had the insight that the only way of thinking with which one could understand this transformation must also adopt this form, or at least take it seriously. In an interview with *Der Spiegel* that took place in 1966 but was published only in 1976, he even predicted that cybernetics would replace philosophy.[28]

In this respect Heidegger's philosophical diagnosis is fundamentally different from diagnoses which discuss 'metrics' or numerical form as a contingent kind of technology. Such diagnoses are legion; think for instance of Jerry Z. Muller's critique of the numerical recording of all human activity,[29] or of Cathy O'Neill's criticism of scoring strategies.[30] While these diagnoses are not wrong, neither is the critique of some of these strategies; but they hardly ask why such a technology has been able to push through. To think that this is just a result of political or economic decision-making is to underestimate its significance. As a reminder, I have argued in chapter 1 that the metric interpretation of society is practically constitutive of the complex social structure of modernity – that society itself had already adopted a digital form that attracts precisely this kind of technology.

Now, we must not confuse the figure of thought of Heidegger's *Ge-Stell* with a historical–philosophical theory and with a kind of historical necessity. Rather this philosophy of technology foregrounds the conversion of our reference to the world [*Weltbezug*] to a cybernetic form. Then the statement that cybernetics will be philosophy's heir means that the ways and modalities of describing what is must indeed make use of certain means if they are not to fail at their very object. This is why I speak of the mutual dependence of means of knowledge and object of knowledge. Ernst Cassirer conceptualized something similar in the formula we do not see objects, we see object-like.[31] Today we see cybernetically, whether we like it or not.[32]

Meanwhile, Heidegger's prediction that cybernetics will replace philosophy has become true. It is not just that information is now the matter through which the world can be explained across all kinds of knowledge. Even more, only information allows those feedback loops to which Heidegger attributed something like inescapability. Like the forester, who is dragged into the industrial processing logic of his activities without any participation on his part, without any motives or intentions of his own, the cybernetic model of the technology that Heidegger speaks of is constructed in such a way that the incommensurable takes place according to the same principle and in the same medium the cybernetic model of the technology that Heidegger speaks of is constructed in such a way that the incommensurable is to be found according to the same principle and in the same medium in each case. This is not about information concerning the world, but about the fact that the world can be described only through information and that this produces inescapable forms of coherence, which Heidegger captured in the concept of *Ge-Stell*.

Now, the object here is not to come up with a philosophical interpretation of Heidegger, but to work out the mode of thinking that provided the foundation for what would later be called digitalization – which obviously means more than expressing everything numerically and translating it into quantitative entities. This is in fact about the function of such an occurrence. A key to answering the question about function seems to be that world references [*Weltbezüge*] are described in their self-referentiality – an idea that is not at all alien to the history of European thought: it ranges all the way from problems of reflection in logic, conceived of as an aspect of the self-reference of propositions and arguments, to the philosophy of consciousness.

Walter Schulz in his epochal 1972 book *Philosophy in a Changed World* has articulated this idea particularly well. The difference from classical philosophy is that this is no longer about understanding a cohesive order; the subject of research is not something external to research – it is created by research in the first place. Schulz, too, places cybernetics in a key position, on the grounds that it is more than a research method or a technique – actually it answers philosophical questions in new ways: 'Cybernetics can no longer be understood through traditional concepts of science according to which science is the grasp of a fixed reality. Cybernetics reveals instead a new concept of science: knowledge is a reflection on possible knowledge, in other words knowledge should constantly overtake itself, in the sense of technological increase.'[33] He sees in Kant that tipping point at which the fight for primacy (so to speak) between the inside and the outside is decided in favour of the former. Since then, he says, we can no longer return to the basic experience of the process that Schulz calls moving towards 'internalization'[34] – either in the history of philosophy, treated as a philosophy of subjectivity and as existential philosophy, or in the history of science, conceived of as priority of method over reference to the subject.

The digitalization of communication

The priority of method over reference to the subject certainly becomes most obvious in communication theory, which laid the groundwork for the distinction between digital and analog forms as early as the 1940s with Claude Shannon and Warren Weaver's communication theory; and what they had in mind above all was a model of the technological transfer of information.[35] Shannon and Weaver demonstrated that communication happens only if there is a certain probability that information can be generated from signals. The degree of probability depends on whether the signals conform to an order that can be deciphered by the receiver's resources and is plausible for the receiver. This means that communication cannot be a simple transfer of information, because the receiver cannot passively receive signals but must be in a position to decode them by him- or herself. Hence there is always room for manoeuvre, which in the technological theory of communication consists primarily in how high the bandwidth of the transmission is. Shannon and

Weaver's ultimate goal was to calculate with precision how much of the signals could be omitted without loss of information. Thus the receiver must calculate the probability vis-à-vis other possibilities, depending on the strength of the signal.

This is not alien to social communication among natural persons. If you want to understand your counterpart, you will organize the signals according to how probable the various possible meanings seem to you. What Shannon and Weaver call '*mathematical* communication theory' is the calculus by which a receiver calculates the probability of the signal.

These two pioneers of communication theory were initially interested in the technological transmissibility of signals and in questions of depth of focus, clarity, and signal strength, in order to enable communication. But the semantic form of communication also depends on probabilities of meanings. We may have known this already from classic hermeneutics; for, if it is possible to understand in different ways linguistic expressions – from a simple utterance made by a fellow human to divinely revealed holy scriptures – then processes of understanding are ultimately subject to some probability management of the appropriate meanings, no matter who or what calculates the degree of appropriateness in each case. And in everyday situations it is enough for communication partners to know the conventional frame in which the communication takes place. After all, when it comes to connections, conventions are nothing but an enhancement of the probability rate. If I hold the door open for somebody, this is a mix of politeness, invitation, and avoidance of collisions – and there is no need to make any of this explicit. Consequently, most communications situations get by with a relatively simple probability calculation, whereas in uncertain situations the strength of the signal must be increased: if I cannot assume that my counterpart more or less knows what I mean, I have to put it under sharper focus, so as to increase connectivity.

Even everyday situations are constructed in a way that resembles Shannon and Weaver's question about the level at which the transmission rate can be reduced. They follow the principle of economy: make explicit only as much as is necessary for dealing with a situation. After all, modern everyday life among strangers depends on the fact that people do not interact as whole persons; only pieces of information get checked against one another. Everyday life is a feedback process – successful communication refers to successful communication and information creates new information, while completely different possibilities are ignored they must be updated, under disturbing conditions. That is why in modern societies humans who play the roles they are expected to play can do without many pieces of information that could have hardly been ignored in less modern social forms.

Here are a few striking examples to illustrate the point: in almost all foreseeable situations, my counterpart's denomination does not matter at all, and there are even more situations in which information about gender or ethnic markers is discounted. Even the intentions of a person may be ignored when it comes to everyday communication, which is practically technified. And wherever this does not succeed, that is where situations render explicit more information than is necessary, this may be increasingly perceived as a disruption; we are more accustomed to scandalizing it. But one must take it into account that 'irrelevant' information of this sort may seem disruptive only because everyday communication in complex modern societies is practically *technified*. It is worth applying here Heidegger's concept of technology as a counterpart to the 'gestalt-facing' form with connotations of 'art' – that is, the analog form oriented towards the concrete gestalt. Simply reducing the other to playing a role in a certain situation actually makes that person a bearer of information. The less I need to know about that person, the more I know about how I can and may benefit from him or her. Everyday roles are actually pieces of information that cast the individual into technological form – technological in the sense that the role is somehow the social–technological form of reducing signal strength in spite of communicating effectively – or precisely because of it.

It is precisely the individual's reduction to being just an information bearer in certain situations – a diminished information bearer in a network of possible meanings – that increases enormously that individual's degree of freedom. It is a high achievement of civilization that we do not have to look at other people in everyday life as complete humans but can reduce them cybernetically, as it were, to a few roles within information streams and hence hold them to be virtually indifferent. If you don't believe this to be an achievement, try putting yourself in the shoes of someone who is always perceived by others in his or here complete 'gestalt', with skin and hair, so to speak. In that situation women will remain restricted to their existence as women, Blacks to their skin colour, disabled people to their vehicles, and homosexuals to their sexual orientation. Shannon and Weaver could not have targeted all this in their communication theory. Nevertheless, in terms of sociology of knowledge, its symbolism should not be underestimated on the grounds that modern society can really be understood only as a cybernetic information machine that has no common gestalt. We are dealing with an entity that actually does not consist of firm analog relations between humans but is a system of mutually reinforcing information and communication streams.

The theoretical means necessary for this must be adequate to the nature of modern society – this is precisely what Heidegger had critically in mind; but an affirmative description is needed if full understanding is to be achieved. Here the internal interconnectedness of theoretical means and subject is taken to extremes, and certainly has reached its peak with sociological systems theory. Luhmann's systems theory was criticized first and foremost for not considering humans to be parts or elements of social systems and for locating them instead within their environment. Luhmann describes systems exactly as communication systems, that is, systems whose internal dynamics are acquired through the succession and hence informational feedback of communications.[36]

In this respect, in the last resort social systems can be described only as *cybernetic* systems: systems that control themselves each in its present act and develop structures because processes become selective: in this way they prove and perpetuate themselves. They increase the probability of certain connections, and thus enable a kind of simplicity and predictability that we call social structures.[37] None of this happens without the participation of humans, but not in their analog overall form – whatever that may be – but in the form in which humans are taken into account in concrete systems. In modern everyday life, humans are always taken into account according to the information-processing rules that are in place in different systems – as payers, consumers, or employees in the economic system, as voters or opinionated speakers in the political system, as conflicting parties in the legal system, as fathers, mothers, or children in the family, as students in the educational system, as participants in concrete interactions, as members of associations or parties, churches, or trade unions. Only such a society can emancipate itself from making, say, gender, skin colour, or denomination into a discriminating criterion for memberships of other kinds. Mind you – it can emancipate itself, but sometimes it does not. But this can be criticized only because humanity does not feature in the gestalt-like compactness of its particular contexts; it features *digitally*, that is, as information value.

I have a claim to a state benefit, for example, because I am entitled to it on the strength of a specific information situation, not because I am judged as a person, in toto. The digitalization of people as information bearers is very much an achievement of civilization, precisely because it makes it possible for the individual not to be tied down too much to one overall shape, which always limits one's degree of freedom. This is why modern law has developed for example the institution of subjective rights, which grants the individual enforceable rights while disregarding the person. And – another example – this is why the decision of early Christianity to dispense with circumcision and strict dietary rules is a universalizing achievement: then it is possible to accept individuals while disregarding the person (notwithstanding that the concrete practice of Christianity has repeatedly undermined this attitude). In this sense Christianity digitalizes the human being by adjusting the transmission rate of communication to external conditions: in the past, being able to accept members of other religions; today, getting along in a pluralist society.

Such examples, which are only hinted at here but are nevertheless clear, demonstrate that there are good reasons, appropriate to the subject, not only for preferring theoretical constructions oriented towards cybernetics and information theory but even for regarding the subject itself as a subject of this kind. The complexity of modern society really necessitates that humans – and, as we are going to see, also other attribution entities – can be described in the form of information. This is exactly why it makes sense to conceive of humans in their compact wholeness in the environment of social systems.

This, by the way, is how you take the individual really seriously, because our lives must be led in a compact fashion. We are tied to our bodies, to physical and mental continuity. Unlike information systems and social systems, human lives cannot be interrupted, they cannot differentiate themselves but are tied to their own linearity and psycho-physical existence. For this very reason, they obviously move at a level of reality that is different from that of social systems, which in complex modern societies do not depend at all on compact representations of humans. 'The human' disappears – or, as Heidegger said with a shudder in the 1949 lecture, '"[t]he human" exists nowhere'.[38] It is rather determined by something that cannot even be expressed in the categories of the human. Sociologically speaking, the dynamics of the social cannot be imagined starting from the human being; they must be described in terms of information technology, as the momentum of a system of communicative connections, in Heidegger's sense.

On the whole, theories of the disappearance of humankind have seen a boom, if we think of Michel Foucault's probably most quoted sentence that the human being is disappearing 'like a face drawn in sand at the edge of the sea'.[39] This is not moral anti-humanism, it is not a rejection of or contempt for the human; at best, it is a kind of methodological and theoretical anti-humanism that pays heed to the fact that the momentum of knowledge, meanings, information, and the like cannot be described using categories of human capability. This still lends itself to being described, with Heidegger, in a gesture of cultural–critical shudder, or with Foucault and his indifference, or with Luhmann and his analytical sharpness – which at the same time has the normative component of considering what the alternative might be: the theory of a strict representation of the human being, according to which 'the human' becomes a regulative idea rather than an empirical category?[40]

It makes sense, then, not to take persons, humans, individuals as elements of social systems, not least in order to describe in greater empirical detail that this way the individual, and I mean the unique single person, is and can be taken considerably more seriously in his or her possibilities and limitations. Placing the individual within the environment of social systems must be considered a subject-related decision, which has much to do with the digitality of the social structure. On this, Luhmann writes tersely: 'Besides, there is no apparent reason why a place in the environment of the social system should be such a bad place. I, for one, would not like to swap.' He warns against any hypostatization of representations of the human, which in most cases are in essence ideals of humanhood: 'All too often, ideas of the human have served to harden role asymmetries through external references and to withdraw them from the social disposition [*sozialen Disposition*]. Here one should recall race ideologies, or the distinction between the chosen and the damned.'[41] And one can ponder that ultimately such 'representations of the human' evade the potentials for uncertainty that complex societies need.

Shannon and Weaver's achievement would be the first to point to the potential for uncertainty in information. They put forward in the end a theory of the *improbability* of communication, and they upgraded the receiver. Even receiving signals is an active process that, against the background noise of possible signals, must identify the one that makes a difference insofar as it may be a piece of information. *The receiver receives according to its own rules of processing that the sender cannot decide!*

This kind of communication theory is not about the conditions for the possibility of connectivity, of connections. It is about the operative aspect of communication, not about its content. This is what Heidegger, referring to Nietzsche, meant by 'the victory of the method': it is not about content, not about form, but about the informational shape of the sort of communication that is capable of feedback. And this was exactly one of Shannon and Weaver's intentions: to be able to figure out, through a mathematical – in other words formal and content-insensitive – communication theory, how much interference is tolerable for communication, so that the technological setup of signal strength, kind, depth, and bandwidth may be calculated on this basis. Thus communication has to do not so much with transmission management in the strict sense as with a particular kind of vagueness management. There is no need to know exactly what the other has said, perhaps it is even *impossible* to know. And indeed, because communication does not depend on this kind of knowledge but, on the contrary, is functionally necessary only because there is no real one-on-one transmission from A to B, communication may be called a 'non-knowledge machine'.[42]

This communication theory does not measure communication by connections, by transmission, by successful understanding, or by agreement but by interruptions, that is, by the places where transmission is not trivial but always generates something different from what was the starting point of the communication. Information is not transmitted, but communication becomes an information problem as a result of interruptions between sender and receiver. Through its mutual character, this kind of communication generates what Heidegger called feedback. In theory, then, only this information game is of real interest; it is to be determined completely independently of content, and thereby is open to every possible content. And it opens the concept of information to the digital world, where the transmission of information, or its processing, are anyway independent of substance and content but start out from internal patterns – that is, from feedback patterns of transmission networks. A classic hermeneutical understanding of communication, whose object is to understand meanings and their cultural relevance, becomes a theory of informational probabilistics.

Once again, it is Heidegger who conceptualizes this idea in a very poignant way:

> Through the leading ideas of cybernetics – information, steering, feedback – principal concepts like ground and consequence, cause and effect, which until now have been authoritative in the sciences, are transformed in a way that one could almost call uncanny. For this reason cybernetics can no longer be characterized as a grounding science. The unity of the thematic field of knowledge is no longer the unity of ground. This unity is in a strict sense technical.[43]

Thus Heidegger sees the classical categories of scientific thought – one could say, everything in Aristotle's table of categories that was relevant as a basic framework of concluding and connecting, of reasoning and argumentative thought – becoming meaningless, at least as a fundamental figure of grasping the world. Rather cybernetics generates in his view a form that is interested in the feedback of information, a development that could 'make one day the historical humanistic disciplines, too, subject to the claim of cybernetics'.[44]

With Walter Schulz, I demonstrated earlier that the character of science changes: it is no longer knowledge of a world that is independent of the knower, but reflection on *possible* knowledge, that is, on a knowledge that arises out of the processes themselves. Thus theory–method and subject dissolve at the same time. Just as a hierarchical world needs a theory form organized into hierarchical levels and a somewhat monotheistic–monologic world with an ensuing preference for the One needs a unity-generating theory form, so, too, a dynamized and complex world needs a theory form that is interested in the dynamic structure of order and in feedback processes.

If we look closely, a dynamic closure [*Geschlossenheit*] emerges between pieces of information that refer to themselves and to each other. In fact such dynamics of unity or coherence have announced themselves already before in philosophy: we need only remember that in modern philosophy the being of the world can be inferred only through the consciousness of the world – as transcendental philosophy, as phenomenology, or as philosophy of language. World carriers, so to speak, emerge everywhere that are characterized above all by immanence – the immanence of consciousness or the immanence of language. Coherence becomes a generator of openness, which is the reason for the problems of justification and description in modern philosophy when it comes to 'reality' – a reality that cannot be immediately accessed. This is why philosophy ended up being a kind of thinking that had to give itself a reflexive account of its own possibilities of grasping the world. Here again, then, we find coherences – but strictly speaking these are coherences in references to meanings, in logical relations, in causal statements, in inner contradictions and their resolutions, and so on.

The dynamic of closure

The above considerations are still searching for the reference problem of the digital, of digitalization, of the triumph of data processing, of informatization, whose theoretical foundations were obviously laid long before their technological implementation. Remarkably, all these theoretical innovations refer to forms and dynamics of unity or coherence. We are no longer dealing with the stubbornness of an imagined, cognition-dependent reality but with a *dynamic of closure* that includes cognition in itself.

- Perception itself is physiologically dependent on translating the diversity of stimuli from the outside into signals, and then relating them to one another. Out of the manifoldness of sensual impressions a world must be formed that appears just like the world.
- The world of consciousness refers to the world by referring to itself.
- The world of signs does not refer to the world but to itself, and thus still to the world. This is the paradox of the sign, which stands for itself and at the same time for the signified.
- The linguistic world refers to the extra-linguistic world exclusively through its own means, namely linguistic ones.
- Meaningful references always refer to something else, but always in the form of meaningful references.
- Systems never operate within their environments but regulate their contact with the environment through self-contact and in the form of self-contact.
- The data world knows its outside only in a given form, as data.
- The priority of the method over the subject reference in science refers to the fact that a methodically controlled science experiences by itself that the modality of its theoretical and methodological constitution creates the subject it finds; this is not to say that it was not already there, but now it is brought to a form adequate to science.

As already indicated in the sign paradox, all these examples call attention to the paradox that in each case the medium stands for itself and for the other at the same time.

In the social sciences and in cultural studies, the term 'constructivism' has come to be used in this context. This is indeed a makeshift solution. The fact that reality must be *construed* comes along, then, with an almost critical gesture, which gives an impression of changeability, of possible alternatives, of a liquefied perception of reality. But the term may as well be misleading. The historical relativity of meanings and the variability of cultural forms is, after all, old hat. Ultimately constructivism is only a variant, perhaps naïve, of an equally naïve scientistic belief that, in spite of everything, in the end one will be able to determine the *ens realissimum* unambiguously. That reality is construed is not the problem – that everything, literally everything, is a result of operations, even a result of cognitive operations, is the real information. The dynamics of coherence I am discussing here point to the operativity of their subject and to the fact that the coherence of operations, quite obviously, is not just a contingent theoretical decision but must have something to do with the current form of processing reality.[45]

The example of the Bach algorithm should be now easier to understand: there is no outside for networked data, they are just feedbacks of themselves within the medium. Information refers to information – this was already stated in Husserl's critique of science, which objected that scientific data and concepts had lost sight of the condition of their own constitution – namely their relation to their outside and to the acts that refer to this outside. And this argument was also upheld by Heidegger, who considered the reference to information to be with other information and thus emphasized the self-implicative nature of information technology.

This epistemologizing perspective of a dynamic of coherence makes visible not only the *observer* but above all *observing as an operation*. And operations of this kind draw attention to the system formation, to technological systems of self-control achieved through internal use of data, to neuronal systems that reproduce themselves internally through interconnections, to mental systems made up of consciousness events, and to social systems made up of communicative events. To some extent, such systems perform internal reference possibilities. They generate the very forms through which they secure contact with reality.

This must not be confused with an Aristotelian theory of forms in which any actual being (*ens actu*, 'being in act') is preformed in a potential being (*ens potentia*, 'being in potentiality'). There is no unmoved mover at work above everything, but operations must somehow develop into reference possibilities. Within shaped spaces they must point to things that can be distinguished, they must provoke information values, and they must carry at least so much unconditionality that they are not considered part of the dull background noise of the world. This is the only way for the medium of meaning to take communicative forms and to alert consciousness to the processes of attention and memory. Both consciousness and communication are addicted to the possibilities of meaningful reference, and their dealers are at every corner. But even these dealers can no more than make promises – empty promises, for even the junk they sell only continues the *dynamic of coherence*, and breaking out of this dynamic, again, does nothing but continue it. There is no escape.

Twentieth-century thought is full of such notions of coherence. Ferdinand de Saussure's foundation of linguistic science is probably paradigmatic in this respect. He conceived of a meaning-generating coherence of language as a reference context. Language contains 'neither ideas nor sounds that existed before the linguistic system, but only conceptual and phonic differences that have issued from the system'.[46] At least since de Saussure, the genesis of meaning has not been tied to any relation of adequacy between sign and signified, but to a language-internal reference context of meanings, which have to create their own representation, so to speak. According to de Saussure, there is no correspondence between sign and thing or sign and signified, but only between a sound or written image and an idea. Admittedly they are not isolated but form a network. It is the difference between signs that can give the individual sign a meaning within a space of meaning – but without any *objective* counterpart in the sense of object reference. The frame of reference is the use of the signs, their relationing, and their testing. What de Saussure describes in this way is a coherence dynamic that substantiates the linguistic–philosophical insight that, in linguistic respects, the non-linguistic can be expressed only through language, or rather that designations know their outside only in the mode of designation.

This idea of closure was even more radicalized by Derrida's deconstruction process. Derrida developed the method of *différance*. Derrida used the French noun *différance* to refer to the distinction between presence (a primordial presence) and supplementarity (the retroactive perception of a primordial presence). In this context he refers to Husserl's *Phenomenology of Internal Time Conciousness* and to Husserl's idea of a present primordial impression that can be perceived only retroactively. Derrida accuses Husserl of claiming an immediate presence with this present of primordial impression and counters that there is always a temporal displacement (*différer*) that complements the presence in such a way that this presence can be perceived only from the displaced position in time. To make it clear that the difference between presence and its perception is irreducible in the first place and, second, is not even to be seen because of its fundamental nature, Derrida changes *difference* to *différance*, which can be recognized only in writing – it cannot be heard.[47]

What remains is always only *the signs of something*; but, paradoxically, this *something* is accessible qua *something* only through its name and, because of the differing temporal and spatial displacement (*différer*!), it is no longer an original something. What remains is only the *sign*, whose difference from the signified cannot be calculated, since the other side of the difference does not have any value.

In our context, the crucial thing is that the method of *différance* creates the 'totality of the sign'.[48] Consequently only the sign can be observed, but not the difference between signifier and the signified.

The result is, as Derrida explains in *Writing and Difference*, 'that the domain or play of signification henceforth has no limit'.[49] Thus, after the deconstruction of the metaphysical presupposition of presence, the sign takes the place previously occupied by that which is prior to the sign: the signified. As a result, a leeway is released whose boundaries are defined only by the game itself. Once the difference has liberated the sign from its subject and from its reference, signs refer exclusively to themselves. The world of the signified is deconstructed into a world of signs.

To understand the cultural meaning, if you will, of the data world, we need these detours into linguistic theory and the theory of signs, into the theory of self-reference and of coherence dynamics. For you will miss the point of digitalization if you take it to be only a technology that implements its most important forms of data or information processing as a transfer of analog signals into electronic data. The medium of 'electronic data' creates possibilities and forms that would be impossible with other media. There is no need to explain it in detail, because in all this time it has become a self-evident theme: the media – from words written in books up to the newspaper, the radio, the television, and even the computer – do not just depict some reality: they use their own means to create a new reality, which is strictly bound to the medium. This has been thoroughly discussed – and the same holds for the data world, whose mediality has hardly been an object of reflection so far. What we have learned in the meantime about the close interconnection of medial substrates and the forms they make possible actually culminates in the theory of deconstruction, insofar as Derrida's theory is able to conceptualize the medium's invisibility to itself. The distinction between medium and form, as Fritz Heider had it,[50] points to the fact that sound can be heard as a form, but not air as a medium, although the sound is constitutively dependent on air as its carrier medium. This is also the case with the relation between language and linguistically communicated meaning – as well as with the relation between electronic data and data form. Data know the world only in data form and are inevitably dependent on themselves, because only what is in data form can register.

The parallel with the cybernetic self-reference of information in the absence of any clear contact with what the information is about should have become obvious. If deconstruction is still somewhat connected to the game of meaningful references, electronic data – information, in Heidegger's parlance – emancipate themselves even from the meaningfulness of the reference. Thus they can be universally deployed: the only thing they refer to is ultimately themselves. It seems that data technology can do even without *metaphysical complicity*, because metaphysical complicity results essentially from temporary illusions of presence.

Initially digitality means nothing but the representation of something in electrically or electronically measurable differences. These electric states radicalize the *dynamic of coherence*, insofar as they no longer allow even the illusion that they might represent anything other than the internal reference context and their probabilistic form of structural formation. Incidentally, this is not a matter of drawing mere parallels between ways of thinking and conceptualizing them; there's more at stake here. This is about the fact that digitalization is not external to our culture but is based precisely on experiences and forms that are constitutive of modern societies. Thus, in terms of a sociology of knowledge, it is neither coincidental nor meaningless that the *technical* formation of digitalization can be found in epistemic discourses. Heidegger's dictum that philosophy will be replaced by cybernetics was not just empty talk but showed high diagnostic potency. Essentially it anticipates the 'totality of the sign', on which the processing of idiosyncratic data lives. For data sets there is no outside, except in data form.

Thus only information refers to information by referring to differences within the reference context: in Saussure's model of signs [*Sprachraum*], to different designations; in Derrida's deconstruction, to the difference between signifier and signified; in data sets, to pieces of information that arise only because there are differences that make a difference, as Gregory Bateson famously put it.[51]

The self-referentiality of the data world

Thus far, this chapter has seen no technological characterization of data – only an epistemological or a sign-theoretical one. Data are forms that refer to a medium. As electronic data, as digital data, they are based on an electric medium whose binary nature will be discussed later. Their crucial feature is that they are idiosyncratic – obstinate. In the columns of numbers, signs, and electric excitation there is only the sign itself and nothing more. I have demonstrated this via the science-like nature of the digital, the operational coherence of self-generated data, and the fact that it is impossible for data to break out of themselves. Information refers, brutally and unyieldingly, only to itself, as Heidegger said, to a form that ultimately has no external contact. What is manifest in the data world, which wraps itself around practices of modern society, is closed in itself. All that data technology can do is find patterns – but not patterns of the world: patterns of the world in the form of its data-shapehood [*Datenförmigkeit*]. This has little to do with the fact that they are only quantifiable data – but a lot to do with the fact that the totality of the sign ensures that data refer to themselves almost self-sufficiently and can combine among themselves almost ad infinitum.

Perhaps the inconceivable potency of the data world already becomes clear at this point, at least in rudimentary form. This potency resides in its radical reducibility to being a sign form. The printing press was such a catastrophe for society because it ensured that the self-reference of the written word created a reality all of its own. Books refer to books refer to books refer to books refer to books – without end.

Thanks to the 'totality of the sign', the sign alone becomes observable – but not the difference between signified and signifier, between sign and referent. As a result, 'the domain or play of signification henceforth has no limit', as Derrida explains in *Writing and Difference*.[52] I remarked a little earlier, in connection with Derrida, that the world of the signified is deconstructed into a world of signs. Well, this is an exact description of what happens with data sets: they are at the same time boundless in their possibilities and radically limited to themselves. Their openness is a function of their closedness.[53] They do not know the world but only themselves, and yet they duplicate the world by what they do.

3

Multiple Duplications of the World

My initial question was: what reference problem does digitalization solve? My first answer was that since the nineteenth century the translation of the world into data and the identification of patterns have served most of all to make the invisible visible. The complexity of society, the multiplication of agencies, the forms of control with demanding requirements, the professionalization of economic, political–administrative, scientific, and (not least) military activities, all required the unveiling of latent structures, an operation for which the introduction of statistic methods is a basic prerequisite. And the condition of possibility for statistic representation is to image the world in the form of countable units and to code analog facts through discrete forms.

In a second step, I then pointed out that the coding of facts in data form is not an imaging of the world, but a process of a rather presuppositional nature. The bridge for this argument was the practices of data technology that I called scientoid because they resemble practical activities of scientific work. This perspective allows us to see that the data form itself – and this is its scientoid feature – develops a life of its own, a momentum of its own that prompted me, along with Heidegger's critique of technology, to interpret cybernetic control as a dynamic of coherence. The world of data is thus a radicalized version of sign immanence, as described in the Saussurean tradition and after that in Jacques Derrida's poststructuralism. Data duplicate the world but do not contain it. With the figure of the duplication of the world, I thus encounter another structural feature of modern societies – which in the final analysis urge their own digitality.

Data as observers

The duplication of the world through digital data is not an extrinsic aspect of modern society. It is not just a simple epistemological variation or gameplay that theoretical forms of a dynamics of coherence were established in the twentieth century in mathematics, in biological sciences, in general systems theory and in cybernetics, in textual and literary studies, in cultural studies and social sciences. This is directly connected to the experience that the description of realities of any kind must always also confront its own perspectivity. The priority of method over object reference in the sciences, the social storing of all actions, the cultural coding of meanings, and the individualization of life experience – all these are examples of the fact that the observer can remain invisible only if one invests a lot of energy in blocking out the perspectivity of one's own view. *Strictly speaking, the observer would have to be not introduced but faded out, because there is no observation without observer.* 'Fading out' is a nice metaphor for the fact that the claim for a non-perspective is a particular kind of perspective, which in turn makes demanding requirements.

Essentially, whoever disregards the fact that any contact to reality is always a certain kind of contact cannot see the complexity of the modern world. I have described elsewhere the complexity of modern society in detail; and I have built my critique of a complexity-forgetful reason [*Kritik der komplexitätsvergessenen Vernunft*][1] around the ideas of perspectival difference and the observer. The observer is ultimately the key to everything. Nothing can be described unless you describe it in an observer-relative modality; and, already with the European philosophy of consciousness, this has finally become an incontrovertible presupposition. Of course, the observer is a form whose significance can be described not just for consciousness. Also organisms, which delimit themselves from their environments, neuronal systems and brains, which process the variety of external stimuli as internal states, but even social systems, which operate with perspectives of their own and have system-specific environments, can be understood as observers.

This is relevant to a theory of digitalization and digitality insofar as even data or their use must ultimately be understood as *observers*. If it is true that data sets are somehow sign-immanent forms of feedback across states, then data themselves are specific kinds of observers, which can deal only with the reality that they themselves generate or that can be processed with their help.

This duplication of the world takes me to the next step on the way to explaining the cultural meaning of digitalization. It is no coincidence that twentieth-century thought theoretically encounters something like problems of representation. From the angle of a sociology of knowledge, the structural reference problem of modern society is the perspectivity of the respective access to the world. The decisive question is no longer what the world is. It is no longer the ontological question of qualities, but the epistemological question of access and representation. Now the world is accessible only in its duplicate – or, more precisely, only *as* a duplicate, which knows the original only in its duplicate form.

Not coincidentally, I formulated the figure of duplication for the first time in 2006, on the occasion of answering the question why art exists, indeed what problem art solves.[2] The function of art, the argument ran, is to call attention to two things. On the one hand, all perception of reality depends on one's own gaze, that is, on the contextures in which I myself perceive; on the other hand, most other social entities want to make this dependence on the gaze, the perspectivity of their gaze, as invisible as possible, whereas art points it out explicitly. In some sense art refers to an original that disappears the very moment it is artistically represented, because access to the original – the template, the world – is opened up and at the same time blocked by the work of art. Thus art points out that all perspectives duplicate the world, but they know the duplicate only from their own gaze.

This is not about arbitrariness and fluid dissolving, but about the opposite: *the fact that all perspectives are radically tied to themselves, to their operational closure.* At best, this duplication function can become reflective, but in reality – *in actu* – it is unescapable and mostly invisible. And precisely this is true not only of all known actors and operators who feature in society – political, economic, media, scientific, organizational and other systems – but indeed also for data, which depend on it in an extreme way, because they know the world only in their own data form and cannot break out of it. Everything that recurs there must itself adopt the form of data.

This is further indication of how deeply the world of data is inserted into the modern world. Perhaps the digital data world is just the radical intensification of a revolutionary mechanism by which signifier and signified move away from each other ever farther and thus the world of signs becomes autonomous, as Derrida describes it and as Niklas Luhmann's systems theory conceptualizes it with even greater precision, as the question of the unfolding of a paradox of self-referential forms. Or, to put it another way, initially the contexture of the data refers to nothing but itself. *Bach by Design* has never heard of Bach but can make his music heard.

In literary and textual studies, the idea of contexture has long been discussed under the heading of the paradox of signs. As it has already been explained, the difference between sign and referent, between signifier and signified, is not a measurable difference, as the signified, in other words the referent, can be represented only as a signifier, in other words as a sign. If we wanted to know whether our consciousness perceives the world correctly, we would have to be able to presuppose a perception-free perception of the world, in order to be able to conceptualize the difference between perception and the perceived, between consciousness and the world. Since such an option is not available to us, we always have to do with a duplicated reality in which the difference between original and image is a difference whose identity we assume but that cannot be bridged. Thus the duplication of the world always creates two halves: one half is the world as it appears to the observer, the other one is the world as it *is*. Then a paradoxical situation arises: this boundary cannot be overcome, yet in practice is always overcome.

This is not a matter of coming close somehow to some presence. It can only be a matter of focusing as sharply as possible on the self-supporting structure of signs. In order to capture this kind of logic in its entire complexity, Niklas Luhmann radicalizes Derrida's thought once again. In its focus on the relationship between signifier and signified, Derrida's deconstructivism still suffers from a kind of metaphysical complicity, as he himself admits. Now Luhmann's radicalization goes as follows: 'So giving form is an act of differentiation, and differentiation is an operation. And, like any operating, it requires time.'[3] Thus the form is self-supporting insofar as it refers to itself. Luhmann goes on: 'The question of what a form "is" is carefully avoided. At any rate, it cannot be something that makes something seem to be "present" (to allude to Heidegger and Derrida again). Operation can only happen or not happen.'[4] The form is paradoxical because it can refer only to itself, and it can stabilize itself only in itself. It contains, itself, that to which it refers.

In reality, data sets contain this form only as internal differences, as internal structures whose paradoxical nature consists in their referring to something else, which they simultaneously contain and do not contain. Duplication is, in a sense, an ironic description, because it calls attention to the paradoxical fact that what looks in practice like a duplication means exactly the opposite: a novel creation of something that exists only by virtue of being duplicated. But this form stabilizes itself, and does so in practice. We stabilize lifeworlds by duplicating the world, and at the same time we pretend that it is as it seems to be in the lifeworld. Otherwise nothing would be possible at all. Epistemologically, the form is a self-supporting structure; practically, it stands only for what it duplicates. This is what makes our society so complex and heterogeneous, both in the lifeworld and in practice.

The same holds for data. Data are highly aggregated forms, and at first they do not represent anything but themselves. In data sets, states refer to states; but in practice, through appropriate processing, they create a surface that can be understood in the lifeworld and thus does not represent a virtual reality, but one that is possible in practice. Precisely in this sense, data are self-referential observers, but observers that can be recombined almost without limit and duplicate the world according to their own rules. And this is exactly the sense in which algorithms are mathematically represented as recursive and iterative functions – which, by the way, are not completely computable, thanks to their self-referentiality.[5]

Duplications

Duplication can be best studied through the example of *writing*.[6] Writing duplicates the world insofar as it represents something without being that thing in the strict sense – hence insofar as it is ultimately something of its own, in which we can both see and not see the doubling. At the same time, writing points to difference from the authoritative speaker, whose speech act can be observed in real time with less immediacy, or rather in a manner that is less time-bound. In this respect the printed word, albeit seeming to have greater authority, finds it in reality more difficult to impose its authority. Writing must be *read*. The *readability of the world* allows itself to be studied through writing, as long as writing strives to be more than perceived: it is always to be read, even though things are positively present in the written form. This is what makes Luther's translation of the Bible, for example, so explosive; for the fact that things are being read now means that they may be read *in different ways,* or else reading would be only perception. Writing is the first digital medium, because it consists of signs that already convey aesthetically the idea that they are not what they stand for. This is particularly true of alphabetic scripts, which do this standing for what they are not in an internal context of reference. The duplication of the world through writing refers to the fact that *something* is not just referred to; rather this duplication generates the cosmos of a written world, a cosmos that has itself a cybernetic character.

In most cases we are not aware of this because the medium of writing – with its digital individual signs, the letters, which are oriented to sounds for the most part (or are the sounds oriented to them?) – has a digital form but in practice represents something exactly. Writing is a kind of duplication that, at least aesthetically, can do without the duplicated, because in a culture of writing things themselves are represented in a written form. Perhaps the strangest digital device in a smartphone, tablet, or data goggles is the *augmented reality* that digitalizes the shape of what you see and then underlays it with subtitles. You fly to New York City, point your smartphone to a house front, and see the words 'Rockefeller Center, 541.3 m' or 'Empire State Building, 381 m', perhaps accompanied by further information, of the sort you see in a museum – say, the Museum of Modern Art, where a plate next to a grey, blurred lithograph reads: *Elizabeth II*, 1966. We are not even aware of the duplication of the world through writing, because we are used to it. Writing is a reality of its own kind, a medium that enables forms, but in these forms it generates a reality of its own, which works only through feedback – basically through the mechanism of one information taking control of itself through another, which thus creates a world of which one can hardly say which is the original and which is the copy.

Language would have to be mentioned even before writing. If speaking is the most human of skills, every kind of human existence is always confronted with the duplication of the world. Even at the beginning of human existence, the world is already there, in the form of data, in the form of abstract information processed by language. Communication is nothing but the to-and-fro of information and understanding, eventfully temporalized in acts of communication, to put it in Niklas Luhmann's language.[7] Now, communication does not merge into language; there are also non-linguistic ways of communicating. But speech makes use of sound gestures that are obviously of a symbolic nature, that duplicate the world, and that can refer to the non-linguistic world, if only linguistically.

The referential contexts of language and writing refer in turn to the matter of social order. The functional differentiation of society, which I already pointed out in chapter 1, means only that modern societies are not homogenous; nor can they be described as social communities, but as systems with internal differentiations, according to different functions. Political, economic, scientific, legal, educational, media, religious, medical, artistic–aesthetic functions differentiate themselves side by side, in the course of a lengthy historical process – and such a kind of society, separated into a variety of functional systems, no longer has a centre and can no longer be explained through a single principle. The theory of functional differentiation of society is a theory that can show how chains of events of their own kind establish themselves *empirically* side by side and develop their own structures, making certain connections more probable. Thus almost everything that happens can be viewed from these different functional perspectives. To put it another way, *in a modern, functionally differentiated society, distinct duplications exist side by side, so that it makes a difference whether something is treated under its economic, political, aesthetic, educational, legal, scientific, or religious aspect.*[8] One can illustrate this with a relatively simple example – namely the question of what a book appears to be, in the context of communication.

From a *scholarly* perspective, one will enquire whether the views are correct, whether the literature cited does exist, whether the argumentation is valid, whether the hypotheses presented deal with questions of truth. As scholarly questions, views do not start from scratch but refer to other research, to theories, to published results, to academic traditions, and so on.

The situation is completely different from a *legal* perspective. There, in the case of a citation, for example, it is less relevant whether a statement is appropriate with respect to truth. What matters is rather whether the material has been quoted or plagiarized, whether quotations have been falsified, whether someone has been defamed, or whether personal rights have been violated. None of these questions can be answered or rendered less legally relevant by the fact that things are extremely convincing at the scholarly level. A plagiarism is not made worse when you plagiarize scholarly nonsense; and it is not made better when you plagiarize sound material.

Once again, completely different questions arise from an *economic* point of view – for example the matter of the price of a book compared to the author's fee. One could ask whether a paperback edition would not sell better than a hardcover, because it is cheaper. Or does it then look less valuable and deter people from buying it? Is there even a market for such books? Was the dust cover necessary? Or the thread binding? As for you, the reader, do you have sufficient economic resources to spend so much time with a book without earning money for the duration?

From a *mediatic* perspective, the book is relevant in several respects. Does it attract an audience? Is the language appropriate for the group it targets? Is it novel enough to be relevant to users or readers? Will it elicit reviews in scholarly journals and in popular magazines? And are there currently any topics in the media that might be counteracted especially for the sake of grabbing attention?

Or we could think of it from an *artistic–aesthetic* angle, which hardly holds here but represents a particular dimension precisely because of this. For example, one may ask whether the text could give the impression of being art, in other words whether it could be literary fiction. One will rapidly come to the conclusion that the answer is 'no' – which, admittedly, is possible only because we live in a society where this question, this aspect, this perspective can be raised at all. 'Non-art' is conceivable only in a place where art is something to be expected.

The same holds for the *educational* aspect. Can this book be used for university teaching, or perhaps even for teaching in secondary schools? Is it too complicated? Too long? Too academic? Or maybe too shallow? Such questions are not about truth but about educational goals, and they may be answered one way or another. Besides, as an author, I do have a presentation problem: the views advanced in a book are placed on a dialectic horizon, for I need to explain certain things in particular detail, given the expected audience, whereas others seem condescending to others, because they are too familiar. These are questions that deal with one and the same thing, namely a specific view, not just as a matter of truth but also as a matter of didactic form.

A *political* angle is also conceivable. Do the views express a right-wing or left-wing attitude, are there among them some that may be used in policy programmes, or that indicate that my next electoral decision should be different? All these questions are conceivable just inasmuch as they can be negated. And one could at least object that the theory of digitalization presented here is astonishingly indifferent from the politically and ethically relevant questions about digitalization.

And there are indeed aspects, albeit less relevant, that break through. For example, *religious* aspects should play a minor role, unless we still lived in a world where scientific theses had to be compatible with the Holy Scripture – which is no longer a requirement, at least in our climes. Even *medical* questions hardly arise.

This somewhat laboured example may serve if we want to imagine a mode of processing that is typical of social modernity. Almost nothing escapes being viewed from these different perspectives. And, even more importantly, these perspectives can hardly be mapped onto one another or get mutually compensated. One cannot improve a book's ideas through literary or artistic quality, or its sense of scholarly satisfaction through a higher price. And a beautiful cover with a sophisticated artistic design will not change the legal position in case of plagiarism – at the most, one will check even more closely whether the publisher has copyright for the illustrations as well.

Here is what I'm getting at: *all these angles and perspectives duplicate the world in such a way as to generate, with their forms,*

worlds in which constellations of problems and solutions reappear.
They produce, each, limited perspectives on the world, by focusing
on one aspect. That they exist in parallel with one another is sympto-
matic of a specific form of order, with which society obviously reacts
to a situation where factual options get differentiated side by side
when they are no longer really compatible with the traditional order
of a stratified society. If out there it was enough to focus on a top–
bottom scheme and to organize worldviews according to these kinds
of hierarchies of levels and strata, which can prescribe something
like an order valid for everyone and everything, in the past 300 years
new forms of connectivity and system building have taken place
right under our eyes, and these could no longer organize society
hierarchically, or with a view to an overall design. The example of
the fictitious book shows how difficult it is to consider any of the
processing rules mentioned so far to be the crucial one, the correct
one, or even the best one. They may be so from their own perspectives, but not if you look at the sum of perspectives as a totality.

We are in the habit of linking the complexity of modernity to the
fact that the functional differentiation of society reinforces all the
elements of this complexity: multiple coding, the growing number of
power factors, the loss of a coordinating centre, the multiplication
of perspectives, simultaneous interaction instead of serial causality,
and so on. Modernity appears to us as the historical exception
that generates complexity, indeed a generator of confusion. But
perhaps it is digitalization and the challenge of data sets, of big
data, of electronic information technology that sharpens our view
of modernity, for there is no doubt that digitalization is a disruption
in the routines of modernity. The catastrophe for the informational
balance sheets of society is similar to the one that the printing press
represented. For one thing, there was clearly a demand for printing
in late medieval society – there was enough of what could be written
down, and it found readers even if this technology had not been
designed for *this* purpose. Had this demand not been existing, the
technological invention of printing would have remained without
social consequences and maybe would never have made it.

The printing press prevailed because, quite obviously, it was
structurally capable of fulfilling a function: a possible problem
encountered a solution. But at the same time the routines of society
were not prepared to deal with the catastrophe that came with it.
On the one hand, through printed and distributed texts it was not
possible to control the reception of information as easily as through
immediate interaction. On the other, special skills emerged for the
description of more complex phenomena and became more and
more independent of place and time, and one discovered different

readings in the sense of a 'hermeneutics', that is, different possibilities of reception with perhaps equal rights.[9] It was a catastrophe
because the possibilities of writing and interpreting multiplied even
as they required new restrictions. At the same time, expertise could
be rendered more independent of concrete experiences, and loyalty
diminished in proportion with the fact that the increasingly growing
sources of knowledge called into question all previously known
compact forms of life or relationships of direct dependence.

Disruptions

It is the forms of duplication that ultimately constitute the routines
of modern society. These duplications generate those institutions
and institutional arrangements in companies and state organizations, in educational institutions, media institutions, and churches,
but also in individual ways of life that make up the user interface of
a society. Behind all this there always lies the logic of duplications, to
which we have become so accustomed that we take them for granted.

To understand digitalization's potential for disruption in all its
radicalism, one would have to attribute to it effects that are similar
to those of the printing press. Or, to put it another way, its radicalism
will be proven only if it turns out that digitalization represents a
catastrophe similar to that of printing. Thus the question is: *Is
digitalization a catastrophe?*

At any rate, it seems that digitalization – or the disruptions we
attribute to it – sharpen our view of the structure of modernity. Just
as the printing press perhaps pointed out the stabilizing function of
stratification and clear hierarchical models, the disruptions caused
by digitalization are likely to clarify, through their duplications, the
ordering and decomplexifying function of functional differentiation.

The next pages contain a few concrete examples.

- Through what is called big data applications, economic routines
  are disrupted when pricing, for example, encounters an audience
  that is offered the most affordable option on comparison portals
  for products and services. Customer loyalty changes as a result,
  so that one can no longer count on limited spaces of attention.
  Comparison portals not only cause enormous pressure on cost but
  also make distribution channels such as retail shops more difficult
  to reach. Business models emerge that eclipse the classic ones, thus
  overriding routines that previously ensured a balance that both
  providers and customers could equally manage. This is neither
  positive nor negative, and it is not really a serious disruption, but

already at this level it interferes with the routines of mutual stabilization of elements on which depends the long-term nature or
predictability of economic transactions. This is the exact opposite
of complete information: limited rationalities that stabilize one
another, each in its own limitations. It is not that the portals I
mentioned provide complete information – but what they create
is, in any case, a different kind of selectivity.

- Data technology is capable of inferring the individual case
  from aggregated data. This enables new forms of surveillance
  and control. Classic routines of interrupting the interdependencies between different fields of activity come under pressure.
  Privacy becomes an even greater illusion than it was before.
  The disruption consists in abolishing for good the illusion of
  the autonomously acting subject, which is attributed everything
  that one does, even as an individual. It is true that, at least since
  the triumph of the social sciences, the culture of modernity
  has seen quite a number of de-subjectivizing parameters such
  as social storage, class position, and constellations of interests;
  however, since then it has also been a popular practice always to
  ignore such social–structural limitations of subjectivity and to
  dissolve them in the fiction of self-determination or attribution to
  the individual. Cultural figures such as competence, authorship,
  subjectivity, decision-making power, and way of life depend on
  such practices of attribution. Now they are patently undermined
  through technologies that are obviously capable of knowing more
  about us than we shall ever know ourselves, because they depict
  our behaviour as a particular manifestation of a general, internally differentiated pattern. The relation between an objective and
  a subjective mind is no longer the relation between a correct and
  a false consciousness but the relation between observer positions.
- Our everyday dealing with digital technology leaves traces that
  serve other purposes than appears at first sight, at the level of
  the user interface. For starters, Facebook is all kinds of things:
  a medium for communication and self-presentation, a space
  of observation and discourse, a mass media distributor, and so
  on. You can go on listing as much as you wish. 'Connecting
  people' was the company's initial slogan. Below this user
  interface, however, the business model of Facebook and other
  companies in the platform economy is 'connecting data', that
  is, collecting and connecting pieces of information that refer to
  one another. It looks as if old Heidegger, with his prognosis that
  philosophy would be replaced by cybernetics, not only predicted
  (post)industrial technologies of control but also uncovered the
  hidden 'truth' behind the technologies of digital data processing:

while at the level of the practical user interface these technologies unfold exclusively in the social dimension, their factual dimension resides in the patterned connection of data. The fact that, for all the rhetoric of responsibility, companies such as Facebook are so insensitive to what happens on their platforms is due to the curious conjunction between the factual and the social dimension in data technology. Digital platforms are only a vehicle for the generation of data that the users themselves produce, practically by doing something else. One buys an automobile in order to go from A to B, or a jumper in order to wear it. Maybe one automobile or one jumper is additionally outfitted with some prestige value that is not directly related to functionality but is visible in the analog mode and can be culturally conveyed. This is no longer so easy to tell in the case of smartphones. Of course, the smartphone is a handy device with very visible functionalities, but the material technology itself includes a condition of production of data that may be used for all kinds of things. Even those who use a navigation app contribute actively, through passive behaviour, to its general functioning, because this way it is possible to measure traffic flows and disruptions. Perhaps even the functionality of the automobile will be changed, seeing that it already requires more and more data technology just self-steering. In the 1980s, when I was a student, I still set the ignition timing on the Volkswagen boxer engine manually, whereas my current car controls this process itself. It can even diagnose its own failure and, in the event of malfunction, it suggests a phone call to the nearest authorized workshop – I don't have to organize even that. The next generation of automobiles will perhaps download new control software to burn fossil fuel in the perfect millisecond without my intervention. But, apart from such self-steering functions, through outreaching data technology, the car will also become a sensor point in the traffic flow in which it moves and to whose electronic control it contributes even without the driver's intervention. The driver still believes she has found the 'green wave' of the traffic lights, or a smooth way through the urban jungle, all by herself, through her own prudent decisions. But individual traffic has long ceased to be individual traffic.

• From different sensors such as these, completely new traces of communication emerge, and they can be used for political, policing, economic, legal, and not least medical purposes. With their help one can predict behaviour, and not only in road traffic. For example, election campaigns can be directed via targeted appeals, or marketing measures can be customized to perfection. Barack Obama's second election campaign in 2012 is now legendary. In that process he managed to pool his strengths by using data processing – that is, information on private house-holds – to focus on potential swing voters.[10] By the end, a *voter activation network* had radically changed the nature of political address – from a collectivist programme to a policy of individual appeal. The disruption consists in changing the semantics of the political; for it becomes even more obvious that the communi-cation between campaigners and potential voters is defined by a political index, and hence that it is about testing market opportu-nities, not (only) about content. Also, this kind of disruption calls attention to the prerequisites of the 'normal case'.

- The rumours about Russian interference in Donald Trump's first election campaign have now been substantiated. This new form of influence is not classic propaganda; it is done rather through a targeted setting of topics, terms, minor information, repeti-tions, and so on. Arguing is not meant to convince somebody, but a pattern is applied that generates attention and in this way changes moods rather than opinions. Decisions of content are then made on this basis. A study carried out by New Knowledge in 2018 summarizes its results as follows: 'It was absolutely intended to reinforce tribalism, to polarize and divide, and to normalize points of view strategically advantageous to the Russian government on everything from social issues to political candidates. It was designed to exploit societal fractures, blur the lines between reality and fiction, erode our trust in media entities and the information environment, in government, in each other, and in democracy itself. This campaign pursued all of those objectives with innovative skill, scope, and precision.'[11] Targeted influence was possible because only information patterns and their feedbacks were calculated, and these, as a user interface, looked by the end like natural communication. This kind of disruption is not only a disruption of the US election campaign by an authoritative regime; it goes much deeper. In reality, this is a humiliation of campaigners and voters alike. It demonstrates that, through a pattern recognition of semantic signals, one can influence the decisions of real persons, decisions that, at the level of self-description, count as one's own. But even this disruption renders transparent the illusion that no previous manipulation of voting decisions had taken place. It is true, though, that targeted incorrect information or misinformation was much easier to account for than the strategies recently applied by Russian 'election observers'.

- Because communication leaves traces, it is technologically possible to spy on communication processes, and also to archive them and to jam them in a targeted way. In January 2019, it became known that the e-mail accounts and electronic diaries of German politicians had been leaked – an action that may result in the destabilization of the political system and in general uncertainty. The political tactic of using private and personal information to blackmail and expose political rulers is nothing new. But the digital society offers completely new possibilities of infiltrating the traffic of personal communications.

- We may expect digitalization to have a most radical effect on work. Classic industrial capitalism was based on work's being the crucial factor in the creation of value; even in the mechanized age, when according to Marx an alienation occurs between work and worker, what produces surplus value out of mechanical power is physical or intelligent work. Digitally controlled automation relativizes or qualifies the uniqueness of work for the production of surplus value. Michael Betancourt comes to this haunting conclusion:

> Digitally enabled automation makes the human labor previously rendered subservient within the productive system itself uncertain, posing a fundamental challenge to capitalism as historically defined through the transformation of *human* labor into a commodity – the use of human intelligence, skill and labor time as a specific form of productive value. The potential for *full automation* emerges with the development of digital automation, one where human labor – human agency – becomes a wasted value.'[12]

Whether the digitalized automation of production will indeed have such a catastrophic impact on the labour market is far from clear. Forecasts range from radical loss of jobs – a line represented for example by Richard David Precht in the German-speaking arm of the debate[13] – to the promise of an employment boom as a result of digitalization.[14] At any rate, it is undisputed that the significance of work is changing, and especially the significance of specific individuals' contributions to the creation of economic value.[15] To quote Michael Betancourt once again,

> By replacing the lowest levels of human labor with automation, greater efficiencies in production emerge, but at the same time that human labor is displaced; some of it occupies (is absorbed by its society into) higher-skilled (greater degree of intelligent agency) positions supported by those automated procedures; however, as that higher-skilled labor is also automated, society's

ability to absorb this displaced labor necessarily creates a new problematic not specifically recognizable as the issue of class struggle described by Marx – a shift from conflict between those who labor and those who do not, to conflict between those controlling the production of exchange values and those excluded from exchange entirely: the human labor whose labor-as-commodity no longer possesses any utility, hence is *not* an exchange value.[16]

- Being exploited – to put it in the classic idiom of labour struggle – becomes visible now as a privilege, because it guarantees that one is assigned a value that can be compensated appropriately. But the position of 'exploiters' becomes precarious too, because their activities are also subject to the danger of automation. This disruption is fundamental to the institutional arrangement of the classic modern industrial society, which was built around this conflict and detained, through work, something of a connective link between economic, legal, and political issues, but also one related to value management.
- One crucial issue is that of information overload. This problem, too, has been around for quite some time; in its classic form it was introduced into the debate by Alvin Toffler as early as the 1970s, as one of the major shocks of modern culture and the future,[17] although routines for dealing with larger amounts of data had already emerged earlier, as operational, organizational, social, cultural and media processes became more complex. Probably the greatest data catastrophe was the printing of books in pre-digital times. A crisis management mechanism developed around the book and its derivates; and this mechanism was able to bring order into a vast set, for example through decouplings and distinctions between different reading audiences, through differential educational processes, through cultural and economic selectivities, and through appropriate form regulations and archiving regulations. Of interest is the turning point at which censorship creates more attention than reading. The information overload caused by digital media does not yet know any routines introduced for dealing with the sheer amount of data – and this at the most diverse levels. What the data obviously need is, again, data-like tools designed to organize them. We may call this 'metadata', that is, data that, in their turn, organize other data.[18] After all, the entire process of dealing with data is characterized by making use of data-like techniques that render these data useful. It is not just the sheer amount of data that matters here but also the disparate nature of the data, which accrue anyway as a result of social

practice in the age of digital modernity. What makes the situation special is that data actually accrue everywhere, in a decentralized manner. But at the same time these decentralized data sets can recombine in a great many ways. Recombinability is not a purposeful form – or, better, a planned one – for normally the data are used for something different from what they can be used for in recombination. This *conversion* is a consequence of information overload. It must be an overload, because only the surplus of data creates the material with which what is possible as a digital solution can be done – as a product and service on markets, as a scientific recombination option, as a control and management option in processes such as traffic, and so on. This is a disruption insofar as the data contain no object that could be converted to data form. Data are completely self-referential, which enables only their extreme recombinability. In the term 'big data', 'big' is taken as *differentia specifica* – the specific difference – but it is the data, in other words the form of representation, that is able to make the disparate comparable. This is an indication of the feedback capacity and feedback structure of the data, which can make everything commensurable by decoupling the meaning from the data structures. Derrida's trace mentioned earlier becomes even more invisible because there is nothing in the data set that refers to what is beyond it.

• Science has always been data-driven. It had to produce regularities out of self-made data, and thus information that could be made into theories; just think of classic cases such as celestial observation, whose data enable a theory of celestial bodies and their orbits only through cumulation. The silver bullet of scientific research is to create the transparent, science-driven continuity of an exploitation chain between the development of a question and the production of a hypothesis, and to do so through the production of data and their evaluation or interpretation. Big data and the availability of accumulated data sets have spawned a discourse on the danger of theoryless research as a self-disruption of science. The editor of *Wired*, Chris Anderson, presented 'The End of Theory' not as a disruption but rather as a promise, and really as a programme – classic scientific methods would become obsolete as soon as sufficient amounts of data existed. He writes: 'Scientists are trained to recognize that correlation is not causation ... Instead you must understand the underlying mechanisms that connect the two. Once you have a model, you can connect the data sets with confidence. Data without a model is just noise. But faced with massive data, this approach to science – hypothesize, model, test – is becoming obsolete.'[19] Now, if that is not a disruption, it is one of the worst mistakes in science to take data sets simply for what they are: primarily, signs that cannot be internally structured any way you like and whose structure can be represented through the corresponding computing capacity. A scientific approach to such data sets practically rules out looking for any statistically conceivable correlation, only to look afterwards for a possible subject-related correlation that might even point to a causal relation – at least a stochastic relation between factors. The handling of data gains scientific quality not merely through the relationship, which can be represented statistically, but through the question, which is itself motivated and substantiated by previous research. An interesting discourse on disruption has established itself within the reflection on data-driven science, and it explicitly warns against the danger that we can now do without theories, without hypotheses and scientifically generated questions.[20] So Anderson recommends consistently: 'There's no reason to cling to our old ways. It's time to ask: What can science learn from Google!'[21] There is one lurking danger: market observers, marketing, targeted advertising, law enforcement, and also technological pattern recognition make use of a technique that looks like a scientific practice – for this reason I called it 'scientoid' earlier – but can do without hypotheses and theories. For here is the peculiarity of such a practice: it identifies correlations that are useful, not correlations that seek to answer questions of knowledge and truth. Parenthetically, let me say that sciences where usefulness is more important than questions of truth in the strict sense, and thus where not knowledge but function is at the forefront, may rather dispense with strict hypothesis formation when dealing with data sets; consider for example the use of statistics in medicine. The one who heals is right; it is not the case that whoever is right is right.

- The availability, in science, of large amounts of data, which must then be organized, stored, catalogued, and structured, creates a completely new question, namely whether this achievement of organization is a genuinely scientific achievement. This is not an abstract question. It has considerable consequences for research funding, for scientific careers, and not least for the assessment of such activities. I owe Kerstin Schill, a cognitive neuro-informatician from Bremen, the wonderful expression 'botanization of data', together with the hint that the botanizing classification of plants was itself defined as a scientific task and achievement. But something here is perceived as a disruption: the expectation of the genuinely scientific tasks that will be taken over by data processing in the future, for example through autonomous and complex cognitive decision-making systems or through algorithms.

- Science is just one of the fields that generate questions of attribution. As soon as data-driven machines – self-driving automobiles or other transport vehicles, support for complex technological systems, algorithms for text processing, buying and selling decisions in the stock exchange, or the mechanization of tax office notices, for example – make decisions, they do something that could also have turned out differently. Such decision-making systems are no trivial machines, because they must check several parameters at the same time; they cannot work via one-to-one transfers but are oriented towards probabilities. Decisions taken by non-trivial machines have the characteristic that they could have been different. Ultimately the sociological concept of action is construed in such a way that one should speak of action in a proper sense, as opposed to mere behaviour, only when the actor could have acted otherwise. Up to a point, we grant the human black box its blackness, that is, the non-transparency of the possibility of an attribution in the form of a granted contingency; and if contingency or deviation are not granted, we have the option of attributing guilt, moral lapse, cognitive insufficiency, pathological characterization, and, not least, coincidence. The rational human being may be granted vagueness, ambiguity, and uncontrollability up to a point. Even more, being 'human' is practically a contingency formula for coping with disruptions. It is experienced as a serious disruption that this kind of fuzzy attribution is hardly possible in algorithms, machines, and cognitive decision-making systems. One will expect higher precision in the decisions taken by such devices, even if it is not always clear that they are really better at it than well-trained humans. At least an attribution to humanity cannot be used as a contingency-coping technique. In this context, the topics with the greatest audience appeal are questions such as whether a self-driving automobile should drive a pensioner or a child to their death if this is only alternative available in a specific traffic situation. In such cases, the human actor will be allowed fuzzy judgement; a rational algorithm will be expected from a machine. The corresponding research questions at the MIT are like this one: Are we ready for utilitarian cars?[22] We would never ask: Are we ready for vaguely deciding human beings? We need not answer this question, because the answer is always 'yes'. The fact that the unambiguity expected of the machine is a programmed unambiguity registers as malfunction when an aircraft's onboard computer draws the wrong conclusions from a certain combination of parameters and instead of pulling the machine upwards makes it go down until inevitably it crashes – as we saw in the crashes of an Indonesian Boeing 737-MAX in 2018 and of an aircraft of the same type in Ethiopia in 2019. The pilots on board, whose reactions were more ambiguous, could not prevent the disaster. Hence the new management of sharpness and fuzziness is perceived as a disruption. This is of course more noticeable in the case of malfunctions – although, cynically, there was no malfunction at all, because obviously the computer did everything correctly. The initial data the computer had to deal with – that's where the error was. The fact that, especially in air traffic, the computer only simulates for the pilot an analog reaction of the flight instruments also indicates this change in the handling of sharpness and fuzziness. The computer makes the pilot's imprecise movements precise and controls them.

• Digitality disrupts the idea of an original, or of the identity of objects. While the unity of an object is still one of the classical categories of our logical notion of the world, digital objects liberate themselves from the materiality of their carriers. By referring to Walter Benjamin's thoughts on the consequences of replicability for the meaning and readability of works of art, Michael Betancourt shows that replicability has attained a new level with digital objects. Unless we still return to Benjamin, we can no longer speak of a relation between original and copy, as the distinction implodes. Copying a file really creates that file for a second time, and does so without any loss. The copy is not a copy, because it is identical to the original, which then disappears as an original. A digital work or object is also bound to a carrier – a physical file or a non-physical repository – but it can be separated from the storage device without any loss. On this point, here is Betancourt again: 'The uniqueness of digital works cannot thus be a result of there being "only one," nor can the uniqueness of digital objects be a result of a solitary (individual) character because all "copies" are identical in every way. In effect, for digital works (as with mechanically (re)produced works before them), there is no first order object, in the way there is a Sistine Chapel.'[23] Strictly speaking, this applies equally to the font, which suffers no loss when the carrier changes and can be reproduced almost endlessly. This is because writing, too, uses discrete signs, not analog ones; but writing is always tied to a medium of visibility. There can be no first edition of a data object. As for the marginal utility that printing already secured for writing, digital data radicalize it so thoroughly that the addition of further 'copies' at some later stage requires no effort and no costs at all, while at the same time it completely dematerializes the information. I remember very well how, in 1985, I handed in my diploma thesis at the University of Münster. It had been written on a computer, which was still rather uncommon in those days, and the two copies for submission were both printed on a printer (at the time, an electronic typewriter with computer interfaces). Thus you couldn't tell from the printed copies which was the original and which was the copy; however, according to examination regulations, the distinction had to be clearly marked. When the lady from the examination office asked which one was the original, I answered that she could have as many originals as she liked. This caused double irritation – on the one hand, at my insubordination to a rigid authority, on the other, because it demonstrated a category mistake that had even found material (non-)expression. The disruption was eliminated by transferring the identity of the two copies into an identity-creating difference. This was done with two seals: 'original' and 'copy'.

- The result is a parallel concentration of capital and data that leads, among other things, to extreme, cut-throat competition among the biggest economic and technological players on the digital information market. This is also due to technology, for some applications work only if as many data with as much internal variance as possible are available. In view of such concentrations, Dirk Helbing even speaks of the danger of *digital fascism* or *digital totalitarianism*,[24] as this is associated with the potential for a radical manipulation of behaviour.

- One of the crucial disruptions caused by the digital is that digital technology makes decisions that, in the classic institutional arrangements of earlier days, were attributed to natural or corporate persons, and this happened in almost all social spheres: preparation of legal decisions through machine-based case processing; medical decisions reached through algorithms that trigger, say, implanted defibrillators; algorithmically automated stock market decisions in economics; moral decisions related to autonomous driving in accident scenarios; political decisions related to the manipulation of election campaigns; scientific decisions based on self-learning algorithms for the detection of structures in data or in texts – and so on. Questions of attribution become relevant mostly in the context of mistake management. But is an algorithm allowed to make mistakes?

This is a long list, and it could be extended even more. It is meant to give only a flavour of the disruptions that stand in the way of the routines of a modern society not (yet) able to deal with these applications routinely. Later on I am going to make the point that, at the latest, such routines develop when things work in everyday life. But initially these disturbances have to do with the fact that, alongside the classic duplications of the world in forms known to us, the world's duplication in the form of data now produces new forms.

Transverse data-like duplications

My initial question was whether digitalization is a catastrophe similar to printing. At any rate, one similarity is that digitalization, like writing and printing, spreads over the whole society, right across other duplications of the world. This accounts for the disruptions I listed. The possibilities of digital duplication are at odds with the clear and practical boundaries of the social structures we are used to – and in this way the digital duplication of the world is at least structurally similar to the duplication of the world through printing.

Ultimately at odds with the incipient modern order of the world, printing was a medium that eluded the social structure insofar as its boundaries were at odds with the logic of the entire differentiation of society. Printing had changed not only religious self-understanding, by allowing for the distribution of the Holy Scripture in the vernacular. It also made legal texts available for public use; as literature, it encouraged the presentation of individual lives through elaborate self-descriptions, endowed personal friendship and love with forms of their own, and demonstrated the art of arguing; it created political spaces of accountability and collectivities, just as, standing in for a political audience, it made it possible to communicate political differences. The book was above all a medium of education – the bourgeois educational medium par excellence, not only on account of the elaborate forms of bourgeois sensitivity and psychologization of images of the self and others, but also as a medium that could make the entire population literate, through compulsory schooling. And the written nature of one's access to the world, as a function of the medium, simulated a common world, made the national state possible, and so on. This kind of textualization of the world covered social practices like a net and created a kind of second reality, which was always present next to the non-mediated practices.

Just as digital data are at odds with the structure of the functional differentiation of society yet do not undermine it, the printed word has partly evaded the clear top–bottom coding of a stratified society. Anyone who can read discovers the argument, and the rank of the speaker fades into the background. And anyone who can set topics by deliberately infecting the discourse with data undermines the power circle of the political system.

It is worth having this demonstrated again, phenomenologically, if we want to get a better grasp of the place of the digital. Not without reason, I started my description of the duplication of the world with writing. Our habituation to it is also reflected in the reality index of writing, which is so high that it has enabled this medium to add another self-referential medium of duplication onto the duplications of the world. The written nature of our culture is reinforced by the world's ubiquitous availability in written form – up to the notion that even divine revelation must express itself in book format to make itself plausible. One could say that the characteristic feature of the practices of a classic modern society is to leave every-where written traces that are themselves the precondition for further operations. One can say that the practices of classic modern society are characterized by the fact that they leave reproducible written traces everywhere, and these in turn are the precondition for further operations.

When we are speaking of a digital modernity, we do not mean primarily that many of the technological devices we use are based on electronic data processing. We mean first of all that the practices of our ways of life and social functional systems leave data traces everywhere, and, to repeat, these are in turn the precondition for further operations. Perhaps this is initially the striking thing about the significance of the written word that can be aesthetically repre-sented. One sees a society in which society recurs in written form. It duplicates itself in such a way that what we find in written texts is not just a copy of society in a different medium and material form; nor is it a society that recurs within society. Rather society creates a trace of itself as part of society. Written and non-written forms start interacting. Recording society in writing also affects its practices. Meaning can be stored, one can deal with earlier connections to the future, one can look at what people said earlier and compare it to what they say today, one can move meaning across time and space, one can decontextualize – and this affects all social practice. The society of writing and of the book is not a society that also features in writing and in books; it is a society that organizes its own connectivities through writing and through books. It is a society of writing and of the book even when books are neither lying around nor being read in multiplied copies (though this area is about to shrink ever further).

Incidentally, we should not forget that even the written nature of self-reflection and the treatment of written material of all kinds – from the diary through the letter and the perusal of educational stories and biographies to the journal or the newspaper and genres of writing and reading with educational aims – were perhaps the most powerful ways of self-tracking and self-improvement. Those who lament practices of self-improvement nowadays should remember that education, especially an education based on writing, was perhaps the most powerful programme of (self-)improvement in our civilization, as it managed to switch from control by others to self-control. This was possible only because the written word introduced a duplication of the world in the guise of its inter-pretation, its normative prescription, and its severance of right from wrong, but most of all through authoritative speech. And at the same time it enabled criticism. The programme of self-improvement of all sorts – for the self was not just individuals but also processes, practices, environments, political associations, even religious experience and aesthetic subtlety – contained the possi-bility of criticism, of questioning the existent, and thus individual attribution only to 'subjects' that could and should be expected to work on themselves. In the language of contemporary critique of subjectivation processes, *the bourgeois world of books, with its practices of self-development, self-criticism, and reflection, was a neoliberal world of self-improvement avant la lettre.*

This ironic description points out how much the practices of social existence of humans depend on the way in which this world duplicates itself for its own information processing. It should also make obvious how really uninformed the criticism of the *neoliberal regime of self-perfection* turns out to be: its normative orientation completely fails to grasp that ultimately this is still about the form of self-development in the old world of the book. Data duplicate the world in different ways, more invisibly, less legibly, less systematically, with fewer hermeneutical instructions. The internal connection between the functional differentiation of society and individualization within the medium of written occasions for reflection is, after all, the classic context of bourgeois society. This *hermeneutic* connection seems to disappear with the nascent digitality of society. In the world of the book, it was possible to produce kinds of moral, communal, political, and emancipatory description that lie transversely across functional differentiation. All of them were unrealistic but could be stabilized through literacy. But we probably become aware of structures only in the hour of their decay and end, which in this context means that the sociological criticism of the data world and of optimization practices of all sorts of tracking still looks like a criticism of the world of the book. The digital duplication of the world can do with less hermeneutics and is more handy, more aesthetic, more selective, and less referential. In the world of the book there was a ubiquitous mistrust of motives, because one had to ask oneself why this had to be written now and in this way rather than any other. The path from God's will (which was passed down in writing) to the author's motive is shorter than it seems.

The self-practices of the digital world get by without motives and without grand explanations. They are self-sufficient, because they are aesthetically convincing and prove their worth in a practical way. This is because hardly any provider of such practices is interested in the practices themselves; only the traces they leave are of interest. It's all about users leaving enough data to be offered new practices. The limitlessness of the demand for data creates exactly this way of duplicating the world and the production of patterns that can then be found. If one still measures this against the demand for hermeneutics in the world of the book, one arrives at the common diagnoses of the quantified self – even though you don't need to understand what the data world is qua data world in order to make such diagnoses.

In a very instructive study, Florian Süssenguth analysed the function of digitalization semantics, in other words not the consequences of digitalization itself, but the way in which digitalization is discussed, especially in relation to organizations' self-descriptions – in politics, economy, and the media. He writes that 'the semantics of digitalization' produces 'a narration of the dissolving of existing structures', a narration

> of disruptive change and loss of control that is due to digital media [...]. If, however, one looks at the effects of the various digitalization semantics within organizations, a somewhat different picture forms. Indeed, the digitalization semantics dissolves existing structures of expectation and makes it visible that, in the context of the spread of digital media, ingrained organizational practices and problem solving can have unintended consequences. But they don't stop at this point; they open the chance for organizations to observe themselves and to transform the indeterminate experience of digital irritation with their practices into decision-making matters and evaluation criteria.[25]

Functional systems had reacted to printing in a similar way. On the one hand, one found out that printing also meant loss of control. Niklas Luhmann writes: 'Printing stepped up the development of a supplementary technology, the technology of reading ability. This ability could no longer be restricted to the subject matter of given functional systems. Whoever could read the Bible could also read polemical religious tracts, newspapers, and novels.' [26] But this need not mean being exposed to complete indeterminacy; new routines developed for dealing with that medium – the book – in all functional systems, in religion, in politics, in law (censorship …). Then the dramatizing reactions of disruptive change released degrees of freedom to find rather continuous solutions, which had to deal, of course, with the strange duplication of the world through printed matter.

This depiction is far too schematic, but it may help to sharpen our perspective on the subject matter when we talk about 'data' – the thing that makes modern society a digitalized society.

The trace of the trace and discrete duplications

Here is the crucial point: *modern digital society duplicates itself once again in the form of data that grow permanently and are at odds with the tried practices of society*. It is now true of digitalization, by analogy with the consequences of printing, that with the establishment of computers as calculating and recombining machines, with the emergence of the Internet as a decentralized network of computers, and with the conversion of social and technological forms of control to data-driven tools, a network takes shape once again that duplicates the world, now in data form; and this network, just like reproduced writing, not only depicts the world but features in it as a duplicate. Even more than printing, the accumulating data create a self-referential structure of forms that can be recombined and are capable of duplicating society in such a way as to affect its rules for the processing of meaning.

The function of duplicating does not depict anything; it is a kind of representing without an original that admittedly contains society in its structure as a trace, a shifted trace, to be precise. As explained in the previous chapter, duplication, and thus data sets too, contain what they refer to only in the displacement of their own representation. Derrida has much to say about this:

> Since the trace is not a presence but the simulacrum of a presence that dislocates itself, displaces itself, refers itself, it properly has no site – erasure belongs to its structure. … The paradox of such a structure, in the language of metaphysics, is an inversion of metaphysical concepts, which produces the following effect: the present becomes the sign of the sign, the trace of the trace. It becomes a function in a structure of generalized reference. It is a trace, and a trace of the erasure of the trace.[27]

ᴅata sets are not presences but only traces of a trace, signs of ᴄne sign – and this is precisely why they are so powerful, so self-referential, so idiosyncratic. These statements are misinterpreted if the 'simulacrum of a presence' is confused with ineffectiveness, instability, or even meaninglessness. Derrida's poststructuralist perspective is indeed capable of conceptualizing the *stabilization* of such self-supporting structures of signs – and this is exactly what our data world, which duplicates society, achieves nowadays when it designates the simulacrum of a presence even beyond writing. Data and data sets are columns of signs whose aesthetic form makes it possible to reshape what they duplicate, giving it completely different, processable forms.

If it is true that the digitality of modernity consists of a data-shaped network that spans the whole society, then we'd have to examine more closely what this network is like. To begin with, the data network is really a network of *data*. It is worth having a look at the sign structure of these data if we want to be able to understand their function. Even writing consists of discrete signs. Mathematically, one would classify writing under discrete maths rather than continuous analysis. While in analysis functions calculate consistencies and continuities, discrete signs denote countable, combinable, and above all encodable units.[28] In an alphabet the difference between A and B is not continuous, and there is no transition: no sign is more A than B or more B than A. The term 'discrete' comes from the Latin verb *discernere*, which means 'distinguish', 'divide'. Discrete states are thus indistinguishable, and for this reason allow free recombinability. They can be detached from their context yet still remain what they are. The A in my first name, 'Armin', is identical with the A in the word *Abend* ('evening'). This feature enables alphabetic scripts such as Latin, Cyrillic, Arabic, or Greek to produce many possible combinations with just a few signs. Such possibilities are reduced for syllabic scripts and completely non-existent for logographic scripts such as the Chinese.

Scripts (and numbers) make use of discrete states or signs, and thus refer especially to the difference between signifier and signified. They demonstrate even aesthetically that they build an independent existence, which is far from the practice they represent – so they not only duplicate it but also influence it. Digital data are the most discrete signs of all, because they make use of the most reductionist form that can be imagined – with regard to their representability as an electronic signal and with regard to their number. Even Aristotle, at the beginning of *Physics* 4, chapter 12, says that 2 is the smallest number.[29] Each given number must always be the other number of another number, otherwise one cannot count; hence 1 would be no number if there were no 2. With digital data the situation is even more basic: the smallest elementary unit of the digital is not a sign but the binarity of two signs, namely the two digits of the binary numeral system 0 and 1. The unit owes its name to binarity. 'Bit' derives from 'binary digit' and consists materially only of the difference between two electric voltages, which can actually express only one binarity, 'yes/no' or 'on/off', such that the content attributions as to which of the three suggested distinctions is *meant* are no longer trivial.

The advantage of the digital form is that its technological prerequisites are increasingly simple; mind you, simpler and less presuppositional than writing – or indeed than spoken language – as a medium of discrete signs. In chapter 2 I have called attention to Shannon and Weaver's communication theory, which dealt with the range and depth required by communication processes and explained what the relation between sender and receiver must be like for communication to succeed. The prerequisites for successful communication (and for its becoming a technology) are made both easier and more capable of complexity as a result of digitalization with binary coding. They are made easier because the difference between stress states is perhaps the most trivial option for a way to mark a difference; and they are made more capable of complexity because the simplicity of their foundation increases almost ad infinitum the possibilities of recombining. A good term of comparison would be the translation of the alphabet into Morse signals: these are easier to transmit than letters, for which one would need twenty-six signs. Letters are binarily resolved and represented. The binary code is thus the condition for simplicity – both in the technological processing and in the technological spread of data.

That they are easy to process technologically creates infinite possibilities of recombination, while the low signal strength required for their transmission and their very simple storage option facilitate the spread of digital data immensely. The difference between music stored on an analog disc and music stored on a digital audio file illustrate this point very well. The analog disc transmits the whole complexity and uniqueness of an analog signal first to an electric data carrier, then to a physical one. The stored signals match the original, then: they are a duplication whose difference finds expression only in the depth, range, and accuracy of the equipment (microphone, tape recorder, embossing machine, record material, record player pickup, amplifier, speakers). The data stored on a digital file, on the other hand, have lost the aesthetics of the 'original'. They are electronic codings whose form is not different from that of other digital data.

Only the combination and the structure of the data are different, and they depend on a certain internal organization of the data set.

Of course, the creation of more complex information such as an audio or video file requires several bits, which of course do not lose their binary structure. The next bigger unit is commonly the byte, which consists of eight bits; thus 256 states can be marked by combining bits. Again, these states can be arbitrarily extended through further combinations. The audio file is, then, correspondingly complex and soon gains size, but remains a *text* made up of discrete characters distributed in a binary structure. Data sets themselves quickly grow to unmanageable dimensions, especially when they have to process complex signals of any kind. At any rate, this is one of the most interesting *material* developments of digitalization. On the one hand, information is practically dematerialized; on the other, file sizes are increased.

Traces, patterns, networks

The simplicity of data is key to their efficacy. The easier the basic coding of the data is, the more possibilities they have to recombine. In the previous chapter I have already called attention to Fritz Heider's distinction between medium and form.[30] Still referring exclusively to human perception, Heider pointed out that all perception depends on carrier media that are not perceived – we see things but not the light, we hear sounds but not the air. So what we can see depends on what we cannot see.[31]

Media are thus inescapable and invisible, strictly matched and idiosyncratically related to themselves; we cannot see them in the medium of light or hear them in the medium of air. Nevertheless 'things' (Heider's term) or 'forms' (the term used at a later stage) can have infinitely many manifestations, precisely because of the particular structuration and idiosyncrasy of their mediatic substrate. Media are indeed tied to preconditions, but then they are no longer available as a constituting entity. Air is as indifferent to sound as light is to what we see. The only limitation is the range of the medium: sound, for instance, travels differently in water and out of water, and light is of service to human perception only within the frequency range available to our perception apparatus.

Beyond strict media of perception such as air or light, the media–form distinction may apply to *digital media* too. Data sets, no matter what they are used for, are strictly matched units whose inalienable character derives from not knowing anything but the internal difference of voltage states: they exist only as bits and bytes. This really simple precondition is the foundation of the wealth of forms that the digital world enables. Binary mediality is the precondition for literally anything that can be digitalized.[32] And it is a big mistake to understand digitalization simply as the *countability* and *quantification of the social.*[33] Thus, in a compendious book, Steffen Mau takes the attitude of the alerting social scientist, speaking of a period when 'the mode of the calculative seems to cover the entire social order, like a kind of colonization process. One crucial driving force in this context is the extension of technologies and infrastructures for the measurement of society.'[34]

Of course, this diagnosis touches on secondary consequences rather than the issue itself: secondary consequences of technological possibilities that, ultimately as a result of the world's duplication through data, have information that does not stop in the face of anything. Perhaps these electronic forms of self-observation and observation of others are only the digital equivalent of the self-reflexivity that modern societies have always demanded from individualized ways of life. I will come back to this later, in chapter 8, when I reflect on the topic of privacy, which in our digital society is changing just as much as it points to continuities. At this point, my first task is to determine the duplicating function of data with greater accuracy.

If we assume that duplication creates a reality of its own kind, data sets are nothing but self-referential structures whose own structure, so to speak, is created by sense impressions. I use the metaphor of the senses on purpose; for the data sets of the digitalized society are made up of data that go back to the fact that social practices leave traces. Bruno Latour used the term 'digital trace'[35] to demonstrate that there is almost nothing that would not leave digital traces:[36] I leave traces as a customer with all sorts of electronic means of payment – from groceries to flight tickets, from the underground ticket to the hotel bill – or with an automobile with a machine-readable licence plate (the only kind there is today); at any rate, as a car owner with a face of my own at airports or in large crowds, with a customer profile available on Internet platforms, or with a passport when I travel to other states (as long as they are outside the European Union); as a patient in my doctor's office – and I mean both my patient file and files of my laboratory findings and examination results; as a participant in social media; as a tax payer at the tax office; as a smartphone user; as a matriculated pupil or student, or even as a tenured professor – and the list could go on indefinitely, because it tends to encompass *all* everyday practices. Such data simply grow, and some of them acquire insights into my own self. My smartphone, for example, registers the number of steps I've taken, tells me whether I've looked at the display for a long time this week, and reminds me of appointments – including appointments saved not by me but by my office manager, who has access to my calendar via the cloud and can add or delete any of them. I use these data constantly in everyday life; for example I can see on an app whether the subway is running, how late a train is, or whether I move up on the waiting list for a flight. The navigation system in my car directs me to another route if it receives data about heavy traffic, and when I am on foot in unfamiliar cities I let my smartphone guide me. Communication with family uses mainly chat software, and even information which has been shared unintendedly is accumulated, such as whether a message has been read or when my addressee was most recently online.

These illustrations, which need not be described in greater depth because most of us are familiar with them, give quite a clear impression that our everyday lives are actually shared by a network of data and their interconnections. The world is doubled by a reality level that does not simply map this world but deals with traces that are left, at the interface between data sets and their environments, through sensors of all kinds – but also through the combinatorics of data sets. It is in these data sets that are calculated those patterns that can be made use of.

In chapter 1 I referred to the *third discovery of society*, by which I meant that digitalization claims precisely the sociality of society. This is its material. Digital technology reckons with exactly the same regularities and exactly the same internal differentiations and deviations that constitute what has been labelled 'society' and 'the social' since the eighteenth–nineteenth centuries. This is exactly what can now be determined with greater precision. These regularities are not there just to be 'calculated'. Rather, digital media are able to draw attention to the very forms they find in themselves as traces of this society. The sensory scan of social practice and the collection of traces of data-dropping practices generate data sets through which one comes across patterns that can be used to do everything that is now possible as a digital social practice – from supporting road navigation through targeting people with market strategies to manipulating election campaigns. *Digitalization discovers society within itself – as a limitation of contingency, as a selective form, as repetitive recombination, as an uncovering of patterns, and at the same time as a generation of patterns.*

Even if data practices seem scientoid, they have in essence no epistemic goals; they pursue only the practical goal of functioning. Ultimately they try out what is possible. Why are personal data worth a mint? Only because they are material for that search for patterns that society keeps an eye on, in conformity with its own processing rules: concerning economic interests or under legal aspects, with an interest in political power or as medical diagnostics, with interests in revealing certain patterns in an athlete's movements – up to the question of the educational use of measuring response speed or types of mistakes. This is another list that could become arbitrarily long. But the crucial information here is not its length, but the hint that the world's duplication though data encounters a duplication through the processing rules of society's functional systems.

Thus the systematic location of digital data is very similar to the location of mimeographed writing, the world of printing. If printing is at odds with social functions, the same applies to digital data. And if writing does not uphold the boundaries of functional systems but positively undermines and disrupts them, the same applies to digital data. It's enough to think of the significance of literary texts for people's political self-understanding or for the intimate experience of love, or of authorial and mediatized reflections on consumption. Multiplied writing is a disruption; it only allows for the self-referentiality of a society that, as a functionally differentiated society, reacts most of all to its own states. Duplicated writing disturbs – and only makes possible – the self-referentiality of a society that, as a functionally differentiated society, reacts above all to its own conditions.

The same can be observed in the handling of digital data: Peter Struijs and his colleagues, for example, point out how much big data, which accumulate through different social practices, affect official statistics.[37] Other examples are the undermining of data protection categories through reuse of data in various contexts,[38] but also new modalities of collecting information, of diversification of media offerings, of medical monitoring, and of price comparison. All these interventions and transversals are experienced as disruptions only because they challenge the institutionalized routines of those stable duplications of a legal, economic, political, scientific, or mediatic nature.

Now I'll sum up and prepare the next step. The first step in my search for the reference problem of the digitalization of society was to work out that the function of digitalization is rooted in the complexity of society itself. Modern society must deal with a high degree of complexity in such a way as to access one and the same subject matter in different ways at the same time, thanks to its functional differentiation, and be aware, in a reflective attitude, that the subject of observation is due to perspective. 'Society' in the form of its own practice knows that it accesses the world simultaneously by different means, even though the 'actors', 'individuals', or 'people' often do not know it or refuse to admit it. It knows by doing it in practice and by aligning its own connectivities accordingly. In the digital society, these connectivity skills and routines are not second-coded by society's digital information processing but are nevertheless empirically changed. This makes a political difference, it makes an economic difference, it impacts right-wing routines, it has an enormous effect on media communication, it opens up new options for political power while disrupting familiar forms of power, and so on. The digital duplication of the world works on the complexity of the world by focusing on patterns it can make use of, whatever they may be.

Thus an entire toolset becomes available thanks to my theoretical suggestion to use the figure of *duplication*. With this toolset, one can avoid viewing digitalization and the data world as something *completely different* from previous social practices. Consequently digitalization, too, is a practice of doubling – with all the limitations, paradoxes, and self-supporting forms to which I have repeatedly referred. Big data creates opportunities for developing a rich combinatorics of elements on the basis of a very simple media substrate (bits and bytes), with which the routines of society can be called upon, and in turn society reacts with its own structures.

My view that digitalization can dock so well with society because it relates to the complex structure of society itself should have become clearer by now. It uncovers those patterns, invisible to the naked eye, that emerge from the same place as their digital measurement and are grounded in the structure of a society whose order seems hardly to be clear – and yet is characterized by a considerable capacity for order, which enables its variety and its wealth of combinations in the first place. In the next chapter I am going to discuss the view that modern society's capacity for order can be best explained with the help of digitality-compatible concepts. This will not lead me to a convenient equivocation. In the next step I will take a closer look at the digitality of society itself. The technological nature of the digital will play a special role here.

4

Simplicity and Diversity

I ended the previous chapter with the claim that modern society itself's capacity for order can best be explained with the help of digitally compatible concepts. And this is exactly what I'm going to do now. My thesis is this: *the relationship between coding and programming in the world of digital data is similar to the relationship between coding and programming at the level of modern society's differentiation into functional systems.* This structural similarity has something to do with the simplicity of programming coded functional systems – in other words the simplicity of digital, binarily coded technology – on the one hand and, on the other, the almost limitless diversity of the possible programming based on it. Social functional systems are based on simple media – for instance money in economy, power in politics, faith in religion, or truth in the sciences – which do not certify anything beyond the conditions for connections. The response to payments in money is payments in money, claims to power must assert themselves against power, matters of faith aim at statements on faith, while maters of truth aim at other, possibly false truths. These possibilities are based on the simplicity of the medium and the code – but it is precisely this simplicity that enables the development of those kinds of diversity and the almost limitless wealth of forms of the most diverse manifestations, cultural and other, which are so striking in modernity. Modernity is at once simple in an almost brutal way and almost unbelievably open to possibilities. This is also true of digital technology. I will explain later what is specifically technological about this; but the digital medium is one of stupendous simplicity and can be applied to anything not *in spite of* this but *because* of it. If there is any reliable indication that the structure of society and the structure of digital technology are at least related to each other, it is in the sense suggested here.

In the introduction to this book I remarked that the fact that the discourse about society *is oblivious of society* often runs parallel to the fact that the discourse about digitalization *is oblivious of digitalization*. Here I would like to overcome this double obliviousness by uncovering a logic in the social structure of modern society that corresponds to the logic of digital technology and thus to the variety of its options. To do this, I will first investigate the digitality of the digital in greater detail, then I will apply the insights gained in this way to the digitality of society.

First of all, *the simplicity of data is the key to their effectiveness*. Their simplicity is the foundation of their diversity. What I mean is the *technological* simplicity of data: not only are they very simple in their structure, namely as difference engines between stress states, but technologically, too, they can be realized very simply. Strictly speaking, the very complex computer machines of our time are so complex and capable of processing so much complexity precisely because their technological realization has very few requirements and relies on relatively free combinability. The minimum requirements are a central processing unit (CPU), a random-access memory (RAM) store, in most cases at least one read-only memory (ROM) store, and a steady energy supply. Of course, RAM and ROM stores vary depending on the physical medium, for instance in size and speed, and the CPU at the heart of the computer is the crucial unit for its performance.

The chips, which get increasingly smaller and increasingly faster, consist of circuits with internal on–off switches (transistors), and these in turn enable logical operations that get increasingly faster, each one according to its frequency. The two computers on which this book was mainly written are equipped with a 3.8 GHz processor (this is a stationary computer on my desk at home) or with a 2.3 GHz processor (a mobile tablet with external keyboard that I use when I'm not at home). The former can perform 3,800,000,000 operations per second, the latter 2,300,000,000 operations per second. The performance of computer chips doubles approximately every 18 to 20 months, which allows for the use of even more complex software and for processing even larger amounts of data. In the summer of 2018, the fastest computer in the world was the Summit computer of the Oak Ridge National Laboratory in the United States: it had 4,608 POWER servers with a theoretical performance of 200 floating point operations per second (PFLOPS).[1] It is used in climate research, in earthquake prognosis, in astrophysics, in brain research and quantum chemistry, and also in artificial intelligence research.[2]

Medium and form

The binary operations of switching circuits or gates on and off constitute the *medium* of computer technology; software and the surfaces and interfaces provided by software constitute its *form*. The medium is as simple as it can be, simple in principle, strictly matched, and ultimately invariable and highly specific. There is no intermediate step between 0 and 1, and there is no alternative to 0 or 1. The states of the apparatus are discrete states. If we bear in mind Aristotle's principle that 2 is the smallest number, their mediality is probably the simplest possible variant of a medium, for it would be reducible only at the cost of the indistinguishability of states, which would then not allow for any form at all. This characterization of data starts at their most elementary shape. Even Rob Kitchin's differentiation of data into nominal data, interval data, and ratio data is one step higher, since technologically all these data must be represented in the discrete form of the basic medium.[3]

Through the binarity of its basic code, this medium is the perfect condition for a wealth of forms of ungraspable and (above all) confusing magnitude. In the case of digital technology, the structure of the relationship between medium and form is particularly striking. This astonishing combination between such a *simple* way of processing and such a *complex* possibility of producing form is probably to be found nowhere else. It is true that even writing, which is the first medium to make use of discrete signs, cannot simply be built in binary form but requires discretely distinguishable signs, the Greek alphabet twenty-four, the Latin alphabet twenty-six, and even twice as many when divided into uppercase and lowercase letters. Such a medium assumes a pluralistic form itself, if not a complex one – whereas the digital medium, with its discrete distinction between 0 or 1, exhausts the possibilities of a maximum of minimalism.

Also, the use of digital 'products' is considerably easier to secure than the much more demanding reading of texts and books, which still requires skills difficult to acquire and to cultivate. The entire developing educational system, with its prolongation of the periods of childhood and learning, the invention of the adolescent, compulsory schooling, and the written duplication of all practices, creates a kind of person who masters the reception and production of text and becomes aware of the textuality of the world. Also here we find a system of signs that are strictly matched. This amounted to an enormous increase in the complexity of meaningful references, which society experienced as a catastrophe, most of all through printing. Printing brought together what was incommensurable, enabled recombinations, and processed meaning in such a way that it could be reworked more slowly, and thus more thoroughly than the permanent dissolution of oral communication would permit. But it created forms of connectivity that were teeming with requirements – incidentally, this process ran roughly alongside the emergence of certain forms of social inequality and stratification. There was no reading at the very top (among the nobility) and at the bottom (among peasants), but after a short time reading was everywhere. What was read and for what purpose, however, became an internal indicator of social inequality as well as of environmental and occupational differentiation. That formal education, together with income or the availability of material resources and money, could become a crucial indicator of inequality is the direct expression of a reading society.

By the way, at the reception end, a reading society can deal with the output of writing and the book in a much more error-friendly way than the digital outputs. Even when there are errors, reading is possible almost without negative effects. A spelling error can be compensated for through reading, given its retentive and protentional connections, which are generated by the reading mind itself. We hardly perceive scrambled letters, because reading always requires a semantically meaningful reference. Missing words can be supplied.[4] So one could say that the medium is matched strictly enough, but not extremely strictly. In digital technology, the opposite is true. Although the fields of application of digital coding are considerably broader and more diverse than the possible combinations of letters, software as a programmed form is not error-friendly. One minor typo can bring down a whole programming, which is why software inaccuracy is almost proverbial and inbuilt.[5] One could say that: software is never complete, because it cannot be made actually error-free, and also because its aesthetics is far away from its application – further than the discrete writing characters are from their analog meaning. Writing can stand symbolically, as it were, for the thing it represents. Just think of letters or of written word figures that are actually figures. This can be particularly well demonstrated by the example of numbers. Probably our idea of 'seven' and 'eight' genuinely corresponds to the numbers 7 and 8, at least more than to an abstract numerical value, or even to an object's 'sevenness' or 'eightness'.

Even the representation of 7 and 8 in binary form can no longer achieve such correspondence: these two forms are 111 and 1000 in binary notation. As early as 1993, Friedrich Kittler pointed out that even the writing of software is still writing, but in its technological form it becomes more abstract than the previous writing. He writes:

> Writing today, as it occurs in software development, is an infinite series of the self-similarities discovered by fractal geometry; except that, in contrast to the mathematical model, it remains mathematically impossible, in physical/physiological terms, to have access to [*erreichen*] all these layers [*Schichten*]. Modern media technology – ever since the invention of film and gramophones – is fundamentally arranged to undermine sensory perception. We can simply no longer know what our writing is doing, and least of all when we are programming.[6]

Here Kittler goes one step further, of course, and complains that a computer's hardware (structured like this for economic reasons) already contains more 'software' than appears at first sight. This is about the question of the freedom of recombining possibilities that is already limited by the hardware, and it points to two distinctions: the distinction between software and hardware and the distinction between medium and form. The technological formatting of the medium is already given, in other words the technological basis already contains pre-programmings, which by the end also include assemblers and other tools, which are somewhat like writing aids. This is ultimately about distinguishing programmable from non-programmable elements of the digital, in the context of which one must concede that the 'soldered' programming, that is, the programming that cannot be changed, is also a kind of programming or programmed thing.

This line of argument does not really take us anywhere – and the critique of capitalist motives is trite. What seems to me decisive instead is that the hardware foundation of programming in the computer chip – in other words the basic pre-structuring of any software production and application – indicates just the freedom of recombining possibilities, and not the opposite, as Kittler believes. Basically this freedom is limited (no doubt for economic reasons, too), also because it is indeed more strictly matched than writing is. More interesting is Kittler's hint at software complexity due to high resolution and aesthetic displacement, as one could describe it. The signifier is so radically distant from the imagined signified that even this distinction seems to implode. Digital data and programs look like pure self-reference – hence it is the production conditions themselves that ultimately ensure that software never seems to be really complete. This is attributable on the one hand to the author's being deconstructed by teams, by constellations of several producers,[7] and on the other to the partial automation of software production. But it also follows from the sheer complexity of the programmed 'text', which is indeed read by machines, and not by consciousnesses in a meaningful context. The constitutional performance of the consciousness, which I illustrated earlier with Husserl's example of the melody, is error-friendly insofar as the consciousness can smooth out the meaning on the basis of earlier structuring. Perhaps this can be explained through the particular function of the reafference principle.

As long as conceptual meanings prove their practical worth, they are completely analogous with what they stand for. We do not ourselves perceive the mediatic, organic, and material substrate of our brain, which is why everything we sense appears to us as analog signals. While we interpret our perception physiologically, the world itself we interpret semantically. Even if the processing of signals is much more complicated, our brain makes us behave as if we perceived the world analogously. As early as 1950, Erich von Holst and Horst Mittelstaedt described (among other things) how this works, and they did so through the so-called reafference principle.[8] Organisms provided with a central nervous system are capable of processing inexact, changing, and unexpected stimuli in such a way that an analogous image of the world is created and can be processed. Thus what happens is not a passive perception of an objectively existing world, but rather a kind of 'self-monitoring',[9] which should be considered an explicit precondition for conscious processes. In layman language, one could say that perception follows pragmatic rather than principled motives, and hence it must be functional rather than justifiable.

The principle of reafference takes care that perception balances disruptions. For example, when I ride my bike over cobblestones, physically I perceive that the horizon sort of dances with the vibrations caused by the cobblestone. The reafference principle compensates for this by simulating a stable horizon. This way, when we walk, we are not disturbed by the fact that with every step we are making an up and down movement.

This principle can also be reconstructed from colour perception. From a physical point of view, the colour of a white shirt, for example, changes with the colour spectrum of the light in the environment: in artificial light with incandescent bulbs or especially under candlelight, there is a high proportion of red, whereas in daylight there is a high proportion of blue. Thus the white shirt reflects quite different colours, but we still perceive a continuity of colours that ultimately ensures that our brain-induced perception is protected against too much environmental variation. To a certain extent, perception uses an image of the world it already knows and compares it to what is added by sensory stimuli. It uses a kind of biological economy principle to create a continuous environment through its own operations. In a way, this is similar to an abductive procedure – which, incidentally, is highly relevant for digital recognition machines, for instance in automated driving or machine learning. The selectivity of the world is a selectivity of its own, which unfolds according to internal criteria and must decide on its own what is taken to be relevant and what is not. This is neither a deduction from general principles nor an induction that rounds up every single perception to something general; it is rather an abduction, which must be understood as a *hypothetical conclusion* whereby an individual occurrence is compared to experiences, regularities, and rules that can be discerned from the latter and is led to results step by step.[10] At the level of immediate operations such as electronic pattern recognition, the precision and exactness that only the simple coding of a computing apparatus can muster still apply. At the level of programming, on the other hand, it is definitely possible that the degree of blur be calculated as well; think for example of photo or film cameras, which are able to balance their own movements independently, by themselves, so as to create a focused or steady image. What is applied here is techniques of fuzzy logic, which deals with the modelling of blur.[11] I will come back later to the techno-sociological implications of this thought. Crucial here is this: neuronal perception feeds on the error-friendliness of its own data processing. As was once formulated two centuries ago, it must make 'the manifold sensual impressions' into a manageable unit, in order to be able to move through the world. Everything is self-supporting.

The key, then, is a certain fuzziness, and it is precisely this fuzziness that's missing from the self-processing of digital technologies, at least at the level of the medium itself. Any software programmer, that is, anyone who wants to create forms on the terrain of the digital medium, will come up against a precision limit, which exists because the strictness of the digital code, with its binary structure, does not permit any fuzziness or, to be precise, does not know any fuzziness. The digital code is perhaps the least error-friendly system one can imagine – and this is the systematic reason why software will never be complete and why work on software requires a kind of unachievable precision that differs from that of other ways of production.

There are social science perspectives on this topic that argue differently. They are focused on the *practice* of writing software and see in it the reason why all solutions are provisional,[12] instead of seeing it rather as a consequence of the strange relationship between the strict need for matches achieved through a binary medium and the possible wealth of forms and complexity of software architectures. Accordingly, Rob Kitchin describes the programming of an algorithm itself as an abductive practice: 'creating an algorithm unfolds in context through processes such as trial and error, play, collaboration, discussion, and negotiation. They are teased into being: edited, revised, deleted and restarted, shared with others, passing through multiple iterations stretched out over time and space. As a result, they are always somewhat uncertain, provisional and messy fragile accomplishments.'[13] And yet you have to say that they *work*, but their production conditions are no longer the same as the production conditions of deductively calculable machines, which themselves had taken the form of deductive–nomological calculations. Software must be written. Now, any complex text, even if it takes a deductive form of argumentation, is written abductively to begin with. This applies all the more to software, whose internal complexity leads to that deplored provisionality. So, at one end, the material basis of software production indeed fosters a provisionality that turns the update into a cultural symbol of a society – namely a symbol that something like a fuzzy mode of simulating stability is hardly possible.

At the other end, the complexity and abstraction of software production is precisely the mechanism that creates the aura of a digital elite that oscillates between digital megalomania and diagnoses of catastrophe. Popular warnings come close to this megalomania, which is less interested in the material and social structure of such digitalization but tends to make overly strong diagnoses. The paradigm for this is the kind of text we encounter in books such as *Homo Deus* by Yuval Noah Harari, whose diagnosis culminates in the statement '*Homo sapiens* is losing control'[14] – no doubt a popular formula for the fascination with a new medium of duplication that changes the forms of compatibility. To a certain extent, this kind of criticism feeds on the aura of that digital elite, whose self-attribution is reinforced by the incredible concentration of capital in the hands of relatively few solution providers (currently these are still concentrated in so called Silicon Valley).

Coding and programming

If we want to describe digitalization as a cultural phenomenon, the complexity of the conditions of production and structure of these new techniques of control, pattern identification, and feedback correlates almost aesthetically with the complexity of modern society, which quite similarly evades the classical cartographies of a stable order in its basic structures. According to the basic intuition from which this book began, the reference problem of the connectivity of digital technology and digitalization can be found in the social structure itself. Let me recall, again, Heidegger's in fact very realistic prognosis that information was to become the fundamental entity of the cybernetic age:

> The world of science becomes a cybernetic world. The cybernetic blueprint of the world presupposes that steering or regulating is the most fundamental characteristic of all calculable world-events. The regulation of one event by another is mediated by the transmission of a message, that is, by information. To the extent that the regulated event transmits messages to the one that regulated it and so informs it, the regulation has the character of a positive feedback-loop of information.[15]

To make this feedback possible and thereby guarantee compatibility with everything and every subject matter, information must not only be the elementary medium of the digital world but also itself adopt an elementary form – a form that cannot be further reduced, no longer has a shape, and differentiates discretely, in an absolute either–or, as it were.

The essentially discrete form of the foundation of all programming is at the same time a condition for the almost arbitrary form of recombining abilities. The same technology can control the most different things; it is stronger even than language, ultimately translatable into almost any situation. It is, in the truest sense of the word, a fundamental symbol of commensurability. And it is precisely here that my intuition and my argument – namely that the reference problem of digitalization is to be found in the structure of modern society itself – can be made more specific. I have already formulated the thesis at the beginning of this chapter: *the relationship between coding and programming in the world of digital data is similar to the relationship between coding and programming at the level of modern society's differentiation into functional systems.*

I need to expand a little to explain this view and flesh it out. Since the beginning of academic sociology, the description of modern society as a functionally differentiated society has functioned as one of the longest-serving and most elaborate diagnoses. The classics of sociology, from Herbert Spencer in Britain to Émile Durkheim in France, Georg Simmel and Max Weber in Germany, and Talcott Parsons in the United States, have understood social modernization above all as a process in which the social structure has displayed differentiation into the most diverse functions, spheres of value, and forms of solidarity.[16] The basic idea is that in the course of the modernization process the most important social entities became more independent of one another but, precisely because of their independence, got bound to one another in a particularly complex way. Accordingly, we observe that the logic of economic processes and the logic of political action have moved away from each other – the logic, mind. The condition for success in economic activity is profitability and monetary gain.

What is called 'capitalism' is nothing but an expression of this differentiation process. The real meaning of being active in business is, then, economic success, which opens completely new possibilities for it. The same can be seen in the sciences, which in the course of long debates and processes of emancipation were able to free themselves from religious, and later also from political forms of legitimation. This does not mean that one cannot impose scientific results politically or buy them through bribery, but that would stand out immediately as an anomaly, as a pathology. Imagine for example the establishment of a special political sphere in which power opportunities are tested and power is shared, distributed, limited, and increased as part of an institutional state arrangement. The political creates decisions of a legal form, but does not merge with the law. It is an aspect of modernization processes that law, which provides normative reliability of expectations, applies to political authorities too.

Such processes of differentiation have occurred over the past three centuries in the course of social modernization, having spread across the entire globe from Europe; ultimately they can also be understood as processes of emancipation. They are for instance attempts to free science from religious legitimation and political patronage, democratic decisions from economic power or proximity to religious dignitaries, and economic decisions from matters of salvation. And rights are granted independently of one's ability to pay, although this ability may contribute to getting justice in a court case. What should not be underestimated is the autonomization of art, which is also spared being compatible with religion, just as it would someday dispense with intelligibility to a larger audience. The privatization of the family is part of this differentiation process too – not least the shift in partner choice, from an orientation towards religious, ethnic, and especially economic criteria to love as a medium of communication in its own right.

Certain forms of social interaction emerge around these different areas. For example, people get accustomed to the idea that one must speak differently in the market and at political meetings, that religious talk is inappropriate in court, and that a scientific standard of expectation must ignore the person's religion or family background. At the same time, a special kind of discourse develops in the contexts of family and intimate love. Authenticity is expected as a staged form of private relations of this nature. Compact patterns of action develop everywhere, and some find expression partly in professional and environmentally friendly forms that are nevertheless tied to social inequality and constitute specific forms of habitual behaviour, sometimes associated with the corresponding gender roles. Then matching professional expertise and special languages, forms of reflection, and, not least, environments emerge alongside these patterns of action.

Sociologically, this diagnosis has quite different manifestations and conceptual solutions, theoretical concepts and traditions. Among themselves, such theories differ especially on the question of how to model the connection between the distinct forms. What holds such a society together, if its central authorities develop mainly centripetal forces? Is there a central authority that stands above the others? The political or the market would make natural candidates, and perhaps also something like common norms and values. Questions of integration arise, and whether such a society can be a unified piece. It is also debatable whether societies have borders, for example national borders, or only one global society exists. There are vigorous controversies on this theme, but the very fact of differentiation can hardly be denied – and it is hardly an exaggeration to claim that this fact is definitely to be found even in everyday communication. As newspaper readers or as users of other media, we can decide competently whether somebody is solving a political or an economic problem. We are trained to recognize that we behave differently at home, in the workplace, or in court. We can roughly identify when we need to switch to legal communication, and it is easy to see that communication with a doctor follows different rules from those of communication with a teacher. It should be just as clear that we literally experience all this at first hand.

In spite of this (or because of it), many observers are still looking for common codes or common principles, for a common morality or some social cohesion – but only because such things are so improbable. Incidentally, a large part of professional observation in the social sciences is looking for such unitary codes – to no avail, of course, but the strongest incentive for intensive search is its futility.

In its most radical and most consequential form, however, the diagnosis of differentiation is only found in those kinds of theories that are really able to take the observer seriously – and this applies first and foremost to cybernetic and systems-theoretical perspectives. Especially the latter have for decades been working with a conception that points semantically, but also conceptually, to the structural proximity between digitality and social system differentiation. Niklas Luhmann's social theory in particular provides a starting point for describing the structural relationship between social modernity and digitalization not only conceptually but also in terms of the structure of its order.

System building refers to operational closeness – elements of one system connect to elements of another system and form something like an internal form of structuring and stabilization. If this seems too abstract to you, imagine a consciousness, a psychic system, which is operatively tied to its own internal processes. Let me recall once more Husserl's melody example. The melody is not simply recognized by the consciousness; it is brought into a context of meaning through cognitive processes, whereby the melody arises within the framework of an internal awareness of time. In fact we should imagine the operational closeness of a mental system as an operator that knows everything external, while it knows everything else only in the form of eigenstates. This figure of thought, radicalized as it is in cybernetics, combines elements of philosophy of consciousness, physiology of perception, mathematics, and systems theory into an operational theory of the observer as an irreducible prerequisite.[17] And perhaps it also became a decisive theoretical innovation in sociology.

Social systems can also be represented as observation systems, systems made up of communications or actions that relate to one another in succession, thus building structures. But systems create order by not linking any element with any other, arbitrarily; they are selective. They impose restrictions on themselves by making certain connections more probable than others – and they are operationally closed, which is why their access to the environment is only observational:

- They impose restrictions on themselves by structuring the connections instead of making them arbitrary. Time itself creates selectivities, because not everything can be done during a unique present, because not everything is possible at the same time. And in this sense, over time, systems create structures while limiting contingencies. They generate order by not operating arbitrarily.
- They are operationally closed because they operate only within themselves, never in the environment. Just as in consciousness only consciousness content can follow consciousness content, so too in a social system only communication can follow communication

and only action can follow action. Just as one can put the world into a consciousness only in the form of consciousness content, so in a social system, too, the world appears only in the form of communication content.

- From this it follows that the environment is accessible only relatively to a system, only in the manner of operation of its own mode of operation.

I'm not trying here to overcomplicate the argument; on the contrary, I want to formalize it in the simplest possible way. Strictly speaking, the idea is very simple. We must imagine the events in one system as unfolding one after the other and as being able to refer directly only to themselves, in succession. To everything else – the environment, the world, other systems – they refer only indirectly, through their own observation. This is precisely what I refer to with the paradoxical concept of duplication. Systems duplicate the world, and in this respect both the original as an unachievable environment and one's own conception of it exist only within the system, only as a differentiation of the system itself. There is no escape from this self-restriction – and this manner of thinking has been constitutive of thinking ever since the observer was discovered – which, by the way, didn't happen yesterday. Classical rhetoric already understood the focus on internal linguistic entities in the description of facts,[18] theology knows God's transcendence only as a function of the immanence of the God-created observer,[19] and the philosophy of consciousness reaches the being of things only as awareness of things.[20] This figure is radicalized here, and it is also found in the idea, developed earlier, of considering the data – just like writing before them – as a duplication medium, which, incidentally, is also closed operationally. *One can connect to data only with data and, even if one extends the data sets, this is possible only with further data.*

But this is not yet the analogy between the social nature of society and the data-form nature of data. I must introduce another piece of theory to move further on the way to the analogy I'm looking for. This piece of theory deals with the question of how, in modern society, functional systems are differentiated. The concept of society is disputed in sociology. What can be said with certainty is that society means the totality of all communications and actions. Society is the complete system. It is the system that unifies all worldwide communication. Such a system, in whose environment there can be nothing social any longer, must create something like a total order within itself, or else would disintegrate.

In earlier societies these were strict upper class–lower class codings, classes, and statuses. Everything processed in such a society was caught up in a hierarchy. There could be no better argument from an underling, it was impossible to find suitable people for positions, what counted most was your descent from social estate and your class, family, or dynasty. Eventually such a society encountered severe limitations, and in the process of modernization experienced at first hand that claims to validity form beyond this indiscriminate top–bottom coding. One experienced for example that the value of money could be at odds with stratification: a coin had the same value, no matter from whom it came. One experienced that the observation of the skies began to contradict religious cosmology, a keyword in the Copernican turn. At the same time, these logics differentiated themselves from one another and became independent – exactly the process I have just described as functional differentiation. Now this adjustment was not an immediate short-term process; it was not a disruptive event. The social system rather adjusted its internal order, at first imperceptibly, then more explicitly, shifting from the all-purpose top–bottom scheme to a kind of cross-differentiation. The primary level of order was, then, no longer formed by classes and social inequality but by the inequality of different functions, which established themselves side by side and formed systems – functional systems: politics, economy, religion, law, art, education. This is not to say that top–bottom distinctions were or are irrelevant. Much to the contrary, modernity, too, knows strong social inequalities – both globally and within state-limited spaces. But this differentiation does not represent the formation of social order in general – which does not mean that social inequalities are thus insignificant or could be neglected; that would be absurd. Rather, it is about the formation of functional systems, which constitute the decisive form of order in social modernity, with its expansive tendencies.

Empirically, the formation of functional systems can be reconstructed as a slow process of emancipation – initially from functional semantics, that is, from ways of speaking, terminologies, and forms of justification and meaning. Then political semantics emerges; this one refers exclusively to economic processes. There are exclusively scientific criteria or legal codes that convey the world, each time in the form of their own logic. In fact this happened first of all linguistically, and thus made possible the operative emancipation of economic from religious or political figures of reasoning, for example, or the detachment of scientific justifications from non-scientific categories. It is, then, the linguistic forms that vary most among themselves – and the printing press has played a strong role here, both in the preservation of such ways of speaking and in their maintenance and further development.

However, the linguistic form alone was able to stabilize functional systems. To understand the problem, we should turn once again to the question of system formation. As has already been explained, systems stabilize themselves by limiting the realm of their possibilities over time, by destroying contingency,[21] and by developing a structure in which they secure structural connections.

Niklas Luhmann faced this problem and was the first to come across *media* that facilitate this possibility to connect. Let's play this out in the case of the economic system: an economic system based on barter would have difficulty separating economic from non-economic operations – one would have to rely more on trust in the other person, difficult negotiations would be necessary, and it would hardly be possible to make economic values independent of the traded goods. The transition to *money* as a medium produces enormous relief. Money requires trust, too, but this is trust in a system, in the economy, rather than trust in your physical counterpart. Money can be modalized, permits comparisons, decouples payer from payment, exempts you from anything that is not an economic feature, and can be stored and transported; in addition, you can deploy something like a generalized pricing mechanism, because money becomes calculable through its numerical form. Money, says Luhmann, is no longer a medium of exchange, then, but a medium of communication through which payment can be connected to payment. Money makes economic communication more independent of extra-economic criteria – and is thus a precondition for the differentiation of a modern economic system. Similar media emerge for science (truth), for politics (power), for law (justice), for religion (faith), and also for the familial and intimate relationships (love). In a reference to the American sociologist Talcott Parsons, Luhmann calls these media 'symbolically generalized communications media': they are symbolically generalized in that they build general symbolic forms, and they are communications media in that they increase the probabilities of communicative connections. Money makes it more probable that payments can be related to one another, and only political power enables political operations without the immediate threat of violence.

But communications media of this sort must be able to relate to an operator, to obtain an operational stability that makes them probable and that allows a modern society on the one hand to attain stability, on the other to provide an unprecedented wealth of forms. In Luhmann's words,

> Symbolically generated communications media require a *uniform code* (central code) for the entire media field. A code consists

of two opposing values, and at this level (naturally not 'in life') excludes third and further values. This converts the possibility – indefinite but tending to increase – of the communicated meaning proposal being rejected into a hard either/or, that is, transforms an 'analog' situation into a 'digital' one; what is gained is a clear choice to be made, the same for both alter and ego. It is not their opinions that are coded but the communication itself; and this is done in a fashion that has to rely on learning ability, namely, on the specification of criteria for the correct attribution of positive and negative values.[22]

Such codes are discretely made, in other words they are binary forms that exclude third values and in turn express a simple enough inclusion or exclusion condition for the operations of a system. Let me test this again on the economic system. The code of the economic system is 'pay/not pay'. This code is unavoidable for economic operations: it grounds the self-referential operational closeness (autopoiesis) of the modern economic system worldwide. An economic operation does pay – or it does not. The negative value is part of this too, for non-payment is possible only as an economic operation. If I am somewhere where payment cannot be expected, I am not even able not to pay. But where a product, for example, is not purchased (because it's too expensive, or unsuitable, or unwanted), there is no payment. This has nothing to do with levels of motivation. I may pay for this or that reason, even for purely extra-economic reasons such as charity, sympathy, or the desire to do something morally worthy. But it is crucial that the economic system registers this exclusively as payment or non-payment. This is how the parenthetic 'naturally not "in life"' in my quotation is to be understood: at the level of coding there is nothing but payment or non-payment, and in the end payments or non-payments are also what constitutes the structure of the economic system. The positive value of the code expresses connectivity, which increases the probability of further operations.

This theory construction responds to the question of system closure, that is, to the differentiation of a functional system – in this case, the economic system – and thus it responds to the complexity of society. The system can differentiate itself only if there is a situation in which the probability of connection is increased by the fact that this is clearly a connection, that is, if belonging to the system is really distinguishable. The ultimate goal is to establish or increase the indisputable character of economic operations. This is by no means a mere theoretical statement; it is rather the empirical problem of how a society that can no longer rely on the hierarchical order of a simple top–bottom coding should succeed in generating order and predictability.

The digital simplicity of society

Systems operate with simple solutions, which are compatible with different possibilities, and any wealth of forms can develop only on the basis of this simplicity. This idea is analogous with the relationship from which I started this chapter, namely the relationship between *simplicity* and *multiplicity*, as it is constitutive of the shape of digital technology.

It is not without reason that Luhmann's theoretical solution describes the issue of stabilizing the system as a *digital* process. The medium is a binarily built, discrete, and inviolable distinction constructed in the same way as *technological* digitalization, which always knows only 0 and 1 – at least at the level of the code, which applies here as well: 'of course not in "real life"'. In real life we do not see 0 and 1 but forms, variety, recombination, and so on. As I have already explained, the wealth of forms and the almost ubiquitous capacity of the digital to make everything commensurable with everything are based directly on the simplicity of the medium – on the simple binary code, which is practically without presuppositions and thus becomes an unavoidable prerequisite.

One has to imagine the relationship between medium or code and form in functional systems in just the same way. It is precisely the digital simplicity of the form that leads to the fact that modern functional systems know almost no stopping rules within themselves, for the only limiting factor is the application of the code. This is why monetary payments can relate to all sorts of things in society, almost ubiquitously. As far as payments or non-payments are concerned, almost anything is monetizable. This is exactly the experience made by modern societies: it is difficult to limit an economic system, for example, because the smoothness of the medium of money and the exclusiveness of the binary code can colonize *everything* – but only within the boundaries of the code.

Diagnoses of economization are in vogue, if only because money is really so pliable and the function of the economic system – scarcity compensation – actually docks in many places. But a diagnosis of politicization is equally conceivable, or one of scientification – in other words a colonization of almost everything in society by the political or the scientific element. Incidentally, this has indeed happened throughout history – in politics, in the form of dictatorship and attempted political uniformization of society;

or, in science, as a warning, very loud in the 1950s, against the total scientification of society.

Anyway, the complexity of modern society can be explained in two ways. One explanatory factor is the differentiation of binarily coded functional systems, which establish an unavoidable difference of perspective in society. Our view of the world inevitably multiplies, and even the attempts to colonize society completely through coding are bound to fail. The other factor is the very simplicity of binary coding, which enables an incredible wealth of operational possibilities. One could say that, because the binary code determines the basic operation in such a radical way, it cannot limit the variety of possibilities. The code is completely indifferent to the question of what is being paid for, thus creating an almost uncontrollable way of increasing the options.

The counterpart to the code payment/non-payment in the economy would be power/non-power in politics and government/ opposition in democracies. In the sciences, it would be truth/ non-truth – and this is not about emphatic truth but about the question of matters of truth. The scientific code is indifferent to what is true and what is false, or what is researched and what is not. We could now go through the other functional systems and look for the corresponding codes, but the argument should be clear by now. Systems-theoretical sociology has a readily available toolset for the description of the simultaneity of stable structure formation on the one hand, radical wealth of forms on the other. The codings are not arbitrary, but the possibilities of unfolding are manifold.

Elsewhere I have frequently used the notion of 'brutality' in relation to the coding of functional systems.[23] This brutality is due to the unavoidability of the codes. Those who are economically active are brutally relegated to the mechanism of payment and are tied to the profitability of economic transactions. Those who want to achieve something collectively binding have no other option than to test power opportunities. Even a politics that criticizes domination needs power to achieve anything. And anyone who displays art is measured by a code like beautiful/non-beautiful, even if his or her art aspires to deny beauty of the traditional kind. As for issues of truth, at some point they will inevitably face the fact that the code of true/untrue is applied and the claim to scientific validity is scientifically negated. The factual brutality of the code makes it so difficult to intervene, in the course of time, in a coordinating fashion because ultimately one can act only from the perspective of one of the decentralized systems, since there are no operations outside the systems. One could proclaim *nulla salus extra systemam*, 'there is no salvation outside the system', but it will be difficult to find *salus* even *intra systemas* – within systems.

As a reminder, the previous considerations are intended to take my argument one step further on the way to justifying the structural digitality of modern society. Now, Luhmann's description does not give us only an equivocation, in other words this is not just about applying concepts (or metaphors) from the field of digitalization or digitality. This would not suffice as a scientific thesis. Rather, it becomes obvious that the reference problem of digitalization is actually rooted in the social structure of modern society. I would like to sharpen my argument in *seven* steps, in the manner of a thesis.

1. The modern social structure of a functionally differentiated society must replace the vanished order of the old world in which everything had a place, in which one could refer to unchangeable traditions, and in which change and innovation were to be ruled out. It must replace it with a different kind of order.
2. Order is always the victory of simplicity over multiplicity. By simplicity I mean the generation of uncontroversial regularities that up to a point can be kept as a basic condition. Diversity is possible only where there is such simplicity. Then diversity does not dissolve in unstable complexity but becomes self-stabilizing.[24]
3. Modern society seems to find this stabilization in the simplicity of the binary codes of its functional systems. Minimum conditions are established such that the operations cannot fall behind them: everything in economy must start from the mechanism of payment, everything in politics must start from the mechanism of power, everything in law must distinguish right from wrong, nothing in science can avoid issues of truth, everything in art is processed aesthetically (i.e. as beautiful or non-beautiful), and everything in religion comes up against the immanence of transcendence. These two-sided forms enforce positioning, they enforce it binarily and hence simplistically, thus preventing an unstable complexity.
4. It is precisely this simplicity that makes it possible to build complexity. Once the mechanism of payment has been established, there are hardly any limits to the unfolding of forms and possibilities. This is why growth seems to be practically inscribed into the economic system, why hardly anything is safe from political power, why science is not only particularly efficient but also inherently contradictory inasmuch as it does not produce any unambiguity, and so on.
5. The reference problem of such a society: it must be capable of handling the relationship between simplicity and diversity.

6. The mechanism for solving this reference problem is not digitalization. Rather the solution has always been a digital one, in that functional systems are presented with a somewhat brutal lack of alternatives for their connection.

7. Efficient digital technology follows the same pattern as functional systems in society: it can achieve its wealth of forms, and thus also its triumphant march into almost all practices of modern society, only because it is also structurally built around the relationship between simplicity and diversity. Its brutally simple coding and its mediality via binary patterns are the foundation of its manifold, hardly limitable use in all realms of society.

But these seven theses must be completed by one crucial general thesis:

• My argument is not that digitalization is also a functional system of society, analogous with the functions I have mentioned. Digitality is a technological form (its technicity will be discussed in the next two chapters) whose structure solves a problem of order similar to that of the functional systems of modern society: how to develop multiple forms on the basis of a simple medium. As digitality is made exactly this way and is capable of doing exactly this, it is in this way compatible with modern society. A society built differently would have had no use for digital technology.

What has been said here should answer my basic question: *what problem does digitalization solve?* In the first chapter I introduced this question as a functionalist one – the incentive was not just to look at the impact of a technology on society but to pursue the idea that only technologies of this kind can establish themselves within a social structure that accommodates them. The answer to the basic question is that *digitalization starts from the reference problem of social complexity.* Thus digitalization is not a foreign object in society but, if you like, it is flesh from the flesh of society.

Increased options

If there is a central topos in the reception and discussion of digitalization and digital technology, it is the experience of boundlessness, loss of control, and ubiquity. This holds for popular diagnoses such as Harari's diagnosis of catastrophe,[25] but academic literature, too, perceives, along with the matter itself, the surplus of digital strategies such as those formulated by Dirk Helbing,[26] Rob Kitchin,[27]

Deborah Lupton,[28] or even Zygmunt Bauman[29] – and rightly so. The basic experience of digitalization is that it stops at nothing, not even at humiliating the human being, who is shown how much better the machine can be,[30] and who gets by-passed whenever possible. In sociology, this is readily associated with quantification, with the power of the digits. To give you the flavour of such diagnoses, I will quote from Steffen Mau again. He explains that,

> although the state and markets were important starting points for the expansion of calculative practices, the language of numbers has since become universalized to a degree that far transcends both these domains and that of science. A new 'quantitative mentality' has arisen, with profound implications for our social environment. This mentality accords numbers an almost auratic pre-eminence when it comes to identifying social phenomena, and is now leading to an ever-widening reliance on all things numeric. Everything can, should or must be measured – nothing seems to be possible without numbers any more.[31]

Whether there is a 'universalization of digits' is open to debate – apart from the fact that numeric values in particular are *universal* per se, because they function relatively independently of context. Nor do I want to discuss whether the thesis that the social is completely quantified is correct – off the cuff, I could cite other trends, such as the qualitative form of the definition of social affiliations in the whole debate on migration, which practically blocks quantifying clarification. Decisive here instead is the basic experience that produces such diagnoses – what Dirk Baecker calls the experience of a 'surplus of control',[32] which is indeed based on metrics, quantifications, forms of comparability, self-tracking, and standardization through fixed measures. The diagnosis of 'universalization' is an expression of the experience of that surplus of control, which ultimately evades control.

At least one should admit that a form of limitlessness is already inherent in digital technology per medium. Per medium means that it is already an integral feature of the mediatic substrate that there is ultimately no such thing as any internal, built-in stop rule. In this respect, the digital is once again comparable to writing, which is indeed limitless insofar as there is no fundamental limit to its capability to recombine. Writing (which is based on language and speaking) does not know any limits at the level of the medium – it encounters limits of sayability, and also limits of time, because it is not possible to write down everything at the same time, but then again, these very limits are occasions to write.

The ubiquitous quality of the digital resides in its simplicity and in its mode of processing signals without presuppositions. This feature has to do not so much with the universalization of 'digits' as with the translatability of everything into the language of the digital, which covers society like a self-referential network of electronic signals. The plasticity of the digital technology consists in its being applicable to everything, and also in a form that combines a strict medium with a loose matching of the capabilities of information technology. Incidentally, it not a negligible detail that the very technology that is said to have an almost disruptive applicability to everything, with rapid consequences of change and dislocation, depends on an almost centralistic definition of global technological standards. It's enough to think of data transfer logs, of file formats that make everything completely accessible to everybody, at least in principle. It's enough to think that certain standard formats and programs had to prevail – which is also true of programming languages and so on. One may believe all these developments to be just the result of cut-throat capitalist competition, but then one must at least explain why there is an obvious demand for such a concentration.

It is one of the winged pieces of wisdom of the self-historicization of the digital word that the best standard does not necessarily prevail; the development of MS-DOS by Microsoft in combination with the rise of the IBM PC to industrial standard is frequently adduced as an example. The fact that such standards prevail is just an indication that the increased options of the digital need a compatible medium – and in this context one has to admit that it is not only the media substrate of the technology itself that has a mediatic function here but also the standard software, which makes possible in the first place the form of the application and its compatibility with other formats. One day the historiography of the digital will tell stories about why it was this software that prevailed and not another, this programming language and not another, these protocols and not others.

At any rate, standardization is the foundation for ubiquity of application and for combinability, for the matching of the data sets. Thus, precisely because of the relationship between simplicity and diversity described earlier, the processing of data makes it possible to monopolize almost every field of practice. As data accumulate and become available – or can be generated and made available – everywhere, there is scope for digital applications, but also necessities related to them.

This is what the social observation of digitalization initially sees: the ubiquitous form of digitalization of the various areas of society, a process that in turn affects social practice. Entire industries have been revolutionized and transformed, particularly by platform-economic models, and lifestyles are co-determined by making data-driven tools available – as an opening of possibilities and as a normative monitoring of one's own living practice. All attempts to limit this come up against limits – technological, legal, economic, political, but most of all the limits of the control mechanism itself. The control surplus caused by the world of data can hardly be controlled. Therefore increased options are, in a way, in the digital nature of things.

At this point a parallel offers itself again between modern society and the digital world. As early as twenty years ago, I pointed out, in the context of studies in the sociology of risk, that a tendency towards increased options is inherent in the functional differentiation of society.[33] The argument was that this tendency towards increased options is directly connected to the binary coding of functional systems.

Once again, the train of thought is as follows. Coded systems are characterized by the fact that their interfaces, that is, the continuation of their mode of functioning, can be seen exclusively in the assignment of positive or negative code values. These are differentiated systems not only because the world exists in them only in the form of self-projections of the codes, but most of all because these codes always connect to operations of their own systems.[34] *Precisely because modern functional systems are coded systems, they lack any built-in stopping rule, and hence the ability of an appropriate self-limitation.*

The only stopping rule that coded systems may know would be that the system comes to an end when the code can no longer be applied. But one can always pay or not pay; everything that happens under the sun can be processed politically, legally, religiously, scientifically, artistically, or pedagogically and never leaves a shortage of options for further behaviour, because this is exactly what society has functionally differentiated itself for. Functional systems where the application of the code is the only condition for their existence – or, better, for their operation – lose self-control, so to speak, because they cannot break out of their code. There are very many examples:

- *Science* cannot avoid or actively forget scientific findings. This is why we will never get rid of nuclear fission or systems theory; and this is why scientific perspectives lose convergence with so-called lifeworld perspectives, as I have shown in the Husserl example. *We* can very well regulate certain kinds of research legally, fight them politically or discredit them morally, but any stopping rule within the scientific system would itself have to adopt scientific forms again.

- *Medical progress* results in a multiplication of medical options, which in turn leads to completely new questions; suffice it to think of the entire set of questions on intensive care medicine, or of the problem of determining time of death for the purpose of organ transplantation, and also of the question whether medicine transgresses the limits of anthropological self-evidence through the use of certain technologies, for example in genetic engineering. Also here belongs the question of overdiagnosing, which can produce the result that the positive value of the systems-constituting distinction ill–healthy, namely 'ill', can hardly be avoided and that the increased options of the medical realm can no longer incorporate health.

- *Economic processes* are, in a sense, the classic example of increased options. What is called 'capitalism' is in a sense the basic factor of increased options, which is why this rather economic cipher could be elevated to being a basic feature of society itself. Incidentally, this category includes the sometimes complete decoupling of the financial economy from the production and trading of goods. Economic actors access options of downright virtual monetary transactions, which have been completely decoupled from the economic needs of entire national economies. That something like growth tendency is inscribed into modern economy, practically for reasons related to the system's coding, is one of the almost unsolvable problems of an economy that can endanger its own foundations by registering success only in economic terms. For example, it is rather blind to the problem of the entropy of its own metabolism.

- Over the centuries, *the mass media* had to fight for the right to report on everything; now they have means of swift and comprehensive coverage that radically increase their options and sometimes undermine their service to society, namely to take care that society is equipped with information. This information tends to get more diffuse because it is more contradicting, more extensive, and, not least, more confusing.

- Ultimately *politics* cannot stay away from any topic in which power could be acquired, secured, or lost. The dictatorships of the twentieth century, but also the boom in authoritarian forms of politics in the twenty-first, are clearly ways of increasing political options that have aspired to, and indeed achieved, a complete politicization of society.

- *Religious* fundamentalism is a modern phenomenon, an increase in the options of the religious in direct reaction to the fact that now religion, too, is just one functional system among others and has experienced a discrepancy between its function of representing the whole and its position in society.

So the essence of my thesis is this: coded functional systems have neither external nor internal criteria that could limit their operations and thereby bring about a measure of self-restraint, of sacrificing one's options, or that could lead in the end to complete transparency in their logic. The result is, first, a logic of the radical increase in options and, second, a radical increase in social complexity. That modern sociality always experiences itself as being in crisis,[35] in a state of mess, and, not least, uncontrollable and out of control is due not so much to loss of meaning, a question relevant to the classics of sociology (Max Weber), to lack of morality (Durkheim), or to the crises of integration of a social community (Parsons). The real reason is precisely the lack of any systematic place for an overall regulation or overall selectivity of the system. To put it in simple words, because of the differentiation structure, there is no place that really organizes and integrates the parts. Integration would mean that the parts could limit themselves, or could be limited, in favour of the whole. But there is no functional position for this. Integration always happens only in concrete presences, only in the here and now, and not in principle. To explain this, I have cited the figure of duplication. There is no place where an original could be found; all operations are duplications of the world, and actually they refer only to themselves.

This theory, and the diagnosis of options amplification, allow us to describe the experience of crisis in modern societies as something much more fundamental than a mere consequence of wrong political or economic decisions. To avoid misunderstandings, I should say that I am not talking here about an almost fateful development, as if there were no attempts at least to hedge in the increases in options of the functional systems; suffice it to recall the attempts to limit political or economic options legally, political attempts to offset the inequality effects of economic or educational systems, or scientific attempts to make rational decision-making situations justifiable. The crucial thing is that an overall integration of society has become impossible, because the differently coded possibilities to connect find, each, their own way out.

Solutions such as the institutional organization of classical industrial society, which was able to bind the centripetal forces of society precisely through such an organizing principle, may be less likely than the impact of the current change in institutional arrangements, which make the structure of social modernity visible. I am convinced that no epoch is currently coming to an end, that no 'next' society is dawning, as Dirk Baecker would have it; or at least this next society would probably be a functionally differentiated society, too. Perhaps it is only now, after the stable arrangement of western industrial society, that the whole structure of social modernity becomes visible – that the efficiency of the social system is secured by the differentiation of functions, with their almost brutally simple possibilities of connection, but that the undermining of internal stopping rules is also responsible for the costs of the system.

Sapere aude – *dare to know* – *as reflected in digitalization*

The structure of digitalization fits almost seamlessly into a society that obviously does not know any internal stopping rules or mechanisms of external control and integration even for its currently existing control authorities. The fact that digitalization is experienced as a disruption relates, of course, to completely new experiences. The duplication of the world through data processing is fed back to the functional systems and possibly even reinforces the option increases. I have referred earlier to those 'disruptions', which is how these feedbacks of the digital on the world we call analog are perceived. It may well be that it is not just the novelty of the technological and socio-technological solutions that is perceived as being disruptive. It may well be that what is new is that modernity is now actually distorting itself beyond recognition: *it can no longer make invisible everything that it represents as a functionally differentiated society and hide it behind an institutional organization that western public discourses and most of the social sciences have held to be the basic structure of society.* The structure is much more radical – it paid for the unleashing of its own powers by making stopping rules impossible, which now requires more intelligent forms of steering and observation. Whether digitalization is more of a problem or more of a solution cannot be decided, because it is already there – sometimes still perceived as an alien, but in its basic structure it is of the same kind as modern society itself.

Perhaps we must place ourselves on the couch for some socio-analysis, and perhaps digitalization is the event that currently forces us to take seriously the displaced structures of a social system whose order involves two things: the *simplicity* of the coding of its control authorities and the radical *diversity* of its practical possibilities and variations. Perhaps this connection was all too hidden behind that ordinary model of a western industrial society with its western institutional organization, which quite obviously suggested more stability than there really was, in a historically highly improbable period after the Second World War. This western model of an industrial society has taken itself to be the normal model of the social and has perhaps perceived the centripetal forces of functional differentiation less strongly than it was experienced in other parts of the world. We may have to let go of this superego – to stay with the metaphor. Incidentally, one indication could be that the Asian region for instance finds it easier than old Europe to cope with digitalization. This is at least an indication of how varied a functionally differentiated society is.

It should be carefully noted that the social West has much to lose – not only in terms of economy and power but also in terms of the achievements of that institutional mode of organizing. It is no coincidence that this danger becomes visible above all in the role of digitalization. The explanation lies in that option-increasing form of digitalization, which is directly connected to the option-increasing possibilities provided by functional systems. Currently the classic institutions have little to offer by way of countermeasures.

The experience with digitalization is primarily not an experience with a colonial master who encounters from the outside well-rehearsed routines with the plan to disrupt them. My argument reverses this figure: digitalization proves to be more of a mirror in which modern society becomes aware of itself when it encounters the control-averse combination of simplicity of medium and diversity of form. Digital technology is in fact similar to the basic structure of the functional systems of a modern society. A theory of digitalization and digital society can hardly afford to remain below this level of analysis if it does not want to find itself in the illusion of control – the illusion of getting a grip on the option-increasing techniques of the digital with the possibilities of control of classic industrial society. The complexity of social modernity becomes visible only now.

It must be conceded that the statements made here do not come from the outside but from within – and can lay claim only on the coding of the scientific. They cannot mark any claims of control over digitalization, but they can mark claims of validity related to its comprehensibility. Looking into the mirror of digitalization could thus be an occasion for a social–theoretical imperative 'dare to know' – *sapere aude*.

Excursus
Digital Metabolism

Digital technology comes unembodied, immaterial, indeed in the form of information. At first glance, one could say that in the age of classic modernity forms of value creation – and not only value of an economic nature – were characterized by mechanical, material machines and large-scale plants. It was all about the physical and chemical processing of raw materials and a tangible metabolism. They are now followed by an immaterial form, almost free of metabolism and based much more on knowledge and information. Between the *historical materialism* of the hunter-gatherer and the large-scale nuclear plant, the path of thought tends to a kind of *historical immaterialism*, from language to electronic information processing, via writing and signs. But the immateriality of data processing refers exclusively to the processing of information or data. My diagnosis that data networks will spread across society in much the same way as did the printing press in the past, and my idea of an increase in options that is built into the combination of *simplicity and diversity* certainly have a material dimension too: digitalization takes place in an analog world, which in turn reacts to it as modern societies do, namely through financing needs, through translations into economic business models, through political regulation, through legal frameworks, and, not least, through educational guidelines for the correct use of data. Digitalization is of this world – just as printing was, and still is. It duplicates the world in data form and must be represented exactly within this world – *meaningfully and entropically*. Meaningfully because the data must always be converted into analog forms, entropically because maintaining the data network consumes energy and thus generates heat. The post-fossil data world shows several fossil dimensions.

That data are the new 'oil', as everyone says, means not just that they are some raw material with which value can be created. They are the new 'oil' because they more than anything else stand for a radical increase in the options of the economy, and thereby also promote a concentration of capital that was one of the causes of the actual distribution of global political interests already in the twentieth century, driven as it was by oil. To this day, many of the conflicts in the region we call the Near East are an expression of that concentration of capital, which stems directly from the need for fossil fuel energy. One could have written at the time that increases in economic options were possible because oil as an energy carrier and its derivates could be used almost everywhere and enabled the highest form of value creation in a short time span. The concrete materiality of oil, its dependence on transport, its regional distribution, and, not least, the colonial and postcolonial network of relations between producer and consumer countries structured industrial capitalism in much the same way as coal had done before.[1] Incidentally, this is by no means just a crisis phenomenon. Modernity, which is based on carbonized value creation, has brought about fantastic technological, medical, cultural, and social achievements. This was a historically unprecedented unleashing of social forces, whose proneness to crisis certainly lay also in the enormous unleashing potential itself. But the standards that are taken for granted in modernity and have brought forth the criteria for this critical attitude are also a result of this social development. In this respect, this development has been a *materialist* one even in its immaterial dimensions, because the driving force of what is called in Marxist idiom 'the development of the productive forces' turned out to be decisive – even if sociologically one can reconstruct with much greater precision the conversions of differentiation to functional differentiation as the basis of material industrialism.

Michael Betancourt contrasts this with the immateriality of the digital and describes the 'aura of the digital' in its immateriality: 'At the same time, the digital appears as a naturalization of the concentration of capital, since the digital itself poses as a magical resource that can be used without consumption or diminishment, leading to a belief in accumulation without production. This shift from a basis in limiting factors and scarcity is inherent to the immaterial form posed by the digital.'[2]

For Betancourt, a critic of digital capitalism of Marxist orientation, any immaterial production is already a phenomenon of crisis in itself, but his diagnosis is impressive in that it sums up very aptly the urge of digital capitalism to increase the options. It is precisely the immaterial form of value creation – that is, information technology – that enables digital products, with their low marginal costs, to strive for an even higher speed of expansion and to increase options even more than was possible for the products of 'material' industrial capitalism. This is perhaps the decisive repercussion of the digital on society: that the conditions of production, reproduction, and processing are simplified because we are actually dealing with the production, reproduction, and processing of information-shaped – or rather data-shaped – forms.

This dynamic, however, comes up against a society that is already there – if you want to put it succinctly. Digital products have limitations of their own, because the low marginal costs[3] suggest an almost infinite form of sales, whereas society, as a material, analog society, simply draws boundaries in the form of customers' ability and willingness to pay, in the form of limits on the manipulative influence on self-optimizing individuals, but also in the form of technological restrictions on what is possible. Once a program is realized, these restrictions prove to be more effective than appeared in its design and intentions.

My argument is that the technology's low marginal costs and simple starting point, as well as the availability of data, suggest a limitlessness that simultaneously ignores and explodes the material and factual limits of an existing society. *The data economy contains no inherent stopping rule.*

The oil era has structured the energy, economic, and political processes around the availability of fossil fuels. One remembers the oil crises of the 1970s, when the political and market-driven reduction in the availability of this source of energy resulted in severe restrictions. The most impressive image was surely that of empty motorways: the events of those days could not have been staged in an aesthetically more dramatic way. If we accept the diagnosis of the *immateriality* of the digital, empty data motorways are hardly conceivable because data, unlike oil, tend to multiply through use. *Data are processed, not consumed.* Nevertheless, they must be collected.

Today the Arabian desert (to name but one important area of extraction) is to be found in California, south of San Francisco, where a concentration of capital and professional virtuosity is becoming the very symbol of immaterial capitalism. Its immateriality does not lie in the fact that no goods are transacted, no traffic routes are used, or no industrial products are made; only the form of value creation is immaterial here. Actually these financially strong companies, whose corporate asssets sometimes reach rather symbolic heights, make their profits through information processing, and often do not even own all the material objects connected to their activities. Uber does not own a single car and Airbnb does not own a single accommodation. All that Facebook, WhatsApp, Instagram, and other media outlets are doing is handling information, and, even for companies that produce material objects, data are the decisive raw material when it comes to improving their products; this is how Nick Srnicek describes 'platform capitalism'.[4]

And yet the discourse of immateriality is correct only in relation to data processing and the technological basis is highly energy-consuming and depends on rare raw materials.[5] When we discuss generating value creation, insight, communication, steering power, and so on with the help of data, we should not forget that the media substrate of digitalization depends on machines that ensure that closed data operations with changing stress states are maintained, that data must be stored, archived, and kept available, that functioning networks interconnect those servers, enabling the constant exchange of data, and that applications are processed in an increasing number of terminals, including mobile ones. For example, a networked terminal such as a tablet in a connected data centre, if it is online, consumes up to five times the energy it needs just for itself.[6]

In addition, we should not forget that digital applications and the digital steering of processes very much control and enable classic energy consumption. Consider for example the transportation sector: global air travel is one of the most data-intensive industries, but also a major consumer of fossil fuels, let alone the production and maintenance of operations. The same applies to car traffic – but also to heavy industry, or heating. The shift to an allegedly immaterial digital value creation does not at all mean the disappearance of material goods and energy turnover. This is not necessarily relevant to a theory of the digital, but very relevant to its practice – including, by the way, what it means for the participation of working people. But this is not the topic here.

There is no really valid information about the share of data processing in the total global energy consumption. Calculations suggest that data centres account for something between 1.1 per cent and 1.5 per cent of global energy consumption. In the United States the share is 2.2 per cent. If we take into account not only data centres but also terminals, communications networks, and their manufacture, one assumes a share of about 5 per cent of the total consumption of electricity.[7]

As far as data centres are concerned, the largest energy consumer in Europe, after Great Britain and France, is Germany. Calculations assume that the demand will increase from 12 billion kWh/year to more than 16 billion kWh/year by 2025, when the energy efficiency of mainframes and data centres will improve significantly thanks to new technologies, especially cooling ones. This also applies to the energy consumption of mobile devices.[8] The energy efficiency of computers has roughly doubled every year and a half over the past fifty years. For example, in 1950 the amount of energy needed to prepare lunch for four people (about 1 kWh) could perform only about 10,000 operations, by comparison with about 1 billion operations today.[9]

Granted, this focus on classic digital applications and terminals by no means conveys the full picture, for the increase in digital options in the technological field can be seen precisely in the fact that the relatively simple, yet highly complex possibility of digital control has found its way into commonplace devices and household appliances of all kinds, which at first sight are not associated with digitalization – from the intelligent fridge and digitally controllable household technology to toys and mundane networking via mobile devices; and this is not just about the devices themselves, but also about their energy-intensive networking. If you include in our calculations the energy consumption of these devices, you will see how electricity consumption is increasing at a very serious rate. A 2018 study by the Borderstep Institute predicts that in the EU the additional consumption of these devices could amount to about 70 TWh/year – which would be almost equivalent to the electricity generated by all active nuclear power plants in Germany in 2017.[10] How valid this information is *in concreto* remains to be seen but, even if it were overestimated by a factor of 3 or 4, this consumption would still have a significant effect on the energy footprint.[11]

In summary, one could say that digitalization, at something around 5 per cent of the world's total consumption of electricity, is far from counting among the biggest energy guzzlers. Possibly the rates will not increase but consumption in absolute terms certainly will, if we assume that economic development in previously less developed regions of the world will also increase their degree of digitalization through computing services of their own. If, however, we look at the digitalization of everyday products and services, the rates are considerable. The fact that all this energy must be generated – from renewable, but also from fossil and nuclear sources – deserves at least some attention. At the same time, it must be conceded that digital energy management may be one of the most important drivers for avoiding CO_2 emissions, both in the production and distribution of electricity from renewable sources and in the management of fossil fuels.[12]

Thus digitalization has in fact a material side, whereby the current form of energy production, energy management, and energy distribution is fundamentally dependent on digital steering elements. Incidentally, digitalization depends on matter not only in issues of energy: its own activities require raw materials that are exceptionally limited. This is especially true of a secondary raw material that is important for running computers and terminals, and also for batteries and charging devices, namely the group called 'rare earths'. Without them, those technologies cannot operate. In Japan, these earths are called the 'vitamins of industry'. The rates of price increases for rare earths are exorbitant, and they repeat a geo-strategic conflict strongly reminiscent of the fatal disputes over access to oil in the twentieth century. Monopoly in this area belongs to China, which is already vastly superior to its competitors as a result of its failure to comply with environmental standards in the mining of these earths.[13] At least as far as the mining of rare earths is concerned – and I mean raw materials such as cobalt and lithium – the mistakes of the oil era are repeated to some extent, when it comes to the question of exploiting raw materials while granting only a small share of the profits to the regions rich in these materials.[14] However, it is assumed that resources will remain limited – forecasts mention an availability of less than fifty years.[15] This resource-related but also geo-strategic 'criticality' of rare earths creates a strong need for research into recycling and substitution measures.[16] Many a consumer will have learned from their mobile services provider that old mobile phones and smartphones have become a lucrative raw material: the reason is the scarcity of rare earths.

The considerations reviewed here are neither an economic nor a technical analysis of the materiality, indeed of the material conditions of digitalization. They are only a pointer in this direction. For digitalization, like everything else, takes place within the entropy of a closed system and produces immaterial kinds of information that are neutral to entropy while its material prerequisites and consequences are not; and this is yet another indication of the immanence of the immateriality of the digital.

5

Functioning Technology

When we speak of digitalization, we refer almost invariably to a technological phenomenon. Yet the fact that digitalization is technology has been mentioned only *en passant* in my argument so far and has not been systematically examined. The focus has been instead on the relationship between medium and form – that is, the electronic medium of the binary code, with its brutally simple structure, and the forms that, precisely because of the simple structure of the medium, not only are exceptionally diverse but hardly come up against any limits to their application. In order to describe this relation of *simplicity* and *diversity*, as I have called it, writing, conceived of as a medium with discrete but by no means simply structured signs, came into view above all as a standard of comparison. Thus I have described the technological raw material of data as a medium of signs. Now I'm changing direction and describe it as a technology. To this purpose, it makes sense to compare digital technology with non-digital technology.

For one, I'm going to develop the argument that digital technology, like any other, should be understood as technology because it is explicitly its status as technology that makes it break through. Although digital technology looks really confusing, unpredictable, and unfamiliar, it prevails most of all because it works. *Functioning exempts it from reflecting and speaks for itself. Doubts about the digital actually dissolve if digital technology proves its practical worth. Precisely because it fits almost seamlessly into society's mode of functioning, it no longer looks alien but accommodates the practice of society itself, at the latest by the time it works in its concrete areas of application.* This thesis, which here appears to be rather vague, is going to be worked out in this chapter. For this purpose, I need first of all to clarify the concepts of technology and technicity, to then be able to understand digital technology better.

The function of the technological

The function of technology was already summed up very aptly by Ernst Cassirer in the 1930s. He understood technology as one of the symbolic forms, namely the one that captures reality 'through the medium of efficacy'.[1] This symbolic form is oriented to the question of what would later be called 'functioning'. The medium of activity is oriented to the question of impact or effecting [*Bewirken*] itself, not to the product. To some extent, technology is a way to achieve a goal – and in this sense it is a method, a form of effecting. One misses the originality of technology if one focuses on the product and not on the particular form of an action or process. Werner Rammert has summarized the situation with great precision, to give us a sociological understanding of technology:

> *Techno-structuration* takes place when the heterogeneous elements of these technicization processes are coupled and transformed into artificial and relatively closed systems in a manner which allows the intended effects to be expected with high reliability. Actual technical systems, like an atomic power plant, can be composed out of acting bodies following skilled routines of behaviour, operating machines causing calculated effects, and signifying symbols aligned by programs. We usually speak of a functioning technology when the heterogeneous elements are closely coupled and interact according to rules. [...]
> We can differentiate between three ideal types of technicization depending on the medium wherein they are moulded. We speak of *habitualization* if we establish effective schemata in routine action of human bodies and couple them strongly with other routines. The behaviour of operators that is produced in this way can be used for practical ends without being conscious of the process involved. [...]
> We speak of *mechanization* when we delegate work or communication routines to physical artifacts, like machines and media, and couple them with one another to construct larger technical systems.[2]

This understanding of technology is not limited to technological artefacts but aims rather at effecting itself or, better, at the process of effecting, at technological practices.[3] For Rammert, however, the *differentia specifica* is its repeatability and reliability in terms of *expected* effects. Then, taken in this sense, technology is a schematism or something even further restricted: a *fixed* scheme. The thrust of this kind of understanding is clear: technology is detached from tools and equipment and attached instead to practices and chains of action. Such a broad concept of technology can then conceive of human actions themselves as being technology too, insofar as they unfold according to some scheme. In this sense, most of our everyday actions are actually caught in a kind of pre-reflexive revision, whereas intelligent phases appear only as *lucida intervalla* – and I'm overstating it a little; at least this is the consequence of this concept of technology. This will play a crucial role later on.

Such *habitualizations* are inscribed into our behaviour and thus appear as self-running programs, as it were – skills that include both physical and cognitive repetitions.[4] In all probability, reading a text can be understood only technologically, in the sense that we should be able to take in written words pre-reflectively, without explicitly decoding every single letter. Mechanization would then be the repetition of this process by means of artefacts whose structure is adapted to the physical conditions that our body is also equipped with – leverage, force development, and so on. Then mechanical systems look like extensions of the human body, ultimately like enhancements of the capability of humans.

The fact that artefacts are, then, in a strange double sense, similar to the human body and its ability on the one hand, yet completely different on the other is currently a popular verdict among social-scientific observers. The supporters of the actor–network theory, and in particular the French sociologist Bruno Latour, emphasize with aplomb that even artefacts are actors, that the materiality of the world has a social meaning. Technological devices as well as other extended objects are symmetrized with cognitive agents. 'An actor', Latour writes, 'is what is *made to* act by many others.'[5] This idea is not new in sociology; it is fact the business foundation of sociological thought that subjectivity is something that comes not from the actor's internal infinity but from the actor's location in 'social' space. What Latour claims to be novel, however, is the figure of thought according to which the 'many others' he addresses may as well be non-human actors: they are offered membership of certain collectives, whose network character jointly creates a world in which observable entities appear as actors.

The *res extensae* and the *res cogitantes*, the realms of the cognitive and the material world, separated in Cartesian fashion at the dawn of modern thought, are brought together again, and thereby the distinction is undermined, or even declared irrelevant. For a sociology of technology, this is a very interesting idea, because it allows us to determine more exactly that the materiality of the world itself acts as an agent by limiting, enabling, and co-determining courses of action. Both the speed bump (a famous example given by Latour) and the super-computer become actors by making an actor do something that this actor would otherwise not do.

This is a captivating idea, yet at the same time quite a simple one; and the fact that it comes as such a surprise to the best brains in social science is perhaps to be laid at the door of practices that prevail in this community, where the material factor has less of a chance to get in the way of cognitive work than in other communities. There is no doubt that the mediators of material form – that is, mechanical machines and their derivatives – are in fact not just apparatuses that somehow affect society from the outside. Rather they themselves become parts, components, elements of social processes, because they decisively shape the courses of communication and action. However, even without the material level, talk of actors is a strong simplification, because social processes are not caused by actors but actors appear qua actors in social processes. Humans become actors by connecting to the other actions and by being connected to their actions. They are addressed, named, maltreated, ignored, held to account, considered relevant or irrelevant: the actor is itself an effect of social processes.[6]

Digital technology

To repeat, Rammert understands technology in Cassirer's sense, as a form of effecting, and formulates an operative concept of technology, which addresses the social relevance of technological methods and starts by arguing for moving the medium of the techno-logical to the second row. Then one can successfully describe both habitualized action routines and the mechanized delivery of power as technology: first, as a subversion of human cognitive capabilities through the partial elimination of cognitive representation; second, as an extension of human mechanical and physical abilities and skills. According to Rammert, both aspects of technology aim for a repeatable schematism to guarantee an effecting.

Rammert also subsumes digital kinds of technology under his definition, when he writes: 'We speak of *algorithmization*, when the technological schemata are completely separated from the behav-ioural and physical context and constructed as sign systems which can be manipulated by following definite procedural rules. Calculation techniques, chemical formulas, and computer programs, like "expert systems," belong to this category of symbolic technologies.'[7]

This sounds plausible to begin with, because in fact such technol-ogies are also oriented to a form of effecting or efficacy. And even here the idea endures that the specificity of this technology consists primarily in building some schematism into social processes. Also, digital technology is able to change the forms of connection between social processes and thus to become not only connectable but also *social* itself – if the social is typically about chains of communications or actions that are socially connected.

- For example, an algorithm on a website that suggests a purchase connects to my earlier practices on this or other websites, and then I may decide to purchase or not, which is registered by the provider, in the accumulation of purchase decisions, as a form of action or effect obtained by deploying a technology.
- Or an intelligent navigation system makes me take a different route from the one I'm on because, by analysing data from other drivers or by assessing databases on traffic streams, its algorithm has calculated that I should better get off the motorway here.
- Or the tracking software on my smartphone signals to me that I haven't yet reached my daily target of 10,000 steps, which may prompt me to get off the underground one station earlier to walk a bit more.
- Or a hotel rating site lets me book a different hotel from the one I had actually intended.
- Or a suitably optimized website catches my eye because, once I put my query into a search engine, this website lands on the first page of the list of search results, which is no coincidence but can be influenced by the website provider through suitably optimized strategies.
- Or my car signals after a while that, from the way I move the steering wheel and with the help of a sensor that evaluates eye movements, it knows that my attention is waning and some oxygen would do me good. Then it makes me drive to a motorway station and do what the display shows in yellow, namely have a cup of coffee (at least that's what it looks like in the car I own).
- Or the algorithm of my word processor alerts me to spelling and grammar mistakes even as I write and learns from my feedback, because I either correct the appropriately marked words according to its suggestions or tell it that the spelling of the indicated word is indeed correct. Through my feedback, the system learns and over time increases its hit ratio. By the way, the German language, with its option of building long compounds, is a real challenge for an algorithm. When deciding whether a certain word exists, the algorithm is in the same situation as learners of German in whose mother tongues words are composed differently.

All these simple examples, with which we are all familiar, show how naturally such algorithmized technological forms of action and effecting are built into our everyday lives. The technological aspect of these technologies is that they organize signs in such a way as to change or structure social processes. And indeed, the attribution to technology contributes to understanding technological systems as attribution points within a social system. This, incidentally, also means that the material the algorithm works with consists of data from the world in which it functions as an attribution point – as for example when algorithms are used in data processing for police profiling and, on the basis of corresponding patterns in the data or of preprogrammed processing rules, they make decisions that are as discriminating or racist as corresponds to the structure of meaning of society.[8] Ultimately what is astonishing about algorithmic decisions is this ordinariness, not some extraordinary feature.[9]

Communicating technology

If it is true that social systems consist of a succession of communications or actions,[10] then such events are sound places for the connection communications. In Luhmann's systems theory, this succession is called an autopoietic process, in other words a process that structures itself successively by connecting communications. Also built into this communication process are technological forms of effecting, which then actually become more or less accountable actors or help to co-determine, by communicating information, how communication processes change. My simple examples have all shown that these technological, algorithm-controlled processes really communicate something information-like and make me do something that I would not have done otherwise. It is not that the algorithms control my behaviour, but they clearly increase the probability of a given behaviour, to which there is then reconnection – through myself, through other people, through other technological processes, and so on.

For example, my yellow coffee cup warning on the display starts flashing more quickly if the sensors do not tell the device that I have had a break, and after a while it adds an acoustic signal. By the way, I have the option of making the device more or less sensitive, or even switching it off. Where I have not been successful yet is in the attempt to make the device think that I am tired and unfocused by deliberately producing steering anomalies and eye movements. Quite obviously, the device is capable of recognizing this kind of manipulation.

The intelligence of the algorithm is, then, to combine parameters as part of a fairly well defined response range, in such a way that it is able to produce an expected output. There must also be appropriate interfaces for connecting the technological, binarily built world of the algorithm with the meaningfully structured world outside the algorithm. These interfaces render what the algorithm does understandable, and thus connectible. This way the unambiguity of the machine's operations is combined with the meaningfulness of the contexts of social use.[11] Such visibility then takes the form of action, for instance when a passageway opens on the basis of information stored on my electronic boarding card or when an intelligent ergometer can adapt a series of tests to my previous performance. Or it takes a communicative form – say, something written on the screen, the yellow cup image on my car's dashboard display, or other appearances on displays. That the digital social world has become a world of displays indicates somehow that surface and depth, user-friendly surfaces and deeply structured forms are different. More than any other technology, digital technology is a black box.

If we compare this digital technology with mechanical machines, the latter can be quite complicated and inscrutable for the everyday user; they only have to work. I have already given an example: you can drive a car without having any idea what you are doing with the two or three pedals. Hardly anyone knows what using the gear lever means for the ratio of the sizes of gears and their shift in transmission, and no one needs to know how a disc brake works in order to make an emergency stop, quite apart from the fact that today, in an emergency stop, most cars do much more than redirecting the mechanical movement of the right foot into a braking process. Today emergency braking is electronically assisted, because hardly anyone presses the pedal full tilt. There is electronic detection software, which recognizes that the driver is about to make an emergency stop and then carries it out. I'm using the car as an example because this is one of the most widespread mechanical technologies, used millions of times in our society. The technology of a car remains invisible as long as it works. In most cases a car's components become visible only when they stop working (one reason being that one must pay to have them replaced).

The function of functioning

The function of technology is its functioning. Niklas Luhmann writes that technology can 'save consensus. What works, works. What proves its worth has proved its worth. Agreement does not have to be reached.'[12] Technology, he says, is *'functioning simplification'*[13] – and this way of understanding technology explicitly includes the habitual, communicative, mechanical, and also information-processing forms described by Rammert. Although in a certain sense technology is always at odds with the logic of social systems,[14] the output of technology can still influence social processes. The development of productive forces, to use Marxist terminology, has been able to co-determine social order; some even claim it to be the crucial driving force of social development. At any rate, the special feature of technology is its 'robustness in absorbing disturbances'.[15] While living organisms and complex systems of all kinds, and especially social systems, are rather loosely matched, technology has strict matches. A living organism must be able to keep its elements within a wide range of variation and to adapt to changes in the environment, and in any case a social system consists of rather loosely matched elements. This means that the wealth of forms of social systems is really limitless.

Technological systems, on the other hand, reduce the variety: they are strictly coupled. In an internal combustion engine, if the pressure in the cylinder rises, there is hardly any variety in the reaction of the piston; also, an algorithmic machine is comparatively strictly coupled to the internal processing rules of binary operations. Hence the function of technology is indeed to function; and because technology reduces variety, it should be clear by now what it means when we give the verdict that by and large technology can do without consensus and agreement.

The medium of technological processes is strictly matched, low variation, and robust; its forms are less so. The steam engine could be used to drive anything, an airplane can be used to fly any fool around, and the possible applications of digital technology are unlimited. Incidentally, these formulations are meant to remind us of what I showed in the previous chapter about the relationship between simplicity and diversity in modern societies: the codes of functional systems are built to be simple in conception and therefore almost brutally robust – and in this way they now prove to be social *techniques* for relieving us of the need to produce consensus and agreement. Modern society *technicizes* itself in the form of the code of its functional systems, thereby simplifying the connections and making itself independent of consensus: the monetary mechanism of payment and non-payment is independent of issues of consensus, and it is inevitable that the political shaping is dependent on power, and that scientific claims to validity operate as matters of truth. Risks of disagreement and a need for consensus arise in the application of codes – but the code itself is not capable of either consensus or of disagreement. It is merely effective. It works.

Low-level technology

This, by the way, is also the key to why functioning technology is so adaptable and can spread so rapidly. If it is true that the purpose or function of technology is first and foremost to function and thus to do without consensus, then it is precisely success, proving oneself, that generates the compulsion to move. At first one cannot imagine there being any demand for certain technological tools, but as soon as a technology proves itself by functioning, it starts to spread. Many technologies that are taken for granted today were originally believed to be unnecessary: we can think of the car or the personal computer, and let's not forget the smartphone without buttons. There is no need to be consensually convinced of such technologies, as long as they just work and prove their worth. Just as the problem-solving potential for technology is built to be very low threshold – if it works, it works – the potential for expansion is also low threshold, as soon as niches for proving itself can be found. This low-threshold condition makes it so difficult to talk about the purpose or danger of technologies because the purpose is first of all their very functioning. Accordingly, consumer habits have adjusted to digitally controlled forms of marketing, distribution of goods, use of search engines, chat programs, self-monitoring software, computer-based assistance systems of navigation, brake applications, or even search functions – not because they are conceptually convincing but *because they work*.

Incidentally, this also applies to all practices of leaving traces. That in our everyday lives we leave behind so many data traces is due, among other factors, to the fact that the use of data-intensive technologies is just as handy at a low threshold. Many are surprised at how carelessly people handle their data, and even security-related issues. There is a great deal of outrage when information is hacked, when data fall into the wrong hands, or when users with criminal, government-surveillance, or economic motives get access to data sets they are not entitled to. But the practices themselves are carefree – and this can probably be best explained by the low threshold in the use of the corresponding technologies.

If it is true that technology can *cut down on consensus*, this means also that, if it works, it does not anticipate dissent or debates. The application of technology is characterized by the priority of practice over reflection – and to this extent carelessness is built into the thing itself, through the low threshold at which it functions.

The entire debate on data protection and the protection of privacy takes place in a world in which digital technology has imposed itself as something other than alien. For its functionality is indeed the condition for the technological infrastructure to prove itself. Here is why we cannot count on human motivations: because, as long as technology is working, it is cognitively undemanding – not for its designer, or for technology itself, but for the user. Digital technology in particular can make this visible even aesthetically, through the figure of the screen, of user interface, and of menu structure. Using digital means, digital technology simulates an infrastructure whose nature is different from what happens within the black box. The user interface is in fact a *virtual reality*, because, as an interface between data processing and a socially effective application, it secures precisely the low-threshold nature of functioning, even in computing operations of the most complex kind.

It is no coincidence that, from the mid-1990s on, browser applications offered the possibility to deny downright, at the aesthetic level, the sign nature of computer operations and to make pictorial representation into the basic symbolism of a computer application. Strictly speaking, all digital applications of technology are just computational programs, which organize patterns and regularities and link them to one another according to more or less fixed algorithmic programs. They carry out operations that function like internal conditional programs. But, as a *technology* for a mass audience, they can be applied only if they are capable of crossing the threshold of low-level functioning. What makes all sorts of digital applications attractive is their manageability in the form of graphically enhanced programs, for example in the form of apps that solve specific problems. What is interesting here is that digital technology, at least for the everyday user, hides the complexity and form of its own structure. A car driver doesn't usually see how the connecting rod turns the linear movement of the piston into a circular movement of the crankshaft, or what leverage forces are at work there; a user of digital technology has even less knowledge of what actually happens inside a computer – and not only because these processes lack imaginable physical, in other words mechanical movements. As early as the 1990s, the sociologist Sherry Turkle saw this as a special feature of 'postmodernism', where the surface has priority over depth and simulation has priority over what happens in reality.[16] Such statements had great public appeal because they enabled a cultural studies environment, critical and reliant on authenticity, to have a relatively easy go at criticizing technology (without rejecting it *in toto*). But then such positions have no interest in the matter itself – otherwise one could not work with such a simple distinction between simulation and reality. But at least they refer to the question of what makes digital and mechanical technologies different from each other.

So what makes digital technology special by comparison with usual technologies, especially mechanical ones? At least the examples I have given do not show any principled difference, for they, too, are to some extent measured by whether they *function*, in other words by whether the form of effecting can remain in the black box, so to speak, as long as it takes only the expected form. For, in Rammert's view, this is precisely the decisive criterion for the technicity of technology – which depends indeed on whether something is attributed to it and, if so, on what that is. Rammert speaks of a kind of effecting that generates repeatable and reliably expected effects.[17] But such an understanding of technology underestimates what digital technology makes possible.

To reiterate, the reliably expected effect is a result of robustness, of the strict matching or coupling of the elements of technological systems. A mechanical machine is strictly coupled, and the more different the actions it is supposed to carry out, the more complex its structure must be. The simplest machine is perhaps a steam engine, which, thanks to its appropriate structure, always achieves a clear result once it has been supplied with water and energy. Even a mechanical calculator with several registers or a mechanical switchboard in a post office knows more adjacent paths of effecting than a steam engine does. Nevertheless, command and execution, and thus also individual mechanical elements, are still strictly coupled here, even if the movable, mechanically controlled elements increase as soon as comma shift operations are executed. Even a changeover from mechanical circuits to transistors fails to change the basic form, but the performance is scalable because the operations are faster.

Thus, as long as a digitalized technology is used for basing computational operations on the strict recombinatorial coupling of information, so to speak, it is not different from mechanical technology. This is, then, just another scaling step, because more and more information can be compared with more and more data in shorter and shorter time spans, to achieve a result that is indeed repeatable and expected. In this respect, the use of digital technology makes much more sense and, above all, is much more widespread than most users may realize and may be seen in everyday life. I refer again to the example of the most widespread mobility technology of the twentieth century: the car. Since the 1980s at the latest, this kind of machine has been packed with digital steering elements that are barely visible and whose output is largely mechanical or physical in nature. Technological assistance systems interfere with the driver's commands without this technology behind the technology becoming visible. But it is not only cars that are digital; even the opening or closing of doors at an airport, for example, is not a simple binary decision of 'open' and 'close' but controls a wide variety of parameters connected to the indoor climate of the terminal building, to walkways, or to congestion avoidance. Such an 'intelligent' control is intelligent primarily because it can process large amounts of data at the same time – so large that no individual or team could process them with the same precision and robustness (mechanics!) or in the required time (performance!). Of course, such systems are relatively simple, deductive machines that either recognize patterns and then convert this 'knowledge' into actions or structure social or physical processes into well-defined patterns.

Even if the actions are difficult to fathom – because of the amount of data and the speed of processing – their logic is indeed easy to grasp: it usually follows deductive algorithms, and the machine is hardly able to do anything other than what it has been very clearly programmed for. Quite similarly to the sign system of writing, the sign system of software or programming duplicates the world according to its own rules, perspectives, and respects. The 'world' is, then, the technologically processed coding of information and actions run for the purpose of steering, or also for 'participation' in communication processes. Internally, such data sets and execution programs have no knowledge of the world, but they are technologically matched to something that can be processed in a socially meaningful way. Here is a catchy metaphor for it: just as the connecting rod in a combustion engine has no idea of where the car driven by this engine is going, so the concrete computational operation has no idea of what is calculated with it.

Now this is a good place for us to recall the thesis, developed in chapter 1, that the reference problem of digitality is the complexity of modern society itself. It offers enough opportunities and develops enough need to connect digitally different fields of action, forms of action, action patterns, and so on. This society consists of regularities and patterns for whose discovery there is obviously some need; and it generates so many connection points through its practice that recombination and pattern creation machines find enough docking sites. I have described the development of social statistical recording from the seventeenth–eighteenth centuries on as the starting point of a *digitalized* society. The strict, *technological*, indeed *mechanical* coupling of the elements of digital systems generates exactly this need, and at this point in my argument it should be even more obvious that this is due to the structure of society and is not an external development.

Demonized technology

As for facts such as that data volumes are growing, computer performance is on the rise, and the availability of technological equipment is improving, indeed becoming universal, I have explained them on the basis of the structure of society: just as there is a radical increase in the options of a functionally differentiated society without internal stopping rules, so too the applications of technology look constantly for new options. And the reason? *Because they can!* At the same time, the costs of this technology are going down by comparison with the costs of non-digital solutions, which is why the boom in pre-digital products is a suitable form of nostalgia in a digitalized society – the record player instead of the digital music library, the dignified pen instead of the electronic pencil for the tablet, the leather-bound calendar instead of the calendar app on the smartphone or on the desktop, the mechanical watch, and so on. Again, sticking with what is the most emotionalized technology in Germany, there would certainly be a market for purely mechanical cars provided with the electrics needed for lighting and ignition, but not with electronic or digitalized steering elements. Such a market would be one for high-priced products; but without digital means no car would be able to comply with the existing emissions and safety standards norms.

The revaluation of simplicity and the romanticizing of nineteenth- and twentieth-century analog technology are somewhat similar to the romanticizing of nature in the nineteenth century, when the urbanized bourgeois discovered the simple life and revalued the previously despised rural life, elevating it to a 'culture' in its own right. At the same time, the critique of civilization and technology flourished among the social classes that benefitted most from urbanistically civilized and technologized ways of life.[18] The critics of cybersociety argue in a similarly demonizing manner when they raise the alarm against the loss of an authentic human form, for example. We are going to be 'cyber-ill',[19] they say, a 'digital exhaustion'[20] is about to set in, and we are going to lose control in the end. I have already mentioned Harari. Perhaps the best-known vision is that of the British philosopher Nick Bostrom, who imagines a superintelligence that will make the Earth (and more beside) into its subject. He writes: 'It also seems perfectly possible to have a superintelligence whose sole goal is something completely arbitrary, such as to manufacture as many paper clips as possible, and who would resist with all its might any attempt to alter this goal.' The consequence would be 'that it starts transforming first all of earth and then increasing portions of space into paperclip manufacturing facilities'.[21]

The basic theme of this kind of criticism is a critique of the increase in options. To cite a classic theme of earlier criticism of technology, Friedrich Georg Jünger's 1946 essay *The Failure of Technology: Perfection without Purpose* identifies the demonic aspect of technology primarily not with the form of the technological itself, but with its tendency to become independent and with its ubiquitous spread.[22] It is mainly a critique of the option increase of the technological: it looks like a threat precisely because of its boundlessness. The increase in options, combined with strict matching, creates an image of mad growth, of senseless enhancement, which becomes uncontrollable by virtue of the very fact that the strict matching of elements makes no room for compromise. Exactly this was one of the functional determinations of technology: to be able to do without consensus – which in the end, once it has become independent, also means being indifferent to contradiction or criticism. Thus Nick Bostrom's paperclip story follows motifs that modernity is familiar with and whose forms are in turn themselves grounded in the social structure, insofar as they rely on option increase and uncontrollable growth.

So then, will digital technology suffer a fate similar to the one that has always haunted technological innovations: the more established it gets, the more its use is taken for granted and the more invisible it grows? This is almost a rhetorical question, for in essence social practice has given us the answer long ago. It's enough to imagine the short cycles of mobile communications technology: the mobile telephone has spread almost everywhere over a good twenty years, whereas the smartphone took only ten years or so to develop.

Nevertheless, one would underestimate digital technology if one were to *normalize* it this way, because the challenge of these technologies and their further development have not been really studied. We are probably only at the beginning of the implementation of technologies that can change and determine social (and technological) forms in their processes and structures, and not only though pattern recognition and computational recombination processes, as indicated. The discomfort with the digital culture has definitely something to do with a qualitative change in technology.

Invisible technology and the Turing test

Niklas Luhmann called our attention to one of these qualitative changes as early as 1997, when he emphasized the particular *blackness* of a computer's black box. Referring to the always elusive relationship between signifier and signified, Luhmann points out that in this way any operation is bereft of its own presuppositions and becomes self-supporting. This is certainly one of the fundamental experiences of our time, that meanings can less and less be traced to a basic ontological presupposition but are a result of their own practices. The basic experience of modernity is that there are only horizons, but no more ground – and where a ground appears, it is the result of a certain horizon, it is limited in perspective, and it depends on an individual practice. What writing has begun – and Luhmann can be read this way – is now continued by the computer:

> In quite different ways, the rapidly increasing computerization of everyday life presents us with the same question; regardless of literary efforts to criticize the metaphysics of being, it is thus a topical issue. For computers veil invisible machines that render their states of circuitry visible only if one enters suitable commands. It makes little sense to describe these invisible machines as 'present'. [...] The dividing line between the invisible and inconceivable calculations of the machine and the occasional, interests-driven elicitation of its states could be well on the way to dislodging the old distinctions between *aeternitas* and *tempus* and between presence and absence from the first place in world construction. There is already talk of 'virtual reality'.[23]

Earlier on I resorted to Derrida to point out the duplicative structure of data or their processing – that is, to the fact that the data world does not represent anything but is entirely self-referential and operates according to internal processing rules. Here the world appears only in the selectivity of the forms of connecting data. Now the angle of vision changes. Once Luhmann has pointed out the invisibility of the data machine, the world of data is seen from the 'outside'. Now social communication duplicates itself into the data machines and looks transcendent just like the other side of the world – namely their outside, which always appears only in concrete recodings. What and how the machine operates is visible only in the current output. Even the input is confusing, if only because a society of omnipresent sensors and permanent data legacies benefits from confusion. One typical feature of big data is indeed that data are brought together and recombined, although they are (or were) not collected explicitly for this purpose. This is why the output is the relevant factor in which the surprise value of invisible machines materializes. What is new about this technology, then, is precisely that it neither follows a fixed scheme nor is repeatable, and above all does not create effects that cannot be reliably expected – to bring in once more Rammert's technology criteria. But is this still a technology, then?

One of the basic ideas of a sociological understanding of technology is to free the concept of technology 'of any humanistic counterconceptuality':[24] this can be treated as consensus, from Rammert's concept of technology through systems-theory to actor–network theory. The conceptually strategic significance of this idea is that it allows us to consider the connections between technological operations and social processes. The *differentia specifica* between technological and non-technological methods consists in the fact that technology is a special form of simplification of processes and methods and that one can do without something like a mode of consensus and understanding with non-technological, in most cases human, attribution points. On this understanding, technology is – technologically speaking – a black box, but the relation between input and output should indeed be calculable and repeatable, if we are to speak of technology. This is plausible especially where human habitualizations or social forms of communication are 'technicized'. In the case of digital technology, this unambiguous relation cannot be assumed.

Even the choice of the term 'artificial intelligence' cannot but define itself, through the counter-term, as a positive negation of a human category; for 'intelligence' refers here especially to those technologies in which the relation between input and output cannot be calculated unambiguously. One could put this in a formula: *technology is characterized by the fact that the relationship between input and output is relatively clear. One does not expect any variation in the forms of reaction to the same input or to invariant output in case of changed input. However, this is precisely what applications of digital technology demonstrate in practice.*

Conceptually, this deviation from classic technology has already found expression in the notion of machine, as it was formulated by Norbert Wiener in his late 1964 book *God and Golem, Inc.*: 'A machine transforms a number of such input messages into a number of output messages, each output message at any moment depending on the input messages up to this moment. As the engineer would say in his jargon, a machine is a multiple-input, multiple-output transducer.'[25] This understanding of the machine avoids the strict

coupling between input and output and turns openness and invisibility almost into a program: on the one hand, the openness of
connections and thus the variability of patterns, recombinations,
and reactions; on the other, the invisibility of the linking principle.
Machine technology is invisible technology – or rather invisible
technology is machine technology in the sense of Wiener's cybernetic definition, which does not reserve the term 'machine' for
material technology in the classic sense but applies it to cognitive
machines as well. For ultimately cognitive systems are exactly what
Wiener describes here: a mediator between input and output – and
their performance is, so to speak, a unity of the difference between
input and output. The cognitive potential of the machine can
be recognized only by the output, which renders its technicality
invisible – or at least makes it appear in a new light, or indeed leaves
it in the dark.

As early as 1950, the British mathematician Alan Turing conducted
a thought experiment that would later become known as 'the Turing
test'. The setup was like this: a human communicates, only via a
computer, with two interlocutors, namely a human and another
computer, hence a machine. If after this communication the user
does not know clearly which of the two interlocutors is the human
and which one is the machine, according to Turing this is proof that
the machine possesses an intelligence equal to that of humans.[26] It
is disputed whether any computer has passed the Turing test to this
day. The most recent candidate is the Google Duplex of 2018.[27]

More interesting is the discussion around the Turing test. It was
in particular the philosopher John Searle who suggested a sort of
counter-experiment, 'the Chinese room'. Here a person with no
knowledge of the Chinese language or script is placed in a room,
to answer questions written in Chinese characters with the help of
instructions in a language he understands. People outside the room
get the impression that this person speaks Chinese, although all he
or she does is execute a formal program where one must follow a
rigid rule and no intelligence in the sense of decision-making skills
is required. Searle wanted to demonstrate that even a Turing test
passed with success, that is, the external impression that something
intelligent is going on in the black box, is not a proof of *intelligence*
in the strong sense.[28] He demonstrated that the *impression* of intelligence can also be created by a purely rigid rule, as long as the
way the output was created remains out of sight. With this, Searle
wanted to show that the Turing test is a necessary condition for the
proof of intelligence in a machine, but cannot constitute a sufficient
test if it is possible to prove that schematic unintelligent behaviour,
too, can look like intelligent behaviour.

Now, a dispute around the intelligence status of a machine could raise two questions. One would be whether such a machine really *is* intelligent, hence an ontological question; the other would be what a machine must be able to do for 'intelligence' to be attributed to it, hence an operative or praxeological question. Logically, one would have to go the other way round, asking how to measure or prove the human ability for intelligence, if one does not want simply to assume it *per definitionem*. In case you find this matter too abstract, in medicine such questions arise sometimes when we have to prove a patient's consciousness, for example. All these tests are similar to the Turing test in that they ask whether the reaction to stimuli is actually the result of intelligence, that is, whether they are of a conscious and intentional sort and act independently, or are just some vegetative kind of reaction that bypasses consciousness. Such tests are particularly difficult with patients who, because of their clinical picture, are not able to show any reaction, even if they want to. This is especially true of coma vigil patients. Diagnostic procedures are difficult insofar as reactions can be inferred only indirectly, for example through scans of brain activity, and the interpretation of these hardly points to one-to-one correlations, even if one would like to elicit such information from the images obtained.[29]

Here, again, the question is to assess the relationship between input and output, insofar as an appropriately *appealing* stimulus is significant for the consciousness test. Confrontation with one's own name has proven to be particularly useful in practice: as soon as the reaction to it is different from the reaction to other linguistic stimuli, this could indicate an activity of the consciousness. Other experiments work with specifically different stimuli, for instance particularly emotional stimuli such Hitchcock films, to test the reaction.[30]

Neuroscientific research on consciousness generally works with such methods, which are rather indirect, precisely because intelligence and consciousness, as operations of the brain, cannot be proven in the substance of the brain itself, and these are not just accidental features of an otherwise material biological operator either – and also because the operations themselves are, quite obviously, processing operations that process the information, whatever that may be in the given case, according to their own rules. These internal processing rules are probably the ones that make a theory of consciousness possible.[31] I will resist the temptation to call these processing rules an *algorithm*, for a formal system of rules seems to be less than what can be attributed to a human consciousness. This brings us back to the Turing test and the problem of which question one should actually ask: the *ontological* one, about what a consciousness is and what exactly it does, or the *operative–praxeological* one, about whom or what we attribute consciousness to – which communications partner or social actor.

In this context, cognitive science works with the concept of what is called theory of mind, which is not a theory of the 'mind' as we understand it in neuroscience or philosophy of consciousness. The theory of mind deals rather with the question of how we ourselves *mentalize* in our everyday lives, in other words how we attribute mental abilities to other objects. According to it, communication and social cooperation are possible only if one can credit the alter ego with some kind of mental activity, even motives in a certain sense. The theory of mind covers, as it were, the topic area of how we deal with non-transparent others and make sense of them. There are parallels to the Turing test – not in the sense that everyday life often gives us reason to check whether in principle the other person has a mind, but in the sense that we do check whether behaviour is intentional and meaningful or is just coincidental, unintentional behaviour. Is a wink an intentional attempt at contact or just a reaction of the eyelids to a speck of dust?

So this is about *mentalizing*, about how one imputes motives to the other and what consequences this has for social practice. In sociology, this topic is approached not so much as a theory of mind topic as via the thought experiment of *double contingency*, which goes back to the American sociologist Talcott Parsons and has been further developed in social systems theory.

This thought experiment goes like this. Imagine that two actors meet and each one makes his or her behaviour dependent on the other's behaviour – this is what the mental construct 'double contingency' means. The situation is mainly determined by the fact that, given the opaque nature of consciousness, neither the 'ego' nor its 'alter' can have any knowledge of each other's motivations, intentions, and other contents of consciousness. It is probable that communication will ultimately fail; for, if both make their behaviour dependent on the other's, they are going to block each other. Hence this symmetrical situation must have some kind of asymmetry built into it, for instance via social expectations, roles, conventions, habits, or norms – or via an attribution of motives. In such situations we try to find out what the other person thinks, wants, intends, and so on: in other words we attribute our counterpart a *mind*, that is, a consciousness similar to our own. The thesis is that, in everyday communication, we always already have an alter ego theory of mind. We mentalize our counterpart through the assumption and attribution of motives.[32]

What does this have to do with our topic? A theory of mentalization such as the cognitive theory of mind or theories of double contingency, let alone the topic of consciousness testing in medical fields, call attention to the ways in which actors attribute each other something like an intentional worldview. This is not simply given – but it remains unobserved, at least for as long as one's own expectations and communication or action processes are too far apart from the other's. One could say: I am confronted with the problem of understanding only when I obviously misunderstand the other.

The problem of double contingency and motive attribution responds to the fact that social processes are not themselves *technicizable*, unless to a limited degree. Typologies, routines, experiences, cultural predictabilities, and so on see to it that this contingency is, by and large, limited. Technology is in essence just an enhancement of this process, which works with more unambiguities and fewer negotiation processes. The social order can then be described as an order that reckons with a certain range of behavioural possibilities and can deal with them. The attribution to humans always includes an indication that this is an operator with degrees of freedom, scope of action, internal infinities, a will, and an individual, indeed unique personality. Perhaps one could even say that social order is a reaction to the fact that people always have more possibilities to act than can be expected to satisfy standards of what is socially acceptable at the time.[33] One could summarize it in this formulation: *humans, human actions, or actions attributed to humans show an enormous potential for surprise, whereas technology is supposed to take care that there are no surprises. Technology works. Its sophistication can take us by surprise, but its output should not.*

The surprise potential of digital technology is higher than that of mechanical and regular technology. Disruptions occur when the attribution routines are disturbed. Already in chapter 3 I have referred to disruptions that are connected with attributions to data processing. Such disruptions are perceived as disturbances because here it is in fact a technology that produces surprises, in other words unexpected or not clearly calculable results. At the latest, the metaphor of *intelligence* would apply to such disruptions when the user of a technology of this kind perceives the contingency of the counterpart, by which I mean, when one is surprised that an automaton takes one decision and not another – because this makes the automaton no longer look like an automaton.

The privilege of making mistakes

Meanwhile, in our everyday applications, we have grown accustomed to automata as alter egos with a high degree of alterity but with a clear ego, easy to read. Obviously more and more scenarios arise in which a technological system creates a situation of double contingency. When a navigation system suggests a route I should take and then changes the route during the journey, so that I have to decide on my own whether to follow the advice or not, this is a classic case of double contingency – but I will not attribute to the device any consciousness. What I attribute to it instead is room for decision-making; and I ask myself whether I really believe that the traffic jam ahead really is as heavy as announced. Nor do I find it unsettling that the system changes tactics as soon as I take a different route from the one that has been suggested.

More difficult are those situations in which it is no longer so clear how the machine reacts and to what, and the output cannot be so unambiguously decoded as the result of a machine operation. One could think for instance of automated news portals, which generate messages from other messages;[34] one could think of medical diagnostic systems in which algorithms compete with diagnoses made by human physicians;[35] one could think even of medical interventions such as implantable cardioverter defibrillators (ICDs), where a computer makes quasi-medical decisions: true, these show some leeway for decision-making, but in the end they are too schematic and cannot reverse their own action – say, in the case of terminal patients – because they lack the algorithmic capability for it.[36]

The best known example is certainly the widespread debate on how a self-driving car will react in a situation of conflict, when confronted with the alternative of hitting either children or a group of elderly people. This is rather a hypothetical example, which presupposes that such a system can recognize this situation. But let us grant for a moment that it can. The first thing that is perceived as a disruption here is that a technological device makes a decision that even a human could hardly make in this situation, and yet one is prepared to attribute to the device less blur than to a human. I am less interested in the moral or technological dimensions of the problem than in the special significance of the form of attribution.[37]

In my opinion, the unease about digital technology stems primarily from the fact that more and more technologies emerge that actually intervene in social processes, co-structure courses of action, and put humans in situations of double contingency. This is now common practice in the highly technologized parts of the social world, where the boundary between human and technological decision-making has long ceased to be drawn with the sharpness it still had in mechanical technology – although there, too, humans were treated as appendages, even part of the machine, primarily with a critical intention. The most iconic vehicle of this idea is Charlie Chaplin's 1936 *Modern Times*, but also forms of critique of technology such as by Friedrich Georg Jünger, mentioned earlier.

This unease is of course at its greatest where technology is no longer visible as technology, that is, when the computer itself becomes an interlocutor in a natural language – this has now passed the experimental stage, for example in companies' telephone hotlines[38] – or when the interlocutor is an algorithm that decides on loan, building, or social welfare applications. In a way, these are real-life Turing tests, carried out and passed. Then the computer or the algorithm is no longer a technological artefact with a potential for attribution; it is a counterpart, an opposite number, which appears either as an anthropomorphic actor (in the case of natural languages) or as a corporate actor (in the case of decision-making algorithms). Not that errors or arbitrariness would not have occurred without such a technology, but to attribute them to a machine is something one is at least unfamiliar with.

The CEO of Google, Sundar Pichai, brings this still unclear situation very vividly before our eyes. In an interview, in response to a question about the conditions under which users would not approve of AI decisions, he produced a memorable statement, which sums up the whole mess of attributions: 'One of our most important principles is that systems are accountable to humans. I think this is an important principle.'[39] Technology is developed to generate better, faster, more efficient, perhaps even more accurate decisions, which are, at least in the provider's understanding, more targeted (more profitable, more just); but the problem of their legitimacy is to be solved through accountability to humans. What becomes obvious here is the fragility of attribution – mind you: of attribution in general, not only to computers. It is a sociological truism that, in social intercourse, attributions work well mainly because their conditions can remain latent, because there is no need to address and renegotiate them each time, because they operate in the background, as it were. Attribution to non-human entities such as algorithms renders reflective and visible all that was previously pragmatically excluded – and it becomes a habit at least when it is already a technological routine. As developed earlier, what makes technological solutions convincing is that they work; and this fact of working dispenses with observation but generates suction through its simplicity. Beyond all the necessary criticism and caution, beyond the fear that algorithms capable of decision-making could make inappropriate decisions, perhaps according to undesired algorithmic rules, it will not be long before such unusual features become commonplace. This is exactly how social change happens.

The condition of decisions stands out when a decision seems to be problematic – and this is when algorithmic technology can be criticized and calls for the human are made. The contingency formula 'human' as a fuzzy operator – fuzzy because equipped with degrees of freedom and fallibility – can serve as a variable in explaining disruptions, conflicts, inaccuracies, and above all *mistakes*. *At least with the digital data and information processing technology – considering its ability to calculate parameters and information at incredible speed, and also the availability of incredible amounts of data – humans should have the outstanding privilege not only to make mistakes but also to be allowed to make mistakes.*

This sounds paradoxical. For, precisely because of the radically strict matching of the digital medium – I mean the binary coding of signs – digital technology is not a particularly error-friendly medium. Digital control does not forgive errors because it cannot deal with errors in a fuzzy way; and the verdict reached by so-called software studies – that it is primarily the production practices themselves that are responsible for the many mistakes in software production and for the permanent need for corrections, new versions, and upgrades – misunderstands the strict nature of the media substrate, which is per se neither error-friendly nor structurally error-free. Thus, although errors are inherent in digital technology, the technological framing does rule them out. Attributions to people almost necessarily include indeterminacy and vagueness, perhaps these features are even constitutive of them, while attributions to technology as a social medium indeed rule them out.

Thus the more complex the internal processes of a technology and the input–output relationships are, the less this technology can expect not to be regarded as a disruption. I have referred to printing several times. Printing had robbed writing of its initially not very suspicious form, because now indeterminacy was built into writing: the more readers, the more ways of reading, and the more indeterminacy (and surplus) in relation to meanings. The relation of digital technology to classic – by which I mean mechanical – technology is similar: while the latter had great potential for power, destruction, and danger, the relationships between elements not only were strictly coupled but also could be clearly determined – even if, in the case of complex technological system failures, it was possible to describe only in retrospect those causal chains – which, above a certain threshold, could no longer be expected in advance.[40]

Even where a digital technology based essentially on deductive algorithms is used, this should also be possible. The output of such machines comes quite close to the criteria of a repeatable technology, fashioned on certainties. It becomes problematic only when repeatability and certainty cannot really be assumed. This is true at least in those fields of AI application that are currently being developed and that aim to process more than deductive algorithms, however complex, self-learning, and quasi-autonomous those may be. From being a rather receptive technology for the discovery of patterns, digital technology is increasingly moving to be a technology that performs operations independently and is thus able to make decisions of its own, which do not occur in the algorithm itself. This is the change from deductive to abductive machines. If we are to discuss this at the level of the logical figure, classic algorithms are nothing but relatively unambiguous reactive forms, which look so complex only because they can perform a large number of calculations – so large that their decisions actually look intelligent. But these are still decisions made within the framework of a well-defined reaction space.

6

Learning Technology

As I have argued in the previous chapter, the invaluable advantage of technology is that it works. Simply by working, a functioning technology suspends claims to consensus and absorbs claims to dissent. The most recent wisdom has it that, even with complex algorithm technology, functioning – the functionality of digital technology – is run along narrowly defined margins. This constellation changes as soon as computers should learn, or rather as soon as they *manifestly* learn. Learning is already inscribed into all algorithms, which can optimize themselves or be optimized through feedback loops: through feedbacks supplied either by the users themselves or by sensors, an algorithm can increase the probability of showing the 'correct' reaction. Intelligence understood this way, as a self-adaptive practice, was operationalized at an early stage;[1] this has already been discussed by Claude Shannon and William Ross Ashby.[2] A new quality is achieved by computers and ways of computing that have recently been called 'cognitive computing' and 'deep learning'. But it remains to be seen whether this really indicates the fundamental paradigm change that such buzzwords attempt to convey.

Image recognition, natural language recognition, object recognition, but also various methods of prognosis such as weather forecasts, prediction techniques for estimating the reaction of molecules in chemical processes or the course of genetic mutations, stock exchange predictions, and the detection of faces and emotions, let alone complex language translation programs – all these applications initially require not only gigantic computing power but also a new way of acquiring information. In a review paper in *Nature*, Yann LeCun, Yoshua Bengio, and Geoffrey Hinton gave expression to the forthcoming paradigm change shift. Here is how they characterize conventional machine learning: this technology 'transformed the raw data (such as the pixel values of an image) into a suitable internal representation or feature vector from which the learning subsystem, often a classifier, could detect or classify patterns in the input'.[3] One could say that the object of a calculation was not an object, and hence not an image either; at first it was the data themselves, which represent something that in the long run makes no difference to the machine. This is exactly the kind of pattern recognition I identified at the beginning of my argument. Digital technology begins where the world can be represented in data, in order to find patterns and structures that cannot be captured with the naked eye and through the perceptual and computational capacities of natural consciousness.

Decisions

But even in this conventional form of pattern recognition we are dealing with learning machines that can expand and refine their pattern recognition capacities by being equipped with metadata on how the variety of the existing information can be put into shape. The framework of such a computational form is largely determined in advance, so that only what we were able to anticipate at earlier stages can be calculated in the final stage, even if feedback loops have the capacity to refine the results. By extension, deep learning is characterized by data being calculated in several steps and layers, according to structures – just as LeCun, Bengio, and Hinton said. In object recognition, for example, the computer looks as it were for different structures, for connections, for different perspectives on one and the same 'object'. These different levels are then connected into nodes that are able to compare their own observations with those of other nodes and to determine, according to stochastic models, the probability of continuing to work with those other nodes' data. This form of activating and deactivating connections between different perspectives and levels has given this process its name: we call it 'cognitive computing' not because the brain is replicated but because here too, just as in a nervous system, this is a matter of structuring by switching certain connections on and off, and their structure then creates an image in the truest sense of the word.[4] Such systems must be trained to structure the interaction of the various nodes and levels.

What is decisive about this method is that the levels addressed here are not pre-programmed but are defined by the learning machine itself. 'The key aspect of deep learning is that these layers of features are not designed by human engineers, they are learned from data using a general purpose learning procedure.'[5]

The classic pattern recognition technology is very powerful at recognizing patterns within data sets and at approaching higher degrees of certainty. Ultimately, this stochastic model is one-dimensional and strives for higher probability rates. The aim is to *recognize* patterns, for example to determine whether an image shows a cat or a dog. 'Cat' or 'dog' must already be present as basic patterns, so that this is a matter of recognition – of course, a recognition under conditions of incomplete information. We could almost speak of a kind of anamnesis technique modelled after Plato's, according to which all learning is a relearning. But when we must work with uncertainties – as when, say, the population is not known and hence we use stochastic models of Bayesian inspiration or likelihood procedures – the learning machine must itself make decisions that had not been intended. If we think for instance of the recognition of natural language or the perception objects for applications of self-steering vehicles, the computer itself must sort the signals according to which piece of information is important and which is not. Natural language, or rather natural speaking, shows higher variance vis-à-vis the grammatical structure of the language, especially when it comes to interference. Then the system must decide what is important information and what is only interference.

Strictly speaking, it is the old ontological distinction between *substance* and *accident* that returns here. Which audio signals belong to language, and which ones are other noise? What kind of variation in spoken language is accidental, and what kind refers to a substantial change in meaning or in grammatical information? It is not enough for such methods to just recognize patterns that are already there, so to speak; they should handle data sets much more selectively than does classic patterns recognition. So we are no longer dealing with the distribution of structures but with stochastic models, distribution probabilities, and prognostic determinations, but all these must lead to current decisions. *Do I or don't I brake? Where does the object end? What perceived objects can be distinguished from one another? Where does a sentence begin and where does it end? Is the phonetic shift coincidental, accidental, or does it relate to another word?*[6]

Such a system can no longer compare its own performance to an already existing pattern or stored image, for this would require too many templates to one image recognition or perception algorithm. How does a computer recognize a crossroads, a passing car, a pedestrian? How can it identify these objects as objects and distinguish them from the background? What signals belong together and what signals don't? This is a mechanism that should first generate the data that are to be sensorially processed, and do so without any pre-selection through metadata or concrete conditionings. Such a system must handle a self-created reality, so to speak, and cannot compare it to any non-self-created reality: this is, in essence, the classic experimental design of cognition theories. How can a self-referential operative system – that is, a system limited to its own operations – perceive its environment, when this is always self-perception?

Object recognition, for example, which is and will remain crucial for many key technologies, radicalizes George Berkeley's famous phrase *Esse est percipi* – 'Being is being perceived'. Berkeley hits the nail on its head: 'There was an odour, that is, it was smelled; there was a sound, that is to say, it was heard; a colour or figure, and it was perceived by sight or touch.'[7] Only being perceived brings the being of things into the world for the perceptual apparatus – and what I described here about the kind of knowledge that takes the shape of consciousness applies exactly to object recognition machines, which similarly cannot operate outside themselves and therefore must decide through their standard tools what to perceive when they steer a car, for example. Here the experimental design, if I can put it this way, falls outside a well-defined and limited laboratory situation: this is a complex world, which cannot be pre-programmed with any clarity. Identifying things, most of all unexpected things, is not trivial; nor is it just a problem of resolution or data quantity but one of principle. For, as Berkeley says, '[t]heir *esse* is *percipi*, nor is it possible they should have any existence, out of the minds or thinking things which perceive them'.[8]

Perhaps the challenge for what cognitive computing means is becoming obvious: higher computer performance is constitutive of it and is certainly a crucial trigger, but it is only a necessary, not a sufficient condition for this kind of the technological, or rather machine-based, processing of information – which must be called 'intelligent' because it has to solve cognitive tasks and to switch to a different kind of logic.

This kind of AI decides increasingly on its own, as it does not look for clear patterns but, by applying detection at several levels, is able to select independently the relevant information for performing a certain task – steering a car, understanding a spoken language, or identifying and separating objects. Then, through multilevel architectures, backpropagation procedures such as error feedback can be used to achieve increasingly accurate results, which the machine itself generates. This is computing from the computed and self-adaption.[9]

However, even models of this kind rely on the basic structure of the machine, on those binary operations that are constitutive of any kind of digital application. It should be even more obvious by now how much digital technology benefits from being built so simply. My thesis was that, because it is so simply built, almost unlimited possibilities of recombinations and forms open up. Even the deepest deep learning is based on this simple digitality – and this is why it creates the possibility of rearranging relations. From this angle, deep learning, cognitive computing, or neural networks have a modified logical structure, but at the same time there is an effect on capacity and scale. LeCun, Bengio, and Hinton write that the classic deductive models look for linear, unambiguous correlations, albeit of a stochastic nature – according to a 'logic-inspired paradigm': 'By contrast, neural networks just use big activity vectors, big weight matrices and scalar non linearities to perform the type of fast "intuitive" inference that underpins effortless commonsense reasoning.'[10]

Abductive machines?

In the end, as I said, capacity and scaling effects are also what enables a change in logical form; and this then looks like a quality leap in the technology itself. 'Whether "strong" or "weak", whether "good old-fashioned" or "nouvelle" AI', as Bernhard J. Dotzler puts it,[11] all these forms have the algorithmic in common – even those neural architectures that Alan Turing had anticipated as early as the 1940s, calling them 'unorganized'[12] machines. LeCun, Bengio, and Hinton speak of 'unsupervised learning'.[13]

The increased computing capacities – and hence also the higher speeds – can perform so many different computing processes in a short time that simultaneous work at different levels becomes possible. This is the trigger for the switch to the recent type of AI. From a logical point of view, the consequence of this technological extension is that now information is no longer extracted deductively from existing data sets but the process has been expanded into an 'extraction of information' 'without the machines' having been programmed for this purpose. This view challenged the theoretical model of any reasoning based on deductive logic. It led to experiments in non-monotonic reasoning (induction and abduction), whose conclusions could be used to explain reality beyond the already known results.'[14]

Charles Sanders Peirce defines abduction as a 'process of forming an explanatory hypothesis'.[15] While induction is a conclusion from something particular to a general law, abduction concludes 'from effect to cause'.[16] The inductive method classifies only in reverse, just like deduction, whereas Peirce describes abduction as a conclusion that creates something *itself*. It is, he says, the 'only logical method which introduces any new idea'.[17]

This is why an abductive reasoning method enables, say, a perceptual operator to identify the very structure of the object and to use earlier perceptions for orientation. Learning systems of this kind improve their accuracy through experience, but are not tied to unambiguous results. The abductive method always yields stochastic solutions, approximations, hypothetical solutions. It always has a remainder of indeterminacy that is not present in rigorously deductive or inductive methods, because there unswerving or axiomatic 'laws', so to speak, are available in the form of concrete determinations. The applications mentioned earlier – language recognition, object recognition, and the like – depend on working with such approximations, because initially the variety of signals is unorganized. To impose a pattern on the signals, one needs to build internal categories somehow through experience.

If we think of an application such as self-driving cars, we must realize that the technological perceptual apparatus encounters a relatively unstructured world, which consists initially of unstructured signals. These signals must themselves be organized and must lead to an assessment of the situation, in a permanent process of internal adjustment. This should be done selectively, and stochastic models and data from earlier selection processes should actually be used to make decisions about how to assess the situation, since a one-on-one mapping of the world is not possible. Let me remind you of my proposed notion of a duplication function of the data, which ultimately have no immediate access to what they calculate and create an image of the world that cannot correlate with the world. This is why the information released through multilevel comparison and multilevel selection ultimately consists of nothing but self-created forms. This kind of AI is, then, a form that must in fact make decisions itself, in the sense of acting like an abductive method that hypothesizes about what the data designate.

It may look strange to attribute decision-making competence to the computer, but these are really decisions, if one takes them as a form of self-determination in relation to futures that remain unknown and that could also have turned out differently. In this kind of technology, output and input are more loosely matched than in the strictly matched mechanical machines. The socio-technical function of those machines is not that they should be understood; it is simply that they should function. But here the machine must not only be understood but also understand itself – if, as with the concept of decision, one cannot expect understanding to imply unambiguous certainty. Understanding always includes the possibility of misunderstanding, failure, error. This is called intelligence – and, as Alan Turing said as early as the 1940s, if a machine is expected to be infallible, it cannot be intelligent at the same time.[18] Luciana Parisi sums up this new experience in digital technology with the formula 'the unpredictable is now the core component of the predictable itself'.[19]

This should at least make it plain that digital technology has not changed in its fundamentals at the level of concrete computational processes, but capacities are now available to increase computational performance to such a degree that abductive multilevel procedures are actually possible.

Distributed intelligence?

Let us imagine for a moment that computers and AI machines are not there. What about offline intelligence? Usually one looks for it in people's heads. Then intelligence is, in a sense, a brain- or consciousness-based problem-solving capacity whose measurement is not trivial.[20] The benchmark for any comparison with AI would then be the person, and almost the entire discourse on the question of AI is ultimately measured against this benchmark. As for classic concepts of technology in this context, it is true of them too that their nature is measured primarily against human capabilities. If we consider what, with Werner Rammert, I have called 'mechanical technology' in the previous chapter, these mechanical forms of technology can be seen as an enhancement of human capabilities. The printing press fills sheets of paper faster, more flawlessly, and especially in bigger numbers than a human does. A wagon can carry more weight than a human on his back. The principle of the lever makes it possible to deploy forces that humans could not deploy without it. A bicycle transfers muscle power to the road more efficiently than the feet. Only through technological progress does the previous technology become a benchmark in technology. The electric stove is faster to switch on and off than a wood-burning stove. A car is stronger than a horse carriage. And a jet engine affords higher flying speeds than a propeller engine.

The social function of technology is its own functioning, to function without consensus. Technology works even in the absence of a response, and its results are well defined. This remains true for a large part of digital technology. And nobody would dream of calling these technologies intelligent, since they do only what they are told to do – physically or mechanically, electronically, chemically.

So then, in the search for an intelligence of intelligent technology, one is really left only with human intelligence, although in the meantime even human intelligence has come under pressure when we question its autonomous status: just consider the question of free will, or of a material foundation to all thinking and consciousness.[21]

But, when we reflect on the intelligence of AI, other benchmarks are also conceivable, for example society. The philosopher Nick Bostrom, of whom I'm going to speak in a minute, is on a quest for the *superintelligence*. In his view, one of the possible superintelligences – that is, an intelligence that exceeds the capabilities of one single human – is something like a 'collective superintelligence'.[22] Bostrom emphasizes that a collective intelligence of this sort depends not only on the quantity of the collective and the quality of its elements but also on their organization. But in the end he does not flesh it out with any details. Sociology certainly has with means to this end. Elsewhere I have described the functional differentiation of society using a metaphor from computer science, namely as a system of *distributed intelligence*.[23]

In computer science, distributed artificial intelligence refers to programs and architectures in which different problems, solutions, speeds, capacities, and operative units are loosely rather than strictly coupled or matched.[24] Loose coupling has produced the result that so-called peripheral devices such as printers, plotters, drives, memory stores, workstations, and so on are no longer subdevices controlled from a central computer but devices that are themselves provided with computing capacity. This makes it possible, for example, to keep the exchange of data as limited as possible, to separate temporal processes, and thus to provide autonomy and also error friendliness in each case. This is because loose coupling allows you for instance to replace a component or develop it further without without having to revise the overall system fully. There is no longer any functional spot for something like the *overall intelligence* of a system with *distributed intelligence*. This is now a matter of interface management, which in a hierarchically structured system with subcomponents still consisted of a simple sequence of commands with relatively non-complex but error-sensitive coupling. *Distributed intelligence*, on the other hand, increases the autonomy of the components; but it also increases interface complexity and reduces the possibility of central control, because one no longer has access to all the processes of the other components. What I have described here about computer components is also reflected at the level of software. Software components are functionally differentiated and must integrate operationally the differentiated elements. And the multilevel AI of cognitive computing mentioned earlier works with similar models.

Where modern society is concerned, it can now be shown that its functional differentiation into *distributed intelligences* amounts not to a collective intelligence but to the separation of components, each with its concrete coding and programming; in the previous chapter I used these terms to be able to describe the fact that the internal organization of coded functional systems is aesthetically and operationally similar to the modus operandi of digital technology, so it is no coincidence that it requires a similar terminology.

The overall intelligence of modern society is an intelligence that separates economic, political, scientific, legal, media, religious, and artistic kinds of intelligence in order to increase the performance of these individual kinds and to enable higher problem-solving capacities. This 'in order to' is not a plan or an intentional strategy, let alone a political programme; it is the result of an evolution that had to deal with the growing complexity of society.

This evolution has also led to a shift from predominantly deductive models to models that can, at least tentatively, be called 'abductive'. Deductive models would be models of a society of hierarchy and deduction. Premodern societies followed a clear top-down scheme – everything could be processed according to *one single* algorithm. The entire world was structured around a top-down scheme. This was true of the classification of people by social layers, by families, and even by their personal relations; and it was true of thought, which always had to deduce the particular from general and highest principles. It also applied to the form of power, which was always hierarchically built. What makes this model special is its simple transparency: the overall structure of society is relatively easy to decode from any angle. Up is up, whether I look from above or from below. And in a system of hierarchical intelligence self-location should be caried out with some clarity.

Modern society must somehow distinguish levels that are no longer top-down differentiations but different kinds of structures. In my view, finding an operational similarity to cognitive computing, neural networks, or deep learning is not a far-fetched analogy. I have shown so far that such multilevel models achieve what they do *in toto* by comparing different perspectives and that, as systems, they can compare the different layers to one another without there being any point in the system that would be able to map this onto overall algorithm. Completely in line with abductive logic, hypotheses are permanently formed and discarded, compared to one another, but never mapped onto one another. Such systems build internal complexity so as to be able to fulfil their tasks. They are not rational machines capable of causally or deductively deriving everything from one principle, but the conditions of their own operations are changing *in actu*. Their *intelligence* is increased by the fact that they do not establish clear if-then relations but rather test and discard hypotheses through stochastic models, work with threshold values, and have to make different computation points for translation services, as it were. Only in this way are they able to complete complex tasks.

A modern society can be described in the same way: as a system of distributed intelligences without a central algorithm, but with all the stronger partial intelligences, which are not rounded up into one total intelligence but enable (and hinder) one another. We must say goodbye to the idea that societies are still based on the hierarchical model of the general and the particular, of integrated large groups or social communities held together by commonalities. Like all social systems, societies are systems that operate in time and whose internal processes depend on the real-time operation of their components. Modern social complexity correlates exactly to the fact that the simultaneity of different logics and the absence of internal stopping rules ensure that masses of situations, pluralities, evolutionary niches, and possible solutions can be tested. This can be told as a history of decay through loss of order – or as the history of a self-adaptive system that oscillates permanently between self-optimization and self-endangerment. Doesn't this capture the state and dynamics of a modern society quite well?

The abductive logic of deep learning systems is ultimately built on the provisonality of all solutions, which is inherent in abductive logic. Such solutions are solutions restricted to a given present; they are extended, corrected, confirmed, or discarded at the next step, which in the end never allows an abductive software anything like a final decision; such a decision is ultimately enforced by the fact that it needs to be made operationally. The permanent dissolution of events, that is, the succession of computing operations performed by an abductive system, consumes time – and at some point requires a decision, a break point, which then becomes the basis for new operations again.

This is *not just a metaphorical description* of a basic experience of social modernity, an experience in which solutions, break points, or events are already experienced as being provisional because the next event, the next speech act, the next action could put them into question again. It is an experience of permanent provisionality, permanent updates, and, not least, absence of final, chronologically stable stopping points. The *unease about modernity* has always been characterized by the *loss of deductive forms of derivation* – by a general culture of the individual life, by general rules for individual action, by universal principles for particular judgements, and so on. Abductive reasoning is more strenuous than deductive derivation, decision-making anchored in the present is more demanding than repeating something that never changes, and self-corrections are less identity-forming than self-affirmation. Modern experience, with its priority of the provisional over the permanent, is exposed to the danger of permanent provisionality, which always puts it in a learning mode (and this includes the explicit refusal to learn).

At the same time, the importance of computations and inferences has shifted in the application domains; consider for instance the debate on the transformation of knowledge structures through an *abductive turn*, which is primarily relevant for *machine-learning artefacts* and for *artificial intelligence* in the widest sense.[25] Such systems of detection cannot work just deductively, because they lack the nomological preconditions; on the other hand they cannot work inductively either, because they cannot just round up individual observations to general patterns. Something like a *heuristic* form of learning arises with these systems, and it relies on adaptation processes.[26] In the last resort this is an imitation of human thought processes, which function rather adaptively. Of course, it is still not certain whether cognitive processes such as perception always really take the route from the smallest to the biggest unit and adapt to the whole starting from the detail.[27] One thing is certain, though: the perception or assessment of situations is an act of calculating from what is already known.

The cybernetician Ranulph Glanville opens our eyes to the fact that our cultural idea of order makes it almost impossible for us to think in control loops, interactions, and non-hierarchical control relationships. Precisely 'artificial', machine-learning apparatuses in particular give us the impression that nature is not built in conformity with the clear top-down principle used in taxonomies and regulations either, but secures structures in self-adaptive ways. What did Heidegger say? The cybernetic idea of the control loop and of a form of order that corresponds to it and ultimately dissolves in complete self-reference will not stop even before the human (and 'nature'). In the words of Glanville, 'we can no longer accept that the controller (or the observer) is "above" that controlled (or observed), since the process is circular. That the controller (or observer) is described as such, as a matter of psychological convenience,'[28] is due to a cultural convention that opened up the world deductively and nomologically, and this then became the foundation of the corresponding scientific ideal.

Abductive machine learning is a cognitive operation that refers to the self-reference of data operations, namely in an operationally closed manner. Just as the brain works only with internal data and adjusts to itself, machine learning, too, is built in such a way that the machine registers the world only in the form of internal signals, thus adapting to an environment that it can know exclusively from its own operations. Then 'data' are, strictly speaking, nothing but those internal states, which can register and calculate 'identities' – that is, certainties – only in the form of 'differences' from other forms. This process comes very close to de Saussure's theory of language, which determines the identity of the concrete phrase through its difference from other phrases. As data sets show built-in structural differences whereby not every datum is connected to every other, so there is a structure, it is also possible to use the internal structure of data sets as an indicator of what these data stand for – hence of what they *duplicate*, and in the meantime I have prepared the ground for this concept. For the natural sciences, and especially for the techno-logical sciences, this is in the first place not a reversal – in the sense of a completely new situation. The fact that the world exists in the form of data is the constituting condition of an empirical natural science that can be mathematized.

Also, deep learning systems are exposed to permanent learning, to the constant redefinition of hypotheses, as they refine their modus operandi over time and ultimately have no in-built stopping rule, because they always find themselves in the provisionality of their own possibility. Granted, this is an all too abstract idea, but it resembles cultural criticism's classic notion of the excessiveness of modernity, of its complete lack of internal boundaries. And, once again, it turns out that digital technology, here in its dynamic, self-learning version, is not at all something alien but something of the same kind, of the same structure, of the same construction of order as modern society itself. Making the latter's intelligence – the intelligence of a dynamic, self-differentiated system that operates in real time – the benchmark for assessing the intelligence of AI could perhaps change the focus. *In this case too, namely that of the architecture of different kinds of intelligence, technology ultimately follows models that are already present in the social structure. As I have already explained in chapter 1, the reference problem of digital technology is in reality the structure of society itself. This is the funda-mental idea of my argument.*

Anthropological and technological questions

Now, how intelligent are smart technologies, neural networks, and deep learning systems? Both the affirmative and the critical assessment of digital technology focus on the questions of intelligence and how to judge its autonomy – and of course on the benchmark of human intelligence and consciousness. That digitalization is experienced as a disruptive technology is due mainly to its being an invisible technology. Invisible machines hide inside computers: 'computers veil invisible machines', as Niklas Luhmann says in the passage I quoted in the previous chapter (p. 154): Luhmann found the special character of digital technology in what I described through the image of a unique darkness of the black box. What is uncomfortable about digital technology, but also its fascination, seems to stem from the fact that the darker, the more invisible, the more non-transparent a black box is, the more variation in attribution can be expected from it. *Anyway, at least in this respect digital technology is more similar to human consciousness, which is non-transparent to the alter ego, than to a visible gearbox with interlocking cogwheels for which there is no possible variation between working and not working.* What happens inside a computer is hard to keep track of – and even the simplest deductively built algorithm can be astonishing insofar as it arrives at its results relatively non-transparently, given the sheer amount of data to be processed. But of course non-transparency and invisibility only incite reflection (and unease).

Intelligent computer architectures or smart objects make autonomous decisions. Whether they really do so is still the question, but what is special about this kind of technology is the attribution of autonomous decisions and, in keeping with the abductive method, the calculation of new features, which were not directly written into the programming. When it comes to the cultural meaning of digital technology, the relevant question is really that of its autonomy. In any event, the modern development of technology is characterized by an increasing dependence of human life on technological devices. This needs no further explanation. But perhaps digital technology introduces a new kind of machinery, which creates a new and different dependence of humans on technology. Certainly, the development of human societies cannot be explained entirely by the development of the productive forces, if only because this development is itself a result of social development. My thesis is that digital technology has been able to achieve such a victory because society itself exhibits dispositions that can be captured only digitally. This applies also to the question of smart technologies. The complexity of big cities, issues of energy process management, traffic, production, stock exchanges, medicine, communication technology, information processing, all this definitely requires technologies that cannot simply be forms of action but whose parameters change in the course of processes. This is why *intelligent technologies* are built into the autopoiesis of society as responsible actors and are accordingly given a different status from that of earlier technologies.

Possibly the discomfort about this technology emerges from the fact that it can no longer be regarded only as a technology – or, if indeed we take seriously Heidegger's *Ge-Stell* figure of thought as I presented it in chapter 2, its technological character becomes exceptionally visible only now, because technology really places people in concrete situations and becomes an almost unavoidable communication partner. Seen in this way, cybernetic technology is the most consistent type of technology, because it has the potential of being itself accountable. Heidegger had also remarked that the cybernetic mode of thinking does not stop at understanding nature and humanity cybernetically, as it were. In his words: 'The world as represented in cybernetic terms abolishes the difference between automatic machines and living beings. It is neutralized in this indiscriminate processing of information.'[29] 'Humanity', he says, 'also has its place assigned to it within this uniformity.'[30]

This criticism is still expressed now in the style of the classic criticism of technology and civilization. But maybe today the question should be asked the other way round. Hasn't cybernetic technology itself attained almost human quality in the meantime – I mean, isn't it so complex that it is no longer visible as a technology but almost conceals its character? The invisibility of the digital machine and the complexity of its possible applications give the impression that what lies ahead is something like the humanization of technology rather than the technologization of humanity. Perhaps 'humanization' is a misleading word, perhaps we should better call it 'mentalization'.

One of the most interesting documents in this respect is the book *Superintelligence* by the Oxford philosopher Nick Bostrom. He defines superintelligence as an intelligence that is superior to that of humans – either simply faster or of higher quality. Both are enabled by machines and both, says Bostrom, radically change the self-image of humans and of society. In his approach, Bostrom tries out the question of whether a superintelligence could achieve world domination. In doing so he does not argue simplistically and naïvely, in the sense that algorithms could become quasi superhumans, invested with speed and cognitive power vastly superior to those of humans. This would be an oversimplistic idea. He reverses the argument and regards the anthropomorphization of technological intelligence rather as a trivialization of the problem. He writes: 'Even if we recognize that a superintelligence can have all the skills and talents we find in the human distribution, along with other talents that are not found among humans, the tendency toward anthropomorphizing can still lead us to underestimate the extent to which a machine superintelligence could exceed the human level of performance.'[31] Bostrom's argument consists in not attributing to AI any human abilities, which in his view always already include something like stopping rules. He does not say it in so many words, but a technology-based superintelligence, even in the form of collective interplay between humans and machines, would be incredibly productive and could achieve its goals most efficiently. He credits technological, artificial intelligence with unimaginable intelligence, conceived of as a problem-solving capacity of the kind that gets tested in intelligence tests with people. He scales it like this: as far as the problem-solving capacity is concerned, the relation between person and machine corresponds roughly to the relation between worm and person: 'The magnitudes of the advantages [of artificial intelligence] are such as to suggest that rather than thinking of a superintelligent AI as smart in the sense that a scientific genius is smart compared with the average human being, it might be closer to the mark to think of such an AI as smart in the sense that an average human being is smart compared with a beetle or a worm.'[32]

But what the machine does not have – and what the worm probably does not have either – is something like *reason*. Bostrom does not make this idea explicit, but it is in the subtext of the conjured threat of technological superintelligence. Reason would be a built-in stopping rule, as it were, judgement's power to terminate processes. Bostrom's examples are always of the sort that refers to missing stopping rules. Computer – or rather AI – world dominance would not be a super-reason to suppress human civilization; it would be more like a well-trained fighting dog doing what it has been trained to do: *fighting*. Bostrom's warning is that AI, the superintelligence, may take on a life of its own and become unstoppable because it does mindlessly and obtusely what it has been programmed to do. His already proverbial paperclip example is a parable of this idea: if a machine has been programmed to do nothing but produce paperclips, its drive to achieve total domination over humankind is not an ideology, or a conviction, or some kind of promise. The dictatorship of this machine is not based on reason, or even a semblance of it, but on the independent and illimitable possibility of producing paperclips until everything has been drowned in paperclips.

This thought experiment is nonsensical, but it captures the character of even the 'most intelligent' machines quite accurately. Bostrom describes rather an unrealistic and fatalistic scenario, which has not much to do with technological reality, but his argument may serve – perhaps unintentionally, but almost dialectically – to demythologize the discourse on the intelligent machine. What he ultimately resists is *a mentalization of the computer*.

I have referred so far to the theory of mind, that is, to the everyday practice of imputing a concept of mind to the alter ego in order to be able to deal with it and understand it. It should not come as a surprise that theories of mind do not stop at non-human entities. The gods, the angels, the animals, and even the stars can be assumed to have intentions – and thus, precisely because of the *invisibility* of computer technology, it is natural to assume that a correspondingly non-transparent technology is endowed with mentality, in other words with room for manoeuvre and decision-making competence, possibly intentions, and perhaps even consciousness. If we refer, then, with Bostrom, to the missing stopping rule of the programmed machine, and hence explicitly to the non-humanity of this actor, what kind of intelligence does it possess?

Experiencing and acting machines

What kind of actor is an algorithm? In sociology, this question is now easy to answer because, at least since Bruno Latour, anything that affects action chains and processes in some way is declared an actor. Latour's idea is to call even non-human entities 'actors' if they influence operational processes and if they make someone do something.[33] But this does not answer the question about the type of actor that an intelligent machine is. This is something to think about when you venture to say what kind of intelligence is inherent in it.

Sociological systems theory offers the distinction between *experiencing* and *acting* for this purpose.[34] This distinction serves to distinguish attribution practices. 'If a selection (by whomsoever) is attributed to the system itself, I speak of *action*, if it is attributed to the environment, of *experience*.'[35] To be clear, this is about what is *attributed* to a system – and if you transfer it to algorithms and AI, you will be able to use this distinction as a rough differentiation. An application that merely detects a pattern in a given data set or in a combination of different data sets is more likely to be an *experiencing* algorithm. The structure of what the algorithm finds is taken rather from the environment, that is, from the data set. Although the process itself plays an active role, the point is to determine a pattern in the data by using digital means. This is how I characterized the beginnings of digital technology: digital technology discovers society by drawing attention to patterns in the environment of technology and by pointing out connections that are not visible to the naked eye.

A deep learning application – what LeCun, Bengio, and Hinton call 'unsupervised learning' – is credited with a selective activity of its own. Such an algorithm does not experience but *acts* by discriminating between different possibilities, by making non-trivial decisions, and by generating unexpected results. We attribute action to such digital systems, and we expect them to act. Action means that we infer an activity intrinsic to the system, and this in turn makes us infer 'intelligence'.

Experiencing algorithms end up fulfilling all the conditions of technology, because they execute repeatable, calculable, and unambiguous operations, as their structure can ultimately be attributed rather to the environment. This does not apply to *acting* algorithms. They even lack an essential feature of the social function of technology, namely the possibility of dispensing with consensus. Classic technology is always consent-worthy – not in the sense that there has never been, or would be, any criticism of technology: that would be a nonsensical point. But, as soon as technology is applied, it can be used without further problems of consent, because it lacks the only thing that makes consent or rejection intelligible: *room for manoeuvre.* In a nutshell, we can (and sometimes must) withhold consent to a particular technology, but the modus operandi of the technology itself is independent of approval.

Acting AI cannot rule out the need for consensus and eliminate it from the communicative process in which the technological object becomes an actor. Do we agree with the route suggested by a navigation algorithm? This may still almost remind you of a trivial machine. But the case is different when it comes to how a self-driving vehicle deals with risk situations, how it assesses tricky situations, what strategy it chooses so as to avoid an accident, and so on. Here the question of intelligence does arise, in the sense that, although of course we do not assume the technological application to have comprehensive or human intelligence, we invest it with a concept of action that has consequences for communicative processes. The question of intelligence is about the relationship between programming and output. To whom can we attribute a result that is naturally reduced to the well-defined tasks of the technological system, but that within this frame provokes questions of attribution, responsibility, legality, and even will?

The question of attribution, especially of a consensual attribution, arises increasingly in the scientific system as soon as *acting* machines (in the sense developed here) are built into the epistemic process and perhaps make an essential contribution to value creation, in other words to the epistemic process. This question does not arise in the deployment of an *experiencing* technology, for example a statistic calculation, a microscope, or an oscillograph. But, as soon as a cognitive machine can, during a data collection process, be credited with decisions of its own that are not clearly comprehensible, the question of attribution arises. What role does the researcher play, then? And what about authorship or the relationship between question and result? Such matters cannot be dealt with here, but these are the questions that arise, at least when the attribution routines can no longer remain unquestioned.[36]

So what kind of intelligence are we talking about here? At any rate, it is primarily a formal system – if we want to distinguish it from a non-formal, living natural system. The concept of formal systems comes from the field of logic. Formal logic covers logical relations, which can be expressed in formal language, completely mathematized – in contrast to sentences in a natural language, which are built on meaningful references and cannot be completely transferred into formal language.[37]

Incompleteness, temporariness, systemic paradoxes

As algorithms must always be expressed in formal language, this intelligence cannot be human intelligence in the narrow sense for logical reasons alone; this can be considered proven since Kurt Gödel's incompleteness theorem in the 1930s. The theorem asserts that in formal systems there are logical sentences that cannot be proven or calculated arithmetically and in terms of the narrower functional calculus – in other words purely formally.[38] It follows from this that not even formal systems can be conceived of as completely contradiction-free, which further means that what we call thinking and human intelligence cannot be represented or simulated algorithmically in its totality – and that ultimately the world is not algorithmically structured either. On this basis, the debate on AI and the status of intelligence comes to a transparent conclusion. The philosopher Julian Nida-Rümelin has recently formulated it as follows:

> Human reason, the human ability to justify beliefs, decisions, and emotional attitudes and, on this basis, to develop a coherent view of the world and a coherent practice, cannot be captured in the model of a digital computer. It will never be possible to fully capture the high complexity of our reasoning adequately with formal methods. Robots and software systems function according to an algorithm, humans do not. This is one of the central differences.[39]

This argument can hardly be countered, at least as far as the qualitative difference between human intelligence and artificial forms of intelligence is concerned – and from an ethical perspective it is certainly valid, at least as a regulative idea. In a way, this is a matter of pointing out the scope of human intelligence or human cognitive capabilities, in contrast with AI's grounding in formal logic. It is this scope, this room for manoeuvre that ultimately the computer cannot cover, because human intelligence is not algorithmically limited.

But, from a logical or, rather, operational point of view, this cannot be the last word on the topic, because the discourse about a coherent worldview is itself a principle of selection. And even if the point is not to express this coherence in formal language, which according to Gödel is impossible, coherence itself is an undemonstrable assumption – it is a transcendental condition of the argument, if you will, that is, a form that cannot be completely proven empirically. It is true that a formal system will never achieve absolute transparency about itself, but this is true of all systems, not only of those that can be modelled in formal language; so, strictly speaking, it is also true of mental and social systems, in which a 'coherent worldview', as already noted, is just a selective aspect and not a complete (self-)transparency.

Along this line of argument it will turn out that the operative differences between formal algorithms and their practice and the operations of meaningfully operating systems such as consciousness systems and social systems are smaller than appears at first sight – but in another respect more extreme than they look.

In terms of systems theory, self-referential systems get entangled in paradoxes because they cannot fully observe themselves in their operations, in which they refer to themselves. From the angle of logical structure, this thought runs along lines similar to Gödel's incompleteness theorem. Systems theory is not about some abstract, theoretical figure; much to the contrary, it is about the theoretical interpretation of an empirical experience. Simply because one must start somewhere and hence the beginning cannot be completely transparent, an operating system must make it invisible.[40]

The empirical question is 'how systems that can observe themselves get to "invisibilize" [*invisibilisieren*] the paradoxes that arise in the process'.[41] The point here is not to emphasize how fragile all perspectives and possibilities have always been for logical reasons; it is rather to ask how, in spite of this fragility, social and mental systems achieve stable, time-proof structures and do not freeze in the face of the paradox but continue to operate. How can a self-observing system, which is a second-order observer, achieve the unity of the system if observation itself is part of this unity? On purely logical grounds, this is impossible – which indicates that logic doesn't take you very far here, at least not a logic construed to be too flexible and non-reflective. At stake here is rather a logic of the process itself of operating, and this logic refers to a unity of the system that is not always already assumed but must be produced operatively. This unity of the system 'is a unity because of the compatibility of the system's own operations, which are self-produced by the system. It is what results when the system operates recursively.'[42] 'What results' means that this unity develops over time and has not always been there preoperatively. And the assumption of a 'coherent worldview' is also subject to this paradox of the operation and the beginning.

Finally, the paradox is resolved by the fact that the system continues to operate. I have elaborated on this in detail elsewhere, calling it *deparadoxification through time*.[43] The resolution of the circle of reflection in a theory of temporalized systems switches over from *substance* to *time*. While traditional solutions to the problem assume an *invariant substance* as deparadoxification, which always already contains the act of self-observation, *event-based, autopoietic systems de-paradoxify through time*. As soon as a new event occurs, the observation that has caused a paradox by simultaneously belonging and not belonging to the system now clearly belongs to it, as a new observation can see. But then it will itself produce yet another paradox. A first distinction can be introduced only operationally, and its own specification remains in the dark. Thus the logical suspension of the paradox of self-reference unfolds through time, in other words it happens *in time*, namely from event to event. The system structures itself, so to speak, from event to event – from thought to thought or from perception to perception in mental systems, from action to action or from communication to communication in social systems. In this way a system feels its way, as it were, to its own assumption of reality. The 'intelligence' of the system is complete and incomplete at the same time – incomplete because it is always selective, complete because it has no support other than itself. And all this unfolds through time – an intelligence arises that is oriented to itself, limited by itself, and enabled by itself. In lay parlance, it stabilizes itself through its own values of experience and tested self-worth. It gets used to itself. It somehow programs itself through its own paths and path dependencies, then becomes what it is. It is not settled and must manage its own scope, explicitly and implicitly. It is status-determined, in other words self-related, and in this mode it addresses its environment.

Now the argument is that deep learning happens the same way: it tests and incorporates not only a factual and systematic level but especially a chronological level, by comparing solutions to its

own solutions, by calculating from what has already been calculated. In point of logical structure, this is not unlike consciousness
or social systems. Thus *acting* algorithms (in the sense explained
here) are also the kind that actually need no beginning. This is
not to say that one turns them on with a switch. They must do the
beginning *themselves*, which is why in this instance I speak of *acting*
algorithms. For example, an object recognition system must begin
somewhere, it must find stability in its own complexity, and then
there must be follow-up selections. It cannot test even a single event
for completeness but must stabilize itself internally, in time, hence
the different levels of concomitant computation.

Luciana Parusi argues along similar lines, pointing out that,
'in Gödel's view, Hilbert's demand for an ultimate algorithm that
could deliver definitive true or false statements about the original
predicative formula it results from has been proven to be futile.
The problem of axiomatic incompleteness confirms instead that no
decision – and hence no finite rule – can be used for determining the
status of things *before they take their course*.'[44]

The intelligence of AI is not a reasoning intelligence. It cannot
make meaningful references, but it can deparadox itself [*sich
entparadoxieren*] through its own practice and thereby arrive at
structures, decisions, and perhaps even something like judgements. It can operate by itself from present to present and thus
to establish its own structure, which becomes the foundation of
its decisions. Neuronal systems and deep learning machines in
particular do not simply process an algorithm deductively but,
with the help of new information, generate new hypotheses that
abide by stochastic threshold values, especially in multilevel architectures. They have to function, not to justify what they do while
they are doing it.

This way they are still *technology*, by the way. One could indeed
question the status of the technological, because this kind of
technology lacks the criterion of simply functioning. But at a closer
look even this, too, dissolves in time. Parisi puts it very nicely when
she says that 'non-monotonic' knowledge-based systems, 'instead of
explaining intelligent learning, simply put into practice'.[45] In such
systems, the primacy of practice over explanation is inherent. It
looks like a latency function that enables its own operations – not
unlike human operational intelligence in this respect. We might
as well describe it as a primacy of functioning over transparency.
This was one of the most important criteria for the technological.
'Whether these machines "think" is neither here nor there. They
function,'[46] Bernhard Dotzler writes, tersely – and one would like
to add that this is also true of most human agents in most everyday

situations, at least as long as the issue of thinking is not (or need not be) addressed.

Even in everyday practice there is latency protection: to work, most things have to be taken athematically.[47] Gödel's incompleteness theorem is valid in everyday life, too: not even natural intelligence and communicative processes can establish a complete formal presence of themselves, if only because they must always presuppose themselves. Now, mathematically this claim is not entirely correct, because, of all things, everyday life is not about David Hilbert's question of the complete algorithm that could become totally transparent to itself. The point is rather that the critique of the idea of a completely intelligent algorithm – whatever that may be – reaches its limits too, namely in the way in which natural intelligence is embedded in its own practice. In the end, the measure of the question about the intelligence of AI is an unrealistic notion of what is counterposed to it as natural intelligence. The latter cannot be fully justified either but is tied to its own practice, which is oriented primarily at the practicability of its own operations; it has no other hold.

A human consciousness is so much tied to its own operations that it cannot survey them completely, because surveying is also part of its own activity as consciousness. It would get caught in a logical paradox – what saves it is time, as I have stated above. The paradox remains unobserved, because it goes on and on, and time cannot be stopped. Everything remains in the state of its own *provisionality*. And this is true not only for natural consciousness but also for the operations of social systems as well as for the operations of algorithmic systems, which abductively approach the solution that, at the next stage, is the foundation for the next stage.

Artificial, bodily, and incomplete intelligence

The fact that ever more meaningful references, ever more practices, ever more structures, and ever more system processes rely on the selection performance of AI systems must lead us to ask what an intelligent use of this technology may look like. At any rate, no functional system can manage without this technology – which is, again, only an indication of the complexity of the social world. Certainly the effect of these machines goes far beyond what the debates on the quantification and metrization of social practice suggest. For a long time now, AI, *acting* machines with their operations, have been points of attribution in the autopoiesis of society, of its functional systems, its organizations, and its concrete practice of everyday life. In this sense, what Bruno Latour so prominently introduced into social science and into public debate has long since become true: that non-human actors, including algorithmic computers, operate at eye level, as it were.[48]

Now, I have no interest in this symmetrization performance, nor am I concerned with adjusting the human to the machine or vice versa. What I want is to dedemonize AI by establishing a rather counterintuitive parallel with the human and social processing of intelligence. At any rate, it is crucial that all intelligent operators, by which I mean accountable ones that *act* in this sense, are closely tied to their operational substrate. AI is and remains artificial intelligence because it depends on algorithms, on formal logic, and on a computer that can be de-energized just as it can be reprogrammed. Although it will not develop *natural* intelligence, AI still is and will be an operational point of accountability (or attribution) for more and more communicative nodes previously created by humans, with a higher computational capacity but a lower possibility of deviation – although this must be put into perspective insofar as the probability of deviation grows with the complexity of the machine itself; and then it can *surprise* more, in that its decisions really make a difference. But the probability of deviation is lower, in the sense that AI can do only what it can do – Nick Bostrom's paperclip parable hits the nail on its head: *a machine that can produce only can indeed do nothing else. And even if we want to create a multitasking algorithm, we should define pretty clearly the tasks to be performed.*

Perhaps the cultural significance of computer-based intelligence will become obvious only where it can be determined with greater precision how much uniqueness and uniformity is generated through computer-based practices and how many possibilities to deviate remain in social practice. What emerges here is a difference between quantity and quality. A statement like the following can be found in Norbert Wiener already in the 1960s: 'It is hard to believe that, as compared with existing computing machines, the brain does not have some advantages corresponding to its enormous operational size, which is incomparably greater than what we might expect of its physical size.'[49] And yet the quality of AI is different from that of natural intelligence.

Perhaps we should reflect on the concept of natural intelligence. At the most, what is *natural* about it is that it is bound to the human. But the intelligence of humans does not depend on their nature; most of all it is due to the circumstance that the material of this thinking and to some extent its content and the structures of meaningful reference are of a social and cultural nature. A sociological understanding of intelligence or cognition in the broadest sense must always take it into account that both the what and the how of human and social cognitions are of social, cultural, and societal origins; in Max Weber, the meaningfulness of motifs is tied to other, cultural meaning, in George Herbert Mead's pragmatism to the ability to play roles, in phenomenological sociology to the structures of meaning of the lifeworld, and in Niklas Luhmann's systems theory to meaning as a context of reference – and these are just a few examples. Although these different theoretical conceptualizations are very different within sociology, there is agreement that the meaningful – in other words significant – material that actors deal with consists in the data that mental and social cognitions work with. These significant cultural references, which are often semiotic (sign-like) and often linguistic (language-based), constitute that 'duplication' material I have mentioned earlier – and this material contains possibilities of recombination that hardly know any limits. For this reason alone, the social and the mental worlds are not completely programmed; and this is why they can incorporate stopping rules, can change orientation, can be *reasonable* in this respect and equip themselves with reasons. Only where social processes are coded unambiguously, in binary form – as they are in coded functional systems – are there no stopping rules.

This possibility of recombining differently, more freely than would be possible through algorithmic programming, is tied to meaningfully operating systems, although it is certainly possible to build algorithms into autopoiesis, into the processes of social systems – be it on stock exchange markets, in medical diagnostic systems, or in bureaucratic rating systems. In all these cases, the process logic is a meaningful process logic of the social system itself and need not be built into the algorithmic technology involved. In AI systems, meaningful references do not occur as such but are conveyed as signs, and thus digitalized – and I have explained earlier that the idiosyncrasy of data is a data-like idiosyncrasy. Even semantically working machines have to decompose the field of semantics into regularities, into patterns that are not themselves based on meaningful references. So you have to formulate it in this graphic manner: *AI is not intelligent in the narrow sense, as a meaning-processing system. At best, it is intelligent in the sense that it can process such a high complexity of recombination possibilities that it becomes increasingly invisible, like a black box, and thus becomes an accountable machine capable of action. But in the end it works only on what it was designed for, even if it achieves results that were not directly co-designed.*

This is the crucial qualitative difference between AI and what may be called, for contrast, *natural* intelligence or the *meaningful* intelligence of mental and social systems. It is no coincidence, by the way, that the particular challenge for passing the Turing test is that the computer must be able to simulate *meaningful* references or decisions – for example the experiment of the Google Duplex test of August 2018 was a phone call in a natural language.[50]

Alongside the question of the meaningfulness of references, a nature mediated in a particular way plays of course an important role for *natural* intelligence. For one difference between the intelligence of machines and the intelligence of humans lies in their *physicality*.[51] If we are to trust brain research, the complexity and performance of the human brain are superior to those of any computer, especially with regard to the neurons' capacity to recombine. I refer again to Michael Gazzaniga, who points out in his book how little aware we are, in our conscious activity, of the brain activities that interact in the most complex ways to ensure the tremendous plasticity of our behavioural responses – with no need or possibility to calculate it formally. We are non-transparent to ourselves. What I have developed earlier at the logical level and with recourse to the problem of the paradox of self-referentiality has its organic counterpart in the depths of the brain. Popular in this context is the iceberg metaphor: Gazzaniga writes: 'Our conscious awareness is the mere tip of the iceberg of nonconscious processing. Below our level of awareness is the very busy non-conscious brain hard at work.'[52]

And all human intelligence is situated in the physical practices of a body that is not only finite but also bound to a physical–practical temporality that is brutally based on the present and cannot be internally differentiated, interrupted, reprogrammed, and brought to a halt – as can social systems or algorithmized systems. Perhaps this is the difference between human intelligence and artificial – but also social – intelligence. *The power of human judgement is situated.* And what appears to the philosopher as a *coherent worldview* is nothing but a correlate of experience and practice that is not completely available to itself. Perhaps it is unavailability that constitutes the paradox of the beginning of human existence – and perhaps it, too, has a parallel in the incomplete calculability of formal systems.

I have pointed out earlier that it is the privilege of human beings to have errors attributed to them and forgiven. If the machine were a physical person, it would probably perceive it as a curse that it *cannot* be error-free on account of its structure and logical incompleteness, yet it is not allowed to make mistakes. But it is after all just a machine, and its sensitivity will be accessible only via a scale effect. The more complex a machine is, the more likely is it that it will be a point of attribution for sensitivity, but in fact it lacks the inner infinity of the brain-and-body existence of the biological machine that is the human being. Perhaps it is too counterintuitive to find the crucial difference between the human and the machine not so much in the cognitive operations themselves as in their mediality substrate. While the medium of the machine depends on the exactness of formal mathematics, which can become invisible only because the internal references become unclear, even the clear references of human existence are bound to the less formally structured connectivity of neuronal networks and physical situatedness. Perhaps it is simply having life as a foundation that makes the two machines different from each other, not intelligence.

Finding forms and theories of reflection for all this – that is, both for the *meaningful social* and for the *sensual physical* difference from the technological machines of AI – is probably one of the most important tasks for understanding the cultural significance of digital machines, but also for shaping digital technology and practices in the digital society. At least it would be an unanticipated irony if digital technology and AI could lead to a *reflective appreciation of non-artificial intelligence.*[53] This need not be laid at the door of humanity itself, but could relate to the ways in which social systems process meaning. As with all new technologies, the question has always been what social leeway these technological unambiguities and pressures have released. This was true of the spoken word after the invention of printing, it was true of non-capitalist forms of exploitation after the invention of technology-induced organized capitalism, and it is also true of those social spaces that elude the formative control of AI.

7

The Internet as Mass Media

Asking if the Internet is a mass medium[1] is a strange question. First, the Internet *is* ultimately not a thing, in the sense that it does not have concrete properties, like an object. It is a *medium* for *forms*. Second, the Internet is, of course, a mass medium. If it is a medium, then in any case it is a mass medium as well, because it is indeed global, a characteristic already inscribed into the name World Wide Web. However, before I get to the question of the kind of mass medium that the Internet itself *is* or *has* within it, a preliminary remark is needed.

The digitalization of an already digital society has made many of its practices suitable for everyday use through the integration of digital technology. This applies both to the taken-for-granted (co-)control of everyday technology (road, rail, air traffic, energy supply, etc.) and to our trust in digitally controlled everyday routines. That we use search engines and work with what they give us is due on the one hand to the fact that the process works – which I just cited as perhaps the decisive criterion in technology's almost invisible predominance. On the other hand, the reason is that we trust this functioning, and we do it blindly. By this I mean that we use the results, be they about making consumer decisions, diagnosing symptoms in our own bodies, or researching this or that. We can even suppress our knowledge, if we have it, that the ranking of the results – what results are displayed right at the top of what search – is not by coincidence. The fact of functioning eliminates all doubt – which is why even technologies that we should perhaps get rid of are not easy to shake, once they have found a place for themselves in our everyday routines through functioning. In a sense, technology becomes part of the habitat; and specific technologies even become part of action and communication chains.

Surplus of meaning businesses

But before we can discuss the mass media forms and functions of or on the Internet, a few remarks on the conditions for the Internet's (semi-)public means of communication are in order. Here again I come up against the function of the technological: functioning eliminates reasoning about technology. If it works, it works. No further information is needed – and, as a result, digital technology is a technology that always means more than seems at first sight. Just one look at conventional or, better, non-digital technology is enough to make this obvious. Again, I'm going to take one of the leading technologies of the twentieth century as an example. What is a car good for? This question is easy to answer: to get from A to B, and to do so in a self-driven vehicle, which allows for individual arrivals and departures at points A and B and keeps coordination among road users to a minimum. What is needed is a reliable measure of expectation that there are functioning rules that all road users stick to, not least because they are legally sanctioned. The technology of the car is flanked by drivers and regulations, through a technology integrated into habits. If we do not act too stupidly, then stopping at a red light, operating the indicator, or giving right of way have become routine – and hence can be taken for granted. Even if the car depends on many conditions – such as road construction, financing of the infrastructure, fuel supplies – its meaning is quite clear. It may be a key technology for the German economy, for example it may be regarded at the cultural level as a symbol of freedom and the right to go ahead, even when you are stuck in a trafic jam – but it remains just an automobile.

The car does not generate much surplus of meaning. It is meaningful, and it has consequences as well as a lot of implications – like any other cultural phenomenon – but it is and remains a vehicle. *I would argue that there are many digital applications and technologies to which this does not apply.* Much to the contrary, the superficial utility value of the technology is just the smallest part of what it could make possible by way of referrals to meaning. This is most obvious in the case of social media platforms, as we call them. At first blush, a platform such as Facebook or Instagram looks like a communications and distribution medium that facilitates making contact with others, sending and receiving information, and creating spaces of attention.

But this technology is not made for a first impression. Its surplus of meaning lies in the fact that, as a result of users' practices, data sets that are not directly related to these practices become available and reveal patterns that can be and indeed are of interest for a wide variety of applications. This ranges from marketing analyses to targeted marketing and advertisement campaigns and to exploitable analyses of the dynamic of topics and semantic forms. Anyone who wants to learn about the mood of a certain group of people, about the conflict situations of certain statistical groups, or about their connectivity conditions can rely on patterns that occur on social networks. The fact that data-intensive technologies like these tend to concentrate on a few players in an almost unprecedented manner, previously witnessed only in the oil market, is also determined by technology. For it is precisely the concentration of huge sets of big data that enables these surpluses of meaning, and hence value creation. It is no coincidence that in 2019 Google, Facebook's competitor, terminated its Facebook-like Google+ service, after eight years of running it.[2] On the face of it a security breach contributed to killing this service, but the fact that it came to this is also an indication of how little profit Google was getting from the whole thing. A social media service like this fulfils its function, or should I say, rather, its expected surplus of purpose, only if there are as many users as can be; otherwise the data are neither sufficient in number nor sufficiently differentiated.

This is how we should understand the trend towards concentration in platform capitalism – a trend that the British economist Nick Srnicek describes in his analysis as a convergence development: 'Instead, platform expansion is driven by the need for more data, which leads to what we might call the convergence thesis: the tendency for different platform companies to become increasingly similar as they encroach upon the same market and data areas.'[3] This makes it at least more probable that the tendency towards concentration will continue, also because a certain mode of classic, demand-oriented capitalism works only to a limited extent on such platforms. Cars that are hardly distinguishable from one another can be charged with identity through their brand values. The benefits of one car are as good as those of any other, but it makes perfect economic sense for different suppliers to compete for solutions, and thus for customers. At any rate, the idea of the car is not called into question on the grounds that there are so many different suppliers. On the contrary. One of the basic rules of classic capitalism is that competition not only stimulates business but also lowers prices.

On platforms, where what matters is not what is offered but what kind of data are produced, an evolutionary process takes place rather than some kind of competition for the better fitting model, which will finally dominate the market. Since the supplier couldn't care less what his product does for the user because this product is only a vehicle for skimming off data for further business, concentration is not the effect of a particularly good offer but rather the prerequisite for the business model. What takes place in this form of capitalism is predatory or replacement competition rather than competitive rivalry – and it depends on such large amounts of capital because predatory competition is still in full swing. If we are to believe Srnicek's analysis, the competition for concentration is still at a stage where it's difficult to predict how exactly it would develop. Accordingly, at the current stage concentration is more important than economic profit. The formula 'growth before profit' summarizes the situation from the angle of the individual player.[4]

In a rousing analysis of surveillance capitalism, the North American economist Shoshana Zuboff writes of a tendency for platform capitalism, especially in the social media, not only to find outlets for products and services – in other words to detect patterns of what already exists – but also to provoke, creating a certain pattern of behaviour by uncovering patterns. Zuboff states:

> Gradually, as surveillance capitalism's imperatives and the material infrastructures that perform extraction-and-execution operations begin to function as a coherent whole, they produce a twenty-first-century 'means of behavioral modification'. The aim of this undertaking is not to impose behavioral norms, such as conformity and obedience, but rather to produce behavior that reliably, definitively, and certainly leads to desired commercial results.[5]

Zuboff does not speak of a surplus of meaning but aims at dispositional behaviour. It is the goal of social media, she says, to create a 'behavioral surplus' – that is, something in our behaviour that holds us imperceptibly in its sway, as it were. She speaks of a 'metamorphosis of the digital infrastructure *from a thing that we have to a thing that has us*'.[6] This is well observed insofar as the concrete practices and the return on these practices for others – namely the providers of data-driven media – are of a completely different kind. What the users do is, in a way, only the trigger for recording data that can then be used to do business and to control the users' behaviour correspondingly.

This should not be mistaken for realizing an intention. Anyway, products, commercial and non-commercial alike, always generate new dispositional behaviours: the book – a reading public, but also a certain knowledge for the sake of control as well as forms of criticizing this knowledge for the sake of control; the railway – thinking over greater spaces; the car – individual mobility; and the washing machine – time for gender conflicts.

This chapter will not be an analysis of digital capitalism, its business models, and its concentration tendencies. I want just to point out that the mass-mediality of the Internet, or mass-mediality on it, can be understood only by emphasizing this surplus of meaning of media practices on the web. But undoubtedly this relationship between practices and surplus of meaning works only because the former have asserted themselves as functioning self-evident realities, and hence as reflection-free and freeing from reflection. The surplus of meaning is an effect of meaning avoidance. What is skimmed off the social media on the web is not visible to users.

In this respect, radical diagnoses such as Zuboff's typically come across an audience that avidly absorbs the critique – a critique of media use on the Internet, but also of other practices that leave usable data traces – but then gets corrupted by the fact that the practice itself is immune to questions of consensus. The fact that something works is the best argument, because that thing is initially unresponsive to consensus and approval. The best criticism of the Internet can be placed on the Internet – if only because dissemination works best there. Incidentally, I read Zuboff's book as an e-book, thus fuelling the topic myself, since my reading behaviour is now detectable; this may have no immediate effect on me but may show the publisher whether it's still worth launching 700-page volumes nowadays – and perhaps why access to them is more difficult than to volumes half the size. In the printed version, contact with the publisher would end with the purchase (and payment); in this case it really began after the payment.

But now I must take a step back and first define more accurately the mediality of the mass media. Usually one starts by saying that the book, the newspaper, the radio, and television have dominated the crucial media formats of modern society – in this order. In social studies classes we learn that modern statehood would not have been possible without newspapers, radio, and television; without the printing press there would have been no reading public for other media to connect to. The cultural self-assurance that nations acquired – by being permanently styled 'nations' in writing, through the news, and through a world of events and persons synchronized via messages and information – and the creation of an audience of political, economic, cultural, medical, and educational impositions would not have been imaginable without these mass media.

The function of synchronization

The social achievement of the mass media is not so much to offer orientation, clarity, and consensus as to provide a place where something like political convictions can be represented, and thereby come into being, and where markets can observe themselves through the publication of rates, prices, unrealistic stories about products and services (i.e., in plain language, advertising), and so on. The informed citizen would not have come into being without the literature and music criticism or the medical and educational information distributed by the media: such citizens were included in society mainly because they can have a say – and all this is appropriately differentiated according to one's economic class and educational and cultural environment. The special achievement of classic mass media is thus a synchronization achievement.

This is what constitutes the modernity of the mass media – if one really wants to call one of the most outstanding reference problems or characteristics of modern society 'the synchronization problem'.[7] This is what I used earlier in order to justify the particular 'digital' form of modern sociality. The basic coding of social functions, brutal and dumb as it is, allows functional systems almost uninhibited possibilities of programming. Anything is possible within the narrow framework of these systems' binary codes. It makes a difference whether we approach the world economically or politically. We see a different world when we look at it as a scientific challenge and when we view it under religious aspects. And the legal regulation of conflicts of norms is different sometimes from that of moral orientations, which again can differ. Yet it is not just factual differences between different logics that make simultaneity difficult but also their different speeds: think for example of the fast pace of economic dynamics versus the sluggishness of democratic decision-making, or think of the time you needed for research and education, while medical issues always arise and have to be solved in the now. Concrete necessities of life cannot wait either, but must be dealt with immediately. These disparities render modern societies temporally and factually complex.

One could go as far as to view the need for synchronization in modern societies as their basic operational problem – and this becomes very clear if we look at it not at the abstract level of functional systems but in concrete forms of life and work. The dynamics of modern forms of life consists precisely in the fact that disparate things must be brought together. The great normative ideas that make us lead autonomous lives and that demand of us, in good Protestant fashion, not only a continuous way of life but also a consistent story to go with it are the result of a discontinuous world. Only where the demands of life no longer fit together must life be actively led and synchronized.

This applies to company or corporation activities as well. The classic example is the economic division of labour. Anyone who wants to assemble half-finished parts must synchronize them – materials, kinds, spaces, activities, and so on. All this must be synchronized precisely because it is not the same. The real achievement of what is called 'management' or 'organization' is making disparate things manageable.

The fact that we are then happy to recharge normatively both our lived life and our organized organization in terms of consistency demands, identity formation, and freedom from contradiction is just an effect of a world that is not made of one piece. It must be made manageable. This is exactly what I call the synchronization achievement.

Synchronization and socialization

Only against this background does it become clear what we expect the social media to achieve. The media do not depict what is – or this is rather a side effect. They synchronize different things in the form of information. Even a newspaper's division into editorial departments reflects this: politics, economy, arts section–sciences, sports, lifestyle–life coaching, and now even the media. Bruno Latour once said that we have never been modern – and he attempted to show it using the example of a newspaper where the departments are neatly separated but all the topics keep recurring in the 'wrong' department, in a somewhat impure form.[8] Clearly Latour has in mind an all too pure form of modernity – but then this is the experience of modernity – that different things must be related, that they cannot be separated without interference, that they must be permanently synchronized. 'Modernity', then, would be the illusion of a division of labour without any friction. Society, of course, is precisely this: the permanent, unstoppable form of friction areas and losses.

This is where the media come in. They separate yet connect, they orient yet unsettle, they report yet conceal, they talk about everything yet are selective, they tell consistent stories about an inconsistent world. They bring things together in the form of information and updates and thus make the world narratable. Niklas Luhmann's statement '[w]hatever we know about our society, or indeed about the world in which we live, we know through the mass media"[9] has meanwhile become proverbial. And the fact that this literally refers to everything also means that we actually match everything with images and semantic forms we know from the media – in other words even our concrete experiences and knowledge, what we perceive directly and not on a screen, what we ourselves interpret and not take from books, even our own feelings and states of mind. We get from the media even our notion of sentiment: we need to know the criteria if we want to classify it as typical or untypical.

An imperceptible form of shaping, like this one, is called 'socialization'. The media are an agent of socialization; this is known most of all to those who use the media to bring their messages to people indirectly rather than directly, through the distribution of images and styles of speaking, of truths and plausibilities, and so on. The modern, individualized lifestyle, with its invention of the autonomously deciding, sovereign subject, is certainly an effect of religious changes, also the result of legal forms of entitlement and protection, and, not least, the outcome of a freely deciding consumer, who is supposed to develop his or her own taste and buying preferences. This lifestyle is first of all the effect of a society whose dynamics really require the individual not to be assigned a consistent place in society. Everything that is normatively expected as a lifestyle, as a consistent biographical decision, as a manifestation of individuality or independence, and, not least, as individual uniqueness is a direct correlate of a society in which the circumstances and biographies of its own members are no longer clearly fixed by the social structure. A modern, functionally differentiated society could not afford this, which is ultimately why it 'invents' the individual as a culmination point.

This individual needs mass media precisely in order to be synchronized with the world. In a sense, the media supply to us the material for individual decisions, a semantic stock for our own thoughts, and a range of variations to make distinctions possible. In sociology, the distinction between primary and secondary experience was introduced to show that the balance we keep between what we know and what seems plausible to us can less and less be traced back to direct personal experience.[10] But perhaps this distinction underestimates the mass media too much; for reading and seeing – text, images, films, and so on – are indeed primary experiences. In this sense, knowledge itself becomes a media format; one has only to watch children play soccer and support their own actions by imitating the intonation and semantics of sports reporters and football commentators.

The media synchronize the diversity of the world into a single perceptible image – and, empirically, they do it in very different ways. They are thereby even misused, restricted, or disturbed, but this does not cancel out their mediality; it happens to them as media. Even media that have been forced to conform fulfil their function, otherwise this enforced conformity would not be worth the effort.

Like all the functions of a modern society, this one, too, is performed in a rather decentralized manner: just as economy has no centre, only more or less powerful and influential enterprises; just as a scientific system structures itself primarily by amassing citations and connections; just as a legal system generates decisions through repetitions and case histories; just as a single work of art cannot change art; and just as in the political system, too, power must always be tested in the circle of decisions and reactions of the political public, even if some degree of centrality can be induced via statehood. The same holds for the media, which accomplish their function in a decentralized manner, at least when diversity of opinion and pluralism of information are democratically protected. The fact that something like a mainstream emerges in the media too, that there are trends not only of topics but also of opinions, that the spectrum of what can be said is inversely proportional to the range of the corresponding media organ – all this is a kind of double media effect, because what is in the media is ultimately also oriented to a large extent to the media.

All this presupposes practices whereby well-trained gatekeepers, along with a corporate structure that provides the infrastructure, ensure methodically controlled forms of distributing information, entertainment, and so on, according to program features and media format. There are program- and country-specific differences here – if you take the same event, the *Frankfurter Allgemeine Zeitung* covers it differently from *Bild-Zeitung*, and commentary from a left-wing journalist is perhaps different from commentary from a rather conservative one. It makes a difference whether something is reported in the specialized press or in a daily newspaper. And what the daily newspaper reports on the day after may explicitly refer to what radio and television have made of it already. I leave it at that. All I want to show is that only the classic, organized distribution media, with their synchronization of information layers and image production as well as with their socialization of the audience, enable something like society's self-awareness *as society*. All this depends on the perceptible and imperceptible selectivity of what is reported, or of what exists and may be presented as information.

To some extent, the selection function of the (mostly profes-sionalized) media generates the forms and trends of thematization and self-description, which are internally more or less differentiated and whose form changes each according to the addressee. And this is the primary space for socialization and experience in a society where it is not only true that its members receive almost all their knowledge from the media: the media are ultimately society's self-experiencing space itself. If things are reordered in society, they are ultimately reordered according to the image that the different social entities receive through the media. To take just one example, in the economic system decisions are made, of course, by observing prices, market rates, supply and demand. And even if decision-makers have access to relevant data on these matters, each decision is made with an eye on what may be said about it and what the others, the competitors and the 'market', will probably do. Mass media exist to provide exactly such forms of information, which are as open-ended as possible, and the difference of contradictory information. They do not create a uniform image of the world, but the contradictory image of the world is represented – nay, created – precisely through the range of statements that are possible in the media. The mass media, of course, perform their service through professional forms of content selection, by selecting topics and offering possibilities of interpretation. *The media cover everything, but selectively. This is not a contradiction.*

Selectivity, mediality, and voice on the Internet

The classical media in the form of text, audio, and video have changed their technological infrastructure. They have migrated to the Internet without having abolished their previous forms of distribution. In Germany, the most successful news portals are Focus online, Bild.de, and SPIEGEL-online, whose range goes far beyond that of print formats. Although the form of some texts has changed as a result – for there is opportunity for much shorter, but also longer formats – one can see even from the providers that all the characteristics of classic media continue to apply here. The Internet is a rewarding distributor of existing formats – not least because it can, through search and archive formats, get hold of texts that one would not have found physically. But in the end this does not change the basic structure of these formats.

Broadcasting has probably changed the most as a result of migration to the Internet. If broadcasting, including television, via terrestrial and 1:1 reception is primarily a real-time medium, the possibility of retrieval from media libraries and centres turns it now into it a time-invariant archive, which will certainly affect the kind and form of contributions. But this does not alter the basic form of the classic media.

This classic form feeds on a clear division line between sender and receiver. The characteristics are:

- a few senders;
- many receivers, organized simultaneously with the sender;
- rather one-sided communication;
- high-threshold access to broadcasting functions;
- professionalization of the sender function.

On the Internet these relations are reversed:

- many senders;
- many receivers, less organized;
- multi-directional communication;
- low-threshold access to broadcasting functions;
- open access to sender functions.

To avoid any misunderstanding: this is not about 'the Internet', which primarily is nothing but a technological infrastructure for connecting servers and for connecting terminals to servers. My concern here is not to explain the Internet, and one underestimates this medium if one believes it to be just a distribution medium for text and images. My only concern here is with the impact that this infrastructure has on *mass mediality*.

The first thing that stands out is that sending becomes easier: everyone can send everything – or rather almost everyone can send almost everything. Some knowledge is required, and at least a computer and access to the Internet. There are legal limitations (but they are difficult to monitor); there are also limits to access – internally the net is by no means one homogenous space but is permeated by boundaries, distribution structures, and, not least, enforcement possibilities (and I'm talking here only about the visible form of communicating with an audience). It is a truism that social structures are represented on the Internet. Almost twenty years ago, the sociological examination of the Internet discovered – small wonder – that structures of inequality, group formation, opportunities for participation, and economic and cultural forms are also reflected on the Internet.[11] Ten years earlier, people still expected the emergence of a virtual community with great promises of being a grassroots democracy, based primarily on the fact that the number of senders would increase, that any user could in principle be a sender, and that any recipient would have a larger pool to choose from. Typical, of course, was the idea that a *community* would develop here, hence a cohesion created through open communication.[12]

There are only a few general rules in the social realm. Everything is historically relative and depends on myriads of empirical constraints. But I would actually go as far as to say that, if there is anything that is completely ruled out, this is open and free communication and the possibility of communitization, of forming or becoming a community. Communitization is rather an effect of being able to do without communication. Even communitization is a selection principle. Analogies between one's direct life experience and social structures should also be treated with reservation; but it is possible to generalize, simply from the experience of close-knit communities such as religious groups, sect-like formations, political associations, strongly integrated circles of friends, and especially families, that the communitization effect is also a consequence of selective possibilities of communication. Communities are instituted most of all by the fact that certain communicative contents, demands, forms, and deviations just do *not* happen.

This is precisely the function that mass media have performed for impersonal forms of communitization since the mid-eighteenth century, and especially the nineteenth. As I have already mentioned, one of the functions of mass media is to create *selectively* something like a common space of communication, through choice and elimination of topics – where choice and elimination can be more or less the result of intentional actions. Not even conformity enforced upon the media by authoritarian regimes prevents them from functioning as media, but calls attention to the limiting conditions of mediality. It is, then, striking that in situations of social conflict trends of topics and of what can be said develop even in liberal, legally secured media constellations.

The impersonal togetherness, or rather responsive collectivism, of media communication – national but also environment-specific, political or bound to some other interests – must above all guarantee sayabilities: a selection principle once again. To some extent, responsive communities must practically define an amplitude of possible communicative peaks and deviations – and expand through trial and error and by testing opportunities to connect. In this respect, the unidirectional form of mass media of classic provenance had not only a technological foundation but also some social meaning: then the public ultimately has only the options of 'exit', 'voice', and 'loyalty', to recall Albert O. Hirschman's famous thesis about how dissatisfied customers may react.[13] The 'exit' option would mean that one stops reading this newspaper; the 'voice' option would mean that one makes a complaint and hopes for improvement; and 'loyalty' would be possible despite being dissatisfied – or else a change of provider, of newspaper, of radio station and so on.

With respect to the classic media system, it is the 'voice' option in particular that is practically ruled out – what remains is 'exit' and in the end 'loyalty' if only because of the limited offer. The Internet, on the other hand, enhances almost to epidemic proportions the 'voice' option, which had previously been the weakest, because receivers themselves become senders. One need not bother with dramatic changes of format to understand this shift. Even the comments columns under newspaper articles on the Internet indicate the significance of the 'voice' option – and they indicate how significant the selectivity of the medial is.

To put it bluntly, free-flowing communication on the Internet knows little selection pressure, because the promise that in principle anyone can say anything also has the effect that community-stabilizing forms of communication are invalidated. Those who say whatever they like will do so – and when they do, communication processes take a confrontational rather than community-creating course. Those who think that this is the diagnosis of a crisis had unrealistic and downright naïve expectations before.

From here one could go on to emphasize, with Zuboff, that it is only the lack of selection pressure that ensures the generation of data with a high degree of variance. This confirms her thesis that practices on the Internet – and this is not limited to social media – are in fact disconnected, in the operational sense, from what they could be used for technologically. Of course, a daily newspaper, too, is not printed only to keep citizens informed. The publisher also wants to earn money with it and may have a social-political interest in distributing certain information, attitudes, or convictions among the population. But all these are relatively transparent connections. That money is to be made can be seen quite transparently from the fact that the newspaper costs money, and how the content was procured can be seen from the contents, no matter how subtly dispersed the attempts at influencing may be.

The situation is completely different in social media. Not only the immediate economic purpose remains relatively invisible, but also the reason why which data, connections, repetitions, patterns, and so on are collected and recombined. Their meaning is not exhausted even at the moment of collection and is not transparent even to the provider; but the user is left completely in the dark as to how multicoded everything he contributes here to maintaining the flow of communication is. Earlier on I described computer technology as an invisible technology because the activities of the machine, and especially the ways in which it achieves its results, are much harder to see from the outside than they are in the case of mechanical machines. The technology behind social media and other trace technologies is even more invisible, even darker, because their meaning is categorically different from what the trace-generating practice signifies socially.

To flesh this out a little, if certain keywords appear and dock in different contexts, an intelligent software can search for combinations and, in the spirit of deep learning strategies, possibly come up itself with connections that no marketing concept or law enforcement authority could find, if it had access to these data. The machine generates a surplus of meaning that is darker than the events of the machine itself, because the practices of the users themselves are in fact irrelevant. If you want to be wicked about it, you can say that such platforms have a hell of a party, as variedly, as differently, and as much as they can. This party is the play material from which the usable data are generated.

Allow me a bold example: if data are the new oil, then the plainly unsuspicious everyday activities of users are like those plants, forests, animals, and soils that in earlier times provided the basis for this viscous fuel and lubricant through their constant decomposition. Today the constant decomposition of communicative events on the Internet and on the sensors that record events everywhere ensures the maturation of the raw material.

So, when we ponder whether the Internet is a mass medium, the first element of this composite is relevant to begin with. The fact that social networks exist at all – and not simply textual content available on the Internet, as offered by book and journal publishers, sometimes still according to business models that are just derivatives of print media – is due not to with what users could do with them, but to what providers could do with the consequences.

Precisely for this reason, a media form is emerging that, in practice, already produces networking. 'In practice' means that the technological infrastructure dictates, as it were, the view that everyone on the Internet will adopt almost automatically. A message from one person to another, or a post to a self-definable group ('friends' only, or a 'public' defined by the algorithm, or 'followers', etc.) is in a different category from an e-mail. E-mail communication is communication between ego and alter ego; a post in a social network is communication in front of, and for, others: *tertii terti-aeque dantur* – third parties are possible!

Watching the watching

Individual statements become *medial* because the communication between a sender and a receiver, who thereby becomes a sender too, *can be observed by a third party*. This is also the principle of what we call social media, in which two principles apply: first, social groups are created on the Internet such that their members are visible to one another (and this visibility is algorithmically shaped by providers and interest-driven). Here anyone becomes a potential sender, even those who are not directly addressed. And, second, a new observer position emerges, namely what is called in systems theory a 'second-order observer' – this has become a popular term by now – or an observer of observers. A public is being socialized that no longer simply sees messages or watches trained observers in the act of observing. The feature section in a so-called high-quality newspaper, for example, is characterized by the fact that it does not just report and reproduce something; the reader co-watches, things are observed in this way and not in any other.[14] But in the social media, observing the observer is elevated to eye level, so to speak. The observer option becomes coextensive with the 'voice' option, thus creating a dynamic form of communication that can hardly be controlled and often goes off course (anyone who makes their comment columns accessible without moderation or consults hot topics on Facebook knows this), as it can certainly take a productive form to communicate in an exemplary manner, visible to others.

Perhaps this is the crucial difference to or the crucial extension of the classic mass media. There is indeed an almost confusing wealth of senders able to offer low-threshold communication. By the way, such senders are not necessarily 'people'; they may as well be algorithms, which are of great interest to some – just think of markets, voters, or other collectives of receivers that look unstructured. But even these simulate, at least as 'persons', attributable communicants who are really watched as they observe. The Internet is a medium where structures emerge that are characterized not so much by a professional sender structure as by a truly evolutionary wickerwork of possible connections.

Also, this function of digitalization encounters a receptive society. The business models of the social media can count on the traces of these practices on the Internet only because they meet a society that has a double experience. For one thing, communication is the raw material of a society whose volatility is rooted in the practically unlimited form of variance formation, in evolutionary communication paths, and in experimentations with connective spheres of communication – but also in the fundamental inconsequentiality of communication. It is often deplored that social media users act really carelessly in putting personal information on the web, and we complain that, in the daily habits of our normal life, we pay so little attention to the disclosure of traces – not to mention that some of these actions are simply unavoidable, if you think of payment transactions, or that we are hanging around in train stations and airports, and so on.

This carelessness is interconnected with the technological function of functioning, which accommodates the primacy of practice over reflection in our everyday behaviour. When you think about it, technology is much closer to our everyday behaviour than practices that are reflexive and cognitively demanding because they rely on deviation reinforcement. Perhaps here it becomes obvious once again why there is such a huge gap between the published criticism and danger scenarios of the digital on the one hand and concrete everyday practices on the other.

Of course, a second explanation says that the Internet, with its possibilities to distribute communicative offerings, encounters a society that has become just as accustomed to *communicative liquefaction* as it has to aesthetic self-presentation. The exponential growth in the number of broadcasters has changed this too. A young generation of digital natives is skilled most of all at presenting itself, in writing and visually, in a form that is visible and appropriate for this medium. This kind of impression management is indeed a specific form of literacy – that is, of the double ability to express oneself and read. The fact that this also gives rise to strange forms deserves a detailed analysis, but is not worth mentioning in connection with understanding the mediality of these media.

What makes this situation of unleashed communication special is indeed the antinomic relationship between an unlimited communication and its tentative meaninglessness. One should look at the timelines of social media to get an idea of how a permanent decomposition of events occurs here and often hardly shows any structure. My aim here is not to examine these practices in greater detail, but I am interested in the fact that the orientation towards the present found in these sequences of events can be seen in the rhythm of the timelines. We are here in the presence of low-threshold connectivity that migrates in real time. And this applies not only to meaningless fiddling around, to self-enhancing forms of reinforced aggression, or to the famous filter bubbles for confirmation bias but also to quite serious discussions even as they take place, for example on Facebook: there, too, one can see, as an observer of communication, what a real-time sequence these communication chains are. If autopoiesis can be observed anywhere, this is the place.

Permanent decomposition is visible in social networks. Things appear, then disappear. The social networks are similar to primordial presences, as I have discussed them in chapter 2 in Husserl's melody example; they develop protention and retention forms, but lose themselves in new presences and come to be literally without base.

Complexity and overheating

Another social prerequisite for the success of the Internet's mediality is probably the basic experience of the complexity of the world. If complexity is taken to mean that nothing can be understood without the idea that it also looks different from different angles, then the Internet is a complexity-generating and a complexity-managing machine in one. It generates unimaginable complexity, because one has access to the most different things, because searches are faster but also take longer, because even more nuances can be retrieved. On the other hand it manages complexity, because here one can, both fast and at a low threshold, come across forms that deal with complexity at a level one could hardly reach with classic mass media, given their selectivities. Besides, this puts the classic mass media, with all their concentrated competence, in a position to serve precisely such rather small groups through the new media formats and to become one player among others there. One can think for example of the success of so-called longreads, which are perhaps more easily distributed and discussed on the Internet than on paper or on the radio. In this sense, the traditional media, too, attract new layers of users to the Internet.

Watching the one who watches – this is perhaps the crucial competence in a society whose complexity is characterized by the need to deal explicitly with differences of perspective.[15] The Internet is a mass medium wherever it enables new forms of processing the difference of perspective. The process of adapting to the formats that are most successful in this respect, for example to the business and income models that may result for publicists and to how distribution channels are to be designed – including whether and how (economic and content-related) forms of centralization and decentralization relate to each other – is currently under way.

In summary, it can definitely be claimed that the Internet is a mass medium. Its function, namely to enable synchronization, is the same as that of other mass media. But the form of delivery is changing. One can formulate it almost in the opposite way.

While, in parallel with the establishment of national states as reference spaces for publicity and decision-making, classic mass media such as the newspaper, radio, and television had to guarantee that something like a relatively uniform view of things was communicated, the reference problem of mass mediality on the Internet is rather the question of how the difference of perspective can be reproduced, organized, and presented via the medium. Thus what the component 'mass' means in the expression 'mass medium' is an open question. It becomes apparent that media events do not change from one form to another, but that the forms that emerge on the Internet, which is used as a mass medium, really presuppose classic mediality, so that the difference of perspective may unfold in a media-conveyed illusion of a common world.

From here on our thoughts can take two directions. The first gives us the Internet as a complexity-processing medium, a recombination medium, a medium that reunites what does not otherwise come together, a productive laboratory for combining forms that otherwise never meet. One not only searches but also finds; one can use algorithms in order to keep up with the complexity of society, at least to some extent, through search engines, expert systems, or other offerings. In this sense, the Internet is not a mass medium, for it reaches the masses like a unity; but it is a mass medium because it makes masses of information adjustable, through individual search movements, to the perspective from which the search is made. The Internet is a breeding ground that generates forms itself. You can find what you were not looking for, and you can adjust your searching strategies even as you find it. In a complex society, this is the perfect problem-solving tool for information processing. The mass medium of the Internet is a medium of pattern recognition and recombination of elements. What you are looking for emerges only during the search. In a sense, the Internet is a medium for the self-observation of society – it is the duplication medium that I have described in detail. The Internet is an inexhaustible source of data in which social practice is documented and instructed. It is a complex observation tool – and probably the only way left for us to get a realistic idea of complex processes, each one depending on the specific issue at hand. Challenges such as climate change or social inequality, the effects of economic, health-related, political, and scientific processes can be tracked on the net; this is where society learns more about itself than ever before. And at the same time this is where it learns less than ever, because the possibilities for recombination and thus variation increase exponentially.

The other direction our thoughts must take is less tempered than the first. It is rather the direction of a radical heating up. Just as this medium provides society with representations of itself, it also provides itself with indomitable permanent attention. Mass media have always been tense, nervous, jittery media. Book printing and the newspaper created tension, visual media and electronic real-time media magnified it, and the Internet went even further. Nervousness means more stimuli than can be processed and filed. Nothing is safe from comments, negative remarks, and the like. Most stiking is perhaps the phenomenon of repetition. Particles of information can be confirmed, passed on, repeated, exponentially enhanced by the millions. No information is lost, although there is a permanent decomposition of events.

In 1962 Claude Lévi-Strauss introduced the distinction between hot and cold societies.[16] Cold and hot societies are different in their attitude to social change: cold societies expend their energies to maintain the status quo; hot societies on the other hand strive for the new, are growth-oriented, are not satisfied with the status quo. In those days, in the 1960s, such distinctions were also an attempt to avoid the all too Eurocentric, derogatory distinction between 'primitive' and 'civilized' cultures – and then in fact to use it after all. The industrialized West was effectively the prototype of hot societies, ready to adjust and change, flexible, heterogeneous, innovative, and above all oriented to cognitive learning styles. When conditions change, hot societies are also ready to change their behaviour. They have what social psychology calls a style of cognitive expectation, and they are ready to learn. By contrast, cold societies maintain a style of normative expectation and stick to established categories.

Printing and mass media are the classic driving forces of hot societies – they compel people to deal with the new, learn, tolerate deviations. They make change visible and appreciate it, because only what is new can be written in the newspaper. A cold society does not need a newspaper. With the Internet, of course, the heat is enhanced. Overheated societies, this is what the net makes possible. Hot societies learn systematically; overheated societies do not learn but collapse from their own dynamics. When the point is neither mere 'cold' preservation nor 'hot' design and strategies, but any detail is an all-or-nothing affair, that is when we are dealing with overheated societies.[17] When every question is about the whole, the only thing that counts is complete orientation to the present, and then events pulsate so strongly that they can hardly be of any information value.

The risks to democratic deliberation processes from this overheating – risks of activation of communication contents, risks of political, scientific, and cultural populism, risks of mood dependence on debates – are widely discussed. Twitter's short message service is perhaps a particularly vivid example of how in principle the mediality and materiality of practices trigger overheating. According to a study from the MIT, fake news spreads faster on Twitter than on any other medium, and considerably faster than true information.[18] It is certainly also the information's being limited to 280 characters that promotes overheating and concentration on practically exclusive circles. Anyone who has ever seen how a Twitter self-confirmation machine boots up in a very short time and how the form of mutual confirmation escalates into a practically unprotected kind of private language in front of an audience has watched overheating as in open-heart surgery. It's not without cause that Twitter is a place where particular groups can establish themselves: these groups look like a true, authentic public because they can be observed by third parties, but ultimately they are only a form of self-confirmation. The fact that this cultural form has emerged is not the result of some media strategy but the result of the very form of communication made possible by Twitter's mediality and materiality, on the one hand, and on the other hand of the provider's indifference to what happens on its platform as long as data are generated.

I have already pointed out in the Introduction that the leading minds in social science are interested almost exclusively in these practices, which ultimately means that they are interested in the personal experience of a group of people whose contact with digitalization is characterized not by the threat of imminent job loss or of new logistical forms, so much as by looking at their smartphones. What you cannot see from this perspective is the strange premise for such practices: that they emerge of their own accord, so to speak, and have nothing to do with the technological providers, who would do everything to keep a data collection machine running.

But the fact that the political tone is getting tougher and public communication is increasingly jittery can be attributed directly to the net. If traditional media had built-in gatekeepers simply as a result of their professionalization and, not least, their materiality, this function is now almost entirely absent. The Internet oscillates between complexity-processing capacities and overheating risks. Just like the servers, the outcomes, too, must worry about an adequate cooling.

The Internet as an archive of all possible statements

Finally, I would like to point out a particular feature of the Internet that in principle counteracts my earlier claim that social media are radically oriented to the present – an orientation that, incidentally, is also a typical feature of traditional media: the newspaper gets thrown away, or starts on a second career as fish wrap or floor protection sheets during renovations.

But on the Internet everything stays – including, by the way, the archives of those whose main job is newspaper printing. The net becomes an exponentially growing archive of all kinds of statements on all kinds of facts. The selectivity of classic media must be constantly re-created from scratch. As (potentially) everything is archived, everything can be found – even what is contradictory. Anyone who has ever used a search engine to research the connection between two *items* will see that there are completely different answers to this question. And even if there is no connection at all, you will find someone who has made this connection and written it down somewhere in archivable format. Among those in Germany who, for whatever reason, prefer German rather than English terms for everything, the Internet is called *Weltnetz* – the world net. If by 'world' we understand the totality of what exists, this is no bad term, because the Internet can indeed access the memory storage and thus the totality of what exists (which is stored in data files). The medium itself does not know any selectivity – but this applies to earlier media as well. Writing is not a selection principle, it is a medium through which one can implement selection principles by writing down this and not that. One does not expect it, but the Internet is much more material than the potentiality of writing.

In the archives of the world things are stored that can be stored via the Internet. In this respect the Internet, too, faces a selection problem if we see it in a mass media form. But the selecting actors have changed: they are no longer just the editorial staff and the forms of sayability in the public sphere; they are people in growing numbers, some of them acting not as biological individuals but as algorithms. If anything is being reorganized right now, it is the question of the selectivity of what may be said, heard, and read.

I have developed here in detail a theorem of the *duplication of the world* that applies to media, to systems, especially functional ones, and also to data. Social media and networks are so attractive to providers because this duplication in data form shows the material with which a profitable surplus of meaning can be produced. And, as I have already pointed out, this applies not only to social media, but to almost all practices that are in some way supported or monitored through technology. This is the material for those intelligent applications that can themselves search for, and find, structure in the data and that no longer limit themselves to answering questions and identifying patterns but can trigger new questions and patterns.

It has been a long way from providing evidence of the *third discovery of society* to reaching this point. The digitalization of society began at a point where the regularities and patterns of social processes could be understood only by digital means. Now it becomes obvious that, with the further development of digitalization, digital technologies no longer just *experience* things and uncover structures but are active *actors*, insofar as *they themselves* generate those metadata-like criteria through which patterns can now be actively created – on markets, on transport routes, in processes of energy supply, and in many other fields. The *cultural* meaning of data practices – including self-practices in data form (self-tracking, self-observation, quantifications of everyday practices) that are the topic of most analyses of the digital in the social sciences – is just the visible part of an invisible technology whose cultural consequences can be considered almost unintended side effects. The surplus of meaning does not need the primary meaning; all it needs is an opportunity to leave behind as many data as possible. This, however, does not make these practices any less meaningful.

Intelligence in the mode of Future 2.0

Since the Internet is the archive of all possible statements, it is also the source of a special intelligence. The archive of all possible statements is produced at a lower threshold than the book, which, at least on the production side, requires an elitist cultural technique, whereas social media are suitable for the masses and their application requires little. This a great advantage, because not only refined semantics is stored but (also) all possible bullshit. This is a great source of intelligence; it shows parallelisms with research on the analysis of technological accidents. In the 1980s Charles Perrow demonstrated that complex technological systems that have been involved in accidents can be well reconstructed from the causal angle. It is thus possible to reconstruct the causal chain of the accident from the remaining components of an airplane crash, for example. But it is not possible to predict accidents from previously known components.[19] Thus, causality is a formula that works only in retrospect, not beforehand.

The archive of all possible statements enables something similar. In the future perfect tense (called *Futur 2* in German), the Internet will demonstrate that mankind has clearly become smarter, more forward-thinking, and wiser. For, for everything that happens in the future, it will be possible to find a fairly accurate forecast in the archives. It is one thing that this is mainly due to there being so many predictions that the right one will always be among them; the fact that all these predictions will now be accessible post factum will be the fulfilment of a promise – even in the future perfect: *We will have known!* And, even better, we do already know, we just don't know *who knows.* At least the linearity of the passing of time cannot be lifted even by the Internet. So, for everything that happens in a present, one will find the right prognosis in the archives. Everything could also happen differently, but it is quite probable that it has been predicted at some time. Then we will know the causal chain of the world's events in Charles Perrow's manner – going backwards.

The great dream of data-based intelligence may be that higher computing resources will be able to project forecasts not only from the past to the present but even from the present to the future. But even if this succeeds, it would not override the mechanism of time. We will know only later whether the prognosis will have really been correct. This is, then, a sort of Future 2.0.

8
Endangered Privacy

If it is true that social media are just an opportunity to detect, store, recombine, and assess individually generated data, and if it is also true that a worldwide network of data really gets formed as a result of the registration of most everyday practices in a wide variety of data sets, then this has considerable consequences for the question of individual data protection. It would be fair to say that the Federal Republic of Germany is one of the most sensitive countries when it comes to the right to informational self-determination. The first data protection law worldwide was enacted in Hesse in 1970. The incentive for legal data protection stems from the classic debate on the individual's rights to protection from the state. Data protection is intended to prevent state authorities from using personal data for inappropriate purposes. It is in a sense a derivative of the principle of inviolability of the home, freedom of opinion, and right to privacy.[1]

Under the conditions of digitalization, the question of data protection is raised in new and different ways, for now it is no longer just state actors who benefit from personal data but actors of very different types. Even the user of a standard word-processing program that stores data in a cloud outsources personal data and files and may not use them. Mobile networks providers have almost comprehensive information about voice and data traffic, and any common smartphone with GPS technology is technically similar to an electronic tag and to a detector of movement profiles – and, if provided with appropriate additional devices, even to a detector of the user's heart rate and blood-sugar profile, not to mention payment transactions, detection of machine-readable number plates, or face recognition in public places. Of course, this does not mean that these data are available to anyone, for no matter what purpose. This is in fact legally restricted and an issue of political debates, and the range of access options varies enormously at the international level. At this point in the discussion one usually points for example to the Chinese model, which sanctions an almost total control of the private individual by the state's morality police.[2] It is of course no accident that this should happen in an authoritarian political model such as China's rather than in liberal democracies. But in principle the possibilities are there.

The improbability of informational self-determination

This is not the place to discuss the legal and political issues of data protection; there is literature galore on this topic. I would like to emphasize something else: the conflict of goals between privacy policies and the dependence of many business models on the avail-ability of appropriate data sets, which are interested not only in the statistically average person – *l'homme moyen* – but in the specific case targeted, whose targeting results from the pattern recognition produced by data aggregated from many cases.

This conflict of goals also lies in the fact that quite a few technol-ogies work only if personal data are available – even if the concrete individual, for example as a potential customer, as a user of social networks, or as a voter, is not ascertained *in persona* but as an element in a cluster. For usually the individual is not a member of a social group, but only of a statistical group – but in this capacity can be individually targeted and identified, if in doubt (and if you know). This can be exploited for quite a few things, including illegal and questionable things in terms of possibilities to control. Dirk Baecker's nice observation that the book world of the reading public has suffered from a surplus of criticism, while the digital world suffers from a surplus of control, finds eloquent expression here.[3] This opens up possibilities that change the way we look at selectivities. If we remember the storms of protest triggered by population censuses in Germany in the 1980s, we see clearly how much the situation has changed. Switching on one's smartphone generates more personal data than any census would have ever been capable of. Just imagine census takers back then asking for the sorts of things that today come up on their own, so to speak.

I am not going to discuss this any further, not because it is not a legitimate and necessary question but because this is not my topic. What interests me is rather the epistemological and sociological aspect of the question of privacy. To begin with, it is worth paying attention to the concept of *informational self-determination*. The term contains a *contradictio in adiecto* [self-contradiction] because, simply on categorial grounds, there can be no self-determination just in relation to information. Information is a correlate of observation.

Whether something is suitable as information or registered as information lies in the eye of the recipient, not in the observed. Perhaps we may put it this way: *Information about the environment is created within the system.* Or *what is observed is created by the observer.* I refer here to my remarks on the *duplication of the world.* Thus informational self-determination is a target variable that is nothing short of impossible, precisely under conditions of complex observation.

Thus privacy is ultimately ruled out on epistemological grounds; one could rather talk about something like control over one's own data. But categorial questions arise even here, for in the course of modern networked everyday life data are generated anyway. Then the question is, again, whom these data make a difference for and what kind of difference it is, or, in plain language, what it is that the data tell. If we think of the widely discussed General Data Protection Regulation (GDPR), which implemented European law in the Federal Republic of Germany in 2018, both the debate generated by it and the operational question itself oscillate between actual control over data and the legal figure of consent. The GDPR and data protection law as a whole actually attempt the legal regulation of data flows, but strictly they only oversee what the law can manage: they implement a *normative certainty of expectations.* For example, through more or less general consent, using the services of providers as a customer is now fitted with a brief obstacle to action [*Handlungshemmung*], such that the consent itself then guarantees all the more clearly that data are legal means of transporting value chains, and not only of the monetary kind. Obstacles to action, as the American sociologist George Herbert Mead put it in his theory of action a hundred years ago, are those points in the process of action at which a concrete practice does not simply unfold, but is inhibited. An inhibition of action occurs only where there are questions of adaptation, decision, or adjustment. Most of our everyday actions get by without inhibitions; what happens is very routine. In sociology, this kind of action is called *practice.*[4] Consciousness, or should I say awareness, becomes involved only when practice is interrupted. Then it becomes necessary to imagine consequences of actions, to assess explicitly how the alter ego would react, or to reason about what to do. Consciousness, according to Mead's wonderful formulation, is not the precondition for, but the consequence of action.[5]

I refer to this theoretical model because it can make clear once again that the question of the adjustability, for instance, of privacy aspects of data traffic can be understood only if we pay heed to the *technological* aspect of the data world. Attempts to implement legal certainty of expectation, as in the GDPR of 2018, interrupt the practices of technological users only briefly. They create something like *lucida intervalla* [periods of lucidity] in the stream of consciousness and practice of users of information-relevant technology. In certain psychiatric clinical descriptions, *lucidum intervallum* is the name given to a short phase of awareness, before the patient returns to the shaded state of his or her morbidity. Now, I don't want to pathologize the users of data technology – that would go too far. But in fact the participation of consciousness or awareness in our everyday lives does resemble such distinct, habitualized phases, interrupted by inhibitions of action. We might as well call these barriers to action conscious reflection (or, in the field of communication, the thematization of things that usually remain anathema) – and this is exactly what the consent solution does in the area of data traffic, for example.

This makes legal sense, is probably unavoidable politically, and certainly prevents some inappropriate use of data. But, strictly speaking, such brief inhibitions are futile, for they must assert themselves straight against the particular potency of technology: *that it works, is consequently resistant to dissent, and does not ask questions.* Functioning is the enemy of reflection – this is why everyday life is possible with technologies one does not see through, one does not understand, one cannot even name, but one is able to apply. Incidentally, this illustrates that tying communication processes to understanding, comprehension, and consensus is perhaps a crude reduction. This is certainly also the result of a fixation on academic social science ideas, which usually get fixated on such goals of communication instead of simply being mindful of the conditions of communicative connections. With the involvement of technology – this applies to digital technology, but also to habitualized forms of technological communication – the elimination of risks of understanding, comprehension, and consensus through simplified connections is central. This includes the coded communication of functional systems, as I showed in chapter 4.

In our digital society, the claim that the rational age of modernity (Auguste Comte) is more transparent and less secretive than earlier ages does not withstand closer scrutiny. Only now the realm of the unknown, of the mysterious, of the dark and invisible can no longer be attributed to gods, demons, fate, or other dark forces but to a technology that dispenses with reflection. A re-enchantment of the world led by technology lacks the magic that one could debunk. What remains is the attempt at control, but this comes up against its limits precisely because information technology is a technology that has to outsource to other observers the usability of its own data. Just as the book world has never got a grip on criticism, almost fetishized it, and upgraded the refusal position from risk status to dignity status, the digital world must wrestle with matters of control, in full awareness that the conditions of observation have changed. At any rate, the classic schema of subject and object – that is, of control of the objective by the subjective gaze through the participation of the subjective in the objective – has given way to a form that increasingly makes the subject into an object of control that, in digital form, operates as self-control.

Most verdicts of surveillance capitalism, of a colonization of the world by digits, or of a self-optimization compulsion pay heed to this section, in which the social-science literature is primarily interested. This lines up with a generational topos of sociological diagnoses that explore the subjectivization of the individual through social 'appeal'[6] – wide-eyed, their proponents express surprise that the individuality of the individual is a consequence of social practice.[7] I cannot deny that most of these diagnoses are in my view hopelessly naïve, for they operate with a strange normative assumption of a self which should be left alone, as if working on the self were not the foundation of a society that is neither able nor willing to condition people completely through group affiliation with no alternative. If digital technologies offer here novel media forms for the operationalization of self-control, namely metric points of comparison, this is merely the digitalizable form of a pattern that has been known for a long time – as if quantified comparison in the form of school marks, or the quantification of results in sports, or educational certificates, or even the comparison of income differentials had never existed and as if the entire semantics of the personality, based on education as it was, had not been a self-optimization program or a means of distinction or comparison, ever since bourgeois society. In any case, a form of *informational self-determination* it was not.

I have already attempted to explain these diagnoses at the very beginning of this book, as a result of the environment created by their authors: in this environment, educational distinction is seen as a blind spot. Education is always taken for granted, which is why the self-optimization practices of the educational program are not perceived as what they are, but rather, perhaps, as the universal human element par excellence, something that this environment likes to attribute to *traditional white elites*, whose members in fact hypostatized their particular position, treating it as a universal model.

This seems to be repeated here – and, just as the traditional citizen sneered at the lower classes and sought to civilize them through education, now the leading minds in social science emancipate the presumptuous citizen, who practises body-, health-, work-, and skills-related as well as aesthetic optimization. The digitality of the digital means that are used to justify this – metrics, quanti-fication, and so on – does not even come into view. This is why, notwithstanding all the justification for privacy policies and for the attempts to avoid data-based surpluses of surveillance and control, a private sphere that may never have existed gets rescued. Then *sensus communis* declares unanimously, unchallenged, that big data endangers our privacy, our private sphere, our personal autonomy. So it repays to focus tentatively on privacy; for initially the debate knows privacy as a space worthy of protection, where power is to be broken. Right now the focus is primarily on re-politicization.[8]

A new structural change in the public sphere?

If the private sphere is the space of our personal autonomy, then the public sphere is the space that moves away from this original form by becoming visible to others – first in the form of bourgeois reading communities, as we know from social history, later on in societies and other associations, and finally in mediatized debating public spheres made up of literate readers; nowadays these are informed citizens who know what is visible about society in public spheres of this kind.[9] Since the beginning of the nineteenth century, the modern nation state has ultimately provided and designed the stages of bourgeois society as a system of needs and as a space of publicly accessible information, but also as a real state and polity, in other words as public order.

There is much debate on the public sphere. Can it release the normative energies that guarantee that something like a democrati-cally formed will prevails? Can it make accessible what in earlier societies was accessible only to the elites? Can it be the corrective for illegitimate power and domination? Can it unlock cultural practices and matters of course by giving us alternatives? Will it deliver the critical citizen, who is still imagined, at least in theories of democracy, according to the model of the Attic agora? And what will happen to the public sphere, if it is mediatized? Only since the printing of books has there been anything like a far-away, imaginary recipient in a preliminary form of public sphere that could be construed as a readership. And it is only through the newspaper that something like the shared reality of a society could be simulated, that a public community of speakers become possible among strangers, mostly within the framework of nation-state order. The media are always the filter that diffuses what becomes negotiable as a topic in public spaces. Thus they are at once enablers and preventers; they are the gatekeepers of publics spheres – and every media revolution brings change to the conditions of what we call the public sphere, hence to the conditions for the system of needs and for the state. This was true for the radio as well as for television, and it is also true for the Internet. And a new medium of dissemination always comes along with both great hopes and great fears.

Concerning the Internet, the range extends from the euphoria of Howard Rheingold, who in 1993 saw a new, democratic culture of 'virtual communities'[10] rising on the horizon, to Sascha Lobo's complaint that the Internet is now broken because in practice it denies these promises. But the main thrust of reflections on the Internet is still the Rheingoldian motif of communitization and the social network, of the possibility of counter-publics and of bringing together sub-publics that could not be reached without the Internet. This is ultimately a discourse on how to exploit the advantage of weak networks: the network brings together people who would not otherwise come together, thus creating addressable spaces that other media cannot create so smoothly. From the public space of bourgeois society, with its desire for one legitimate taste, one legitimate way of life, one socio-moral intuition, and standardization among political lines of conflict, there emerges a *pluralism of communities* that form themselves anew, operationally, and no longer represent society but essentially their own spheres, each with its thematic, aesthetic, and socio-moral intentions.

Until recently, activists celebrated the Internet expectantly and with great confidence in the new forms of communitization and democracy, while academic observers of the Internet, albeit displaying a certain scepticism, were still predominantly interested in the matter of opportunities for new forms of communitization. Social science observers remain in the end advocates of a better world, which they imagine primarily as a world with a high rate of consensus and a simultaneous diversification of possibilities. What is more, new practices almost blur the private and the public, the personal and the factual, merging them into new forms of authentic occasional communication on the Internet and pushing towards a network society in which we can live differently. Meanwhile Howard Rheingold started speaking of 'smart mobs':[11] these are not restricted to virtual communities of individuals but may encompass collaborative systems with a collective intelligence.

Big data is different. Perhaps big data really creates something like a collectivity – but ultimately only in the form of collected collectivities. Big data does not create social groups – only statistical groups. Even on the Internet, social groups are *analog* phenomena

– in other words they are visible, clearly addressable, identity-forming, oriented to natural language and everyday practices. Big data turns analog users into *digital* phenomena. Big data digitalizes the traces of analog practices – movement profiles on the street and on the Internet, purchasing behaviour, health data, leisure behaviour, participation in social networks, and so on – in such a way that it is possible to recombine data that have not been collected for recombination. On the other hand, this creates *statistical groups* that do not exist at all in the analog world – such as potential buyers of certain products, suspects in manhunts, or health risk and credit risk groups. This is where the argument changes direction. Big data is what the invisible siphons off from social networking on the Internet. While this was still driven by the dream of taking resources from private, authentic communication and feeding them into public communication, thereby making society into more of a community again, now the Internet is intruding from the outside into the private sphere, where it has no business to be but where there is lots to find.

Hazards

Perhaps this verdict of *risk to privacy* is the turning point at which the debate leaves the circles of experts and acquires the density we are currently observing. The feature pages provide us with techno-logical details and information about economic strategies, political possibilities, military innovations, medical options for observation and control, and so on: all these use the accumulation of collected data and their recombination and processing as their foundation. Social media become suddenly visible as business practices, and there develops an awareness that all this looks more harmless than it is. There are warnings about a concentration of power, and also warnings that it is no longer possible to distinguish between economic and political actors.

Thus the everyday reaction to the big data threat is very tradi-tional: it is an attempt to protect one's own private sphere against interventions from the outside, to demarcate one's personal space from the public sphere, so to speak, and to be able to determine for oneself, at least there, what can and what may pass through the often invisible membrane between the private space and the world. Privacy is in the end the normative criterion in the critique of the Internet's new possibilities and of the new search and find practices underpinned by big data. Private space is ultimately the world in which we want to live securely in our lifeworld – and so all criticism of the new media loses its abstraction when this private space comes under attack and under surveillance.

Behind this lies a narrative we are now accustomed to: that there is a clear boundary between the private space of self-determination and of idiosyncratic lifestyles and the public space of accessibility to others. From the perspective of lived lifestyles themselves, society appears in fact as a concentrically shaped form in which the significance and uniqueness of individuals decreases with increasing distance. Lifestyles are tailored to families, networks of friends, and physically accessible people, whereas the space of 'society' looks like a public space where rather universalistic rules apply – from politeness routines through traffic rules to a general set of behavioural standards for that space we tend to call the public sphere. The boundary between these spaces is marked architecturally by the front door and socially by the visibility of idiosyncrasies. This way one may even succeed in being private among the multitude, as proven by communication practices such as volume management, deliberate non-listening, and tact in private matters. Private is that which is not made accessible to others – in a sense, it is the space of least generality and greatest specificity. And it is experienced as the space of an immediate, original life, truly experienced by the concrete individual.

Our idea of privacy is, as it were, the embodiment of an ethical life, as expressed in Hegel's philosophy of law. Hegel distinguishes three levels of ethical life: the family, bourgeois society, and the state. In his system the family, which is the original form, represents the most particular form of ethical life – one in which distinct individuals come together to the point of physical symbiosis – whereas in bourgeois society, in the 'system of needs', (economic) subjects represent their interests and appear as self-confident individuals. On the other hand the state, which represents the 'idea of morality', demands from these individuals not self-confidence as much as voluntary submission to something general: submission as a gesture of freedom. Like Hegel, we imagine the reconciliation of these three levels of ethical life in such a way that submission to the state comes ultimately at the price of our leaving behind the symbiotic form of the family and finding our livelihood and income in bourgeois society. Here privacy and the family are conceived of as the most particular but also the most original, most sensual form of ethical life. This thing, the authenticity and originality – one could almost say, the most direct humanity – that finds expression in this particular sphere of ethical life, supplies something like the basic intuition in public debates on the protection of privacy. This basic intuition covers the fact that

privacy is a space almost free of society – if not in reality, then at
least as a normative idea.

Privacy is therefore worth paying more attention to. Or let me
put it this way: anyone interested in Privacy 2.0 should start by
getting better knowledge of what Privacy 1.0 actually was. It is one
of the fundamental experiences of social evolution that discourses
on current changes often imagine an astonishingly simplistic picture
of the past, to be able to conceptualize change more clearly. If I
am to put it strongly, one often laments the loss of, or attempts to
save, something that never was. For example, quite a few complaints
about secularization or the ungodliness of the modern world make it
as if earlier times had truly been integrated into the religious sphere.
Criticisms of the complexity, division of labour, and confusion of
the modern world often take off from a very crude idea of shared
worldviews and almost conflict-free forms of life in the premodern
era. The critique of acceleration, currently very popular, which likes
to pose as a new variety of critical theory, imagines earlier times
as quieter times. The critique of industrial production frequently
believed that the survival strategies of earlier, scarcity societies
created less alienated relationships. The critique of urbanity has
always been based on a romantic idea of rural idylls. A free will
that was previously unknown in this form gets rescued from brain
research and its sometimes shocking results. And the critique of
technology willingly ignores what afflicted earlier social forms. The
critique of Privacy 2.0 could follow a similar path, which is why I
will first devote myself to Privacy 1.0 – and, by the way, I'm doing
this not in order to falsify or manipulate the critique of the threat
that big data poses to privacy, but quite the opposite – in order to
get a sound knowledge of what we are criticizing and defending.

Privacy 1.0

Privacy has been a matter of public debate for quite some time.
That the private is political was one of the most effective criticisms
of social movements such as the cultural revolution of the nineteen-
sixty-eighters, as we call them, or of the feminist movement later
on. They discovered, as it were, the sociality of the private, where
the mediation of the general and the particular is obvious – which
is almost inherent in Hegel's legal hierarchy of the three kinds of
ethical life and is still discussed in this spirit today, when lifestyles or
forms of life and their legitimation are explicitly claimed not to be a
private matter.[12] But precisely the conflict-laden nature of this claim
confirms the basic intuition that the private sphere is something

withdrawn from social access, the very 'other' in which we are who we really are.

To track down the development of privacy as we know it, I would like to draw on Michel Foucault's *History of Sexuality*, since sexuality appears to be the most private area of society, especially in bourgeois society, which is characterized by a strange juxtaposition of prudery and sexualization. The fact that in bourgeois society sexuality contributes to individualizing the person is linked to the fact that sexual desire is considered the most authentic and individual form of desire – most recently today, in bourgeois and anti-bourgeois queer studies that search for authentic desire, as long as it does not follow too conventionally the dictate of compulsory heterosexuality.

Foucault describes how the bourgeois society of the nineteenth century was a 'society of blatant and fragmented perversion'[13] in which the containment of sexuality within marriage ensured at the same time the build-up of something like counterforces, against which certain social techniques were in turn expected to help. Foucault cites confession as the decisive technique. Foucault tells us that around sex 'they constructed … an immense apparatus for producing truth'.[14] Precursors of the modern confession are for example the way in which the Fourth Lateran Council of 1215 organized the sacrament of penance, along with other methods of investigation such as the Inquisition, which did not want simply to prove guilt but sought a confession from the accused. The new authority that assumes this task is now science – a *scientia sexualis* that furnishes the confessor with criteria for what does and does not constitute perversion, thus creating a specific power. This is the power to give shape only to the kind of sexuality that can be considered a socially acceptable variant of a truly authentic private lifestyle and to turn the ubiquitous perversion into an occasion for confessions, in which the individual becomes the kind of subject who rules him- or herself and shows common sense – shows it in such a way that society can earmark a sphere of life labelled 'private'. You can close the front door to your house or apartment and leave the space behind it unsurveilled only if it is known that the subjects behind that door observe themselves. They become bourgeois subjects by ruling themselves or by wanting what they should want. Incidentally, Hegel's legal hierarchy, which connects the particular with the general, also had an eye on this reconciliation between want and should. Just as Marx reversed Hegel from his head onto his materialistic feet, Foucault (implicitly, of course) converted Hegel from connecting the mind to controlling the body.

What seems to be the citizen's basic intuition about freedom and the absence of outside control is, in Foucault's interpretation, the result of a new social type that must justify itself. *Its representatives are free to do what they want, but they should want what they should do.* Hence they are frequently exposed to situations in which they have to give information about themselves – about what they want. Foucault writes very clearly: now 'the agency of domination does not reside in the one who speaks (for it is he who is constrained), but in the one who listens and says nothing; not in the one who knows and answers, but in the one who questions and is not supposed to know'.[15]

On this view, Privacy 1.0 is the result of surveillance techniques that use data to produce something like normality and a normalization of individual lifestyles. What Foucault describes with his famous topos of the *biopolitics of the population* is literally a collected collectivity, that is, in his own words, 'the administration of bodies and the calculated management of life',[16] mediated first of all through organizational membership of schools, military barracks, companies, and the like. Foucauldian turns of phrase, for instance that biopolitics is about the 'vitality of the social body',[17] are frequently quoted with a kind of pleasant shudder about a by-gone period in the discipline. But, much to the contrary, they could not be more up to date. That sexuality was the greatest producer of power in bourgeois society and that the obsession with sex from traditional moral authorities such as churches still prevails may be due to the particular historical situation. Today body control has long left the narrow field of sexuality and is oriented towards beauty, health, authenticity of will and desire, and, not least, the ability to experience a subjectivity that is exhausted and in need of recuperation – exhausted by the speed and complexity of the world and, not least, exhausted as a theoretical and normative concept for explaining the world. The subject is a result of self-techniques that are a reaction to external expectations and to collection techniques.[18] Both the order of subjectivity and the order of privacy are expectation-led normalization strategies that ultimately owe their being to structures of expectation brought on by big data.

Privacy 1.0 as a result of big data?

Strictly speaking, what I, with Foucault, describe as Privacy 1.0 is the question of the application of big data. The biopolitics of the population can be described in almost the same categories that are used to describe today's big data strategies. The development of state authorities of control and normalization, the collection of data on the population, the supervision of collective behaviour, the data-driven form of social planning, the care for populations that depend on the division of labour for the production of consumer and substitute goods – all this required a collection of data for which new authorities were sought, and those did exactly what Foucault described: they did not speak, but remained silent. Just as in the past the confessor used to listen and thus exerted power, now it is the state that collects in silence, then draws conclusions. When the Statistical Office of the German Reich – Statistisches Amt des Deutschen Reiches – was founded in 1872, the data it collected were classified as state secrets, and not without reason. They were not made public, because one knew very well that data are the actual instrument of power for the control of society. And one had to get used to the fact that statistical data revealed strange regularities, although people do everything they do of their own free will. It was big data that first created the 'people' to be lead. Up until then, one knew nothing about a people: It just was there. Now it was created.

The people, too, or the population is now becoming what I called earlier a *digital* phenomenon. The superficial political ideologists treated it as an analog phenomenon – the people was promised meaning and grandeur, recognition and community. The abstract human of human rights became the citizen of a concrete analog community called nation, while the administration and what Foucault calls biopolitics turned him or her into a digital phenomenon that can be controlled, guided, and shaped.

With this I return to the basic idea of the first chapter. There I demonstrated that already in the nineteenth century society was measured, namely in relation to patterns that remain hidden to the naked eye. This 'eye' was the gaze of a calculating elite capable of setting normative standards and disciplinary rules to standardize the measured life, which was also a reaction to the fact that the modernization of society increased the probability of deviation in concrete lifestyles or forms of life. The disciplining calculation is also a reaction to the incipient unpredictability of now free citizens – and the form of disciplining citizenship is the form of ethics, which reacts to the transformation of external leadership into internal leadership.

The discovery of society through digital practices of this sort is an uncovering of regularities in everyday practices that, as in Shoshana Zuboff's description of *surveillance capitalism*, is a 'means of behavioral modification'.[19] Data are not collected in order to get knowledge of something, or even in order to do something; they are collected in order to make others do certain things. Strictly speaking,

ever since the beginning of modernity, bourgeois Privacy 1.0, and
hence the privacy of retreats and protective rights, the privacy of
inwardness and subjective uniqueness, has been flanked by Privacy
2.0 of collected collectivities, so that astonishment at the power and
techniques of big data today on the one hand is itself astonishing
and, on the other, is a kind of Enlightenment project.

Our unease about big data is very productive. It confronts us with
the naivety with which we set ourselves up in this world. The critique
of big data is superficial, if it really believes that one can claim state
protection rights against the state, although we know that since the
eighteenth century the statehood of the modern state is grounded
precisely in the fact that it supplies itself with digitalized data –
and this actually since there has been some kind of centralized
population planning. On the one hand, the strange regularity in the
behaviour of free subjects brings down the concept of subjectivity
as an individual principle, on the other hand it is exactly its starting
point. Subjects can be free only if they are rational – and the
most important generators of rationality in the history of western
modernity have been professionals such as doctors and lawyers,
teachers, professors and social planners, the police and the penal
system. It is no coincidence that these are the authorities who owe
their own rationality, their own criteria, their instructions, and their
expert knowledge to the big data from statistical boards and scientific surveys and, not least, to powerful 'listening'. They knew about
Privacy 2.0, they possessed *digital data* about collected collectivities,
and their professionalism consisted in translating this knowledge
into *analog instructions* that turned clients into reasonable human
beings: patients who care about their health, legal subjects who
abide by normative rules, punished individuals who accept rehabili-
tating punishment, students motivated to do well, and so on.
What belongs to the normal course of life in classic modernity – a
protected childhood, long periods of education, motivation to work
for the sake of working, the will to pursue a career and to start a
family, loyalty to democratic decisions, a sense of community, and
solidarity among strangers – all this is not simply given but must be
demanded – morally and with professional kindness and rationality,
but also with rigour and strictness – by those who know how to play
the game, that is, by those who have access to big data.

Big data and Privacy 2.0

Privacy as we know it today and defend against the strategies of
big data – what I have called Privacy 1.0 – is itself the result of a

data-processing strategy. The state and the public could forego direct control over private life only because one had to deal with staff that, through relevant asymmetries between agents of normalization of the paternalistic type – doctors, teachers, military personnel, social, urban, and hygiene planners, the police and the law courts – and their clients, produced something like a self-controlling person who on the one hand continued to exercise in private life the self-control already learned but on the other found a possibility to escape it to some extent; the parallel existence of prudery and perversion may be an indication of this. When the social physicist Adolphe Quetelet, mentioned in chapter 1 as one of the first to apply statistical methods to society, marvels in the nineteenth century at the regularity of human behaviour, for example vis-à-vis marriage, this is already the result of a normalization strategy that also gives expression to a high degree of normativity. Quetelet saw deviations from the normal distribution as disruptions and ultimately was fascinated by the *homme moyen*, by the average person who can be fittingly worked out and constitutes the basis for all those practices through which people are shaped into self-responsible individuals.[20]

It is only against this background that the special nature of today's big data strategies becomes visible. It should be obvious by now that the idea of middle-class privacy has been from its very beginnings the result of social and statal control strategies. On the one hand, these are control strategies that induce people to reveal information about themselves. The idea of self-justification can be released from a privacy that seems chaotic from the perspective of social control only if it is implanted into the subjectivity of the individual. And one may be sure that the normative idea of leading a life in the image of the *homme moyen* can really be assumed only where a conscience and forms of communication related to inwardness emerge. The entities that introduce people to this normalization are authoritative spokespersons in the form of professionals and experts provided with something like benchmarks and thresholds from which we can extrapolate the criteria for correct behaviour. One should definitely not underestimate the importance of these authoritative professional spokespersons to the formation of private lifestyles. They produce only clients to whom a rational privacy is tolerable.[21]

Granted, today's big data strategies are different from the classic ones since nineteenth-century social physics and social statistics. If those strategies focused on the *homme moyen*, and thus on a somehow supraindividual normative structure, new big data strategies are interested in individual cases or in special groups. If we think, for example, of services providers who use big data to investigate the credit status of potential bank clients,[22] this is not a matter of averages or benchmarks but of individualization of information. Data on previous consumption behaviour and payment habits, but also on people's networks and contacts, connection details, lifestyle information, possibly including health behaviour, will all create a personal profile that serves to evaluate that person's credit status. The big difference from earlier data is that data are now assessed that have not been collected for this purpose. The data traces come from completely different contexts and become information for a specific purpose only in retrospect. Current big data is capable of making very different data sources compatible with each other.

This is ultimately the only place where the special capability of the computer-based form of calculation comes into its own. This form is characterized by the fact that only the digitalization of data provides the basis for their recombinability. Big data recombines data that in the final analysis were not intended for each other; and it creates surplus value only through this recombination. In the case of credit status, for example, health-related data can be used to determine a person's state of health, or even state of regular lifestyle. This is not so much about secret data from health insurers, or even doctors – it would be illegal to use those. The point is that increasing numbers of people leave such data themselves, in clouds or social networks, for example through health apps on their own iPhones that are used for self-monitoring. More and more data regarding Internet users come from the users themselves anyway, for all network-based monitoring programs leave traces.

In this data matrix,[23] it is almost unavoidable that daily practice typical of our society leaves data behind. What gets discussed is the question of data preservation, but this is only the second step; first there is a *data collection* that contains in it the resource for new questions. These questions are developed only at a later stage, by the provider, and are generated by recombining independent data – for example, from a service provider who scrutinizes the credit status of potential debtors, or from government agencies for counterterrorism, which seems to legitimize almost any surveillance practice. Precisely because the data are not collated, scanned, and stored with specific intentions and questions in mind and can be passed on to entities that ask quite different questions, these data collections are a lucrative commodity.

But the real irony is that a large part of these data is not just unintended traces, which are indeed unavoidable if one does not want to give up the usual cultural techniques. Foucault had described how power lies now with those who remain silent and observe, not with those who speak and pour information about themselves. But giving information about oneself is one of those practices that have by now become really unavoidable.

Perhaps the crucial difference from the earlier privacy is that this is no longer a matter of whether one is able to remain silent, thus exercising power in the sense of Foucault. Remaining silent is no longer an option, because everyday practices yield information inevitably, even without meaningful referrals, without intentions, without concrete speech acts, without any performance of their own. Foucault imagined someone who could speak but refuses to do so. Today we are dealing with people whose linguistic and intentional actions are no longer relevant, because the social meaning of their practice, reflected in the accruing data about them, goes far beyond anything that the action can know about itself. The point would then be that the social can no longer be imagined as something that depends primarily on the will and intentions of actors, but rather on a kind of 'assemblage'. This means that entities are connected to more and more other entities, as Bruno Latour says. He is 'interested in mediators *making* other mediators *do* things. "Making do" is not the same thing as "causing" or "doing": there exists at the heart of it a duplication, a dislocation, a translation that modifies at once the whole argument. It was impossible before to connect an actor to what made it act, without being accused of "dominating", "limiting", or "enslaving" it. This is no longer the case. The more *attachments* it has, the more it exists.'[24]

What Latour describes here captures that strange link between the activity of everyday actors and the recording of their data, which generate links that do not exist at all in the activity itself. Against this background, the fantasy of a privacy that is always prior and must be protected looks like an anachronistic idea, because the private form is also a constellation that has become obsolete, having an almost unlimited capacity to recombine – a capacity enabled above all by the low-threshold technology. Digital technology, with its investigative functions, is a mediator that makes me do something I myself could not control. Perhaps this is where my initial idea becomes plausible – my idea as to why the term 'informational self-determination' is self-contradictory. The surplus of meaning is always manifest elsewhere, not by the meaning producers themselves.

Rescuing privacy?

What kind of privacy are we trying to rescue now? It is probably futile to try to rescue something like an unobservable, authentic, autonomous privacy – this has never existed. Private lifestyles have always also been the result of surveillance and confession techniques, of attribution techniques, and, not least, of strong social regulations; and it is these techniques that enabled the image of the autonomous, private person in the first place. Perhaps we can speak of embedded privacy, especially since external coercion was not at all perceived as direct coercion. The threats to private lifestyles posed today by big data are quite similar to those of earlier practices and at the same time are an enabler of these lifestyles, because the practice of leaving traces on the net should not be treated simply as an accident, an anomaly, or a deviation, especially in the generation of so-called digital natives. Perhaps we should get used to the fact that the matrix of the net has become an extension of our person similar to authoritarian speakers and expert cultures in the past – and those, too, used to lay a sort of net over society and sold heteronomy for autonomy.

Perhaps big data and its consequences can currently be read as the opportunity for a major self-enlightenment, a self-enlightenment about the fact that private lifestyles have always been more 'social' than we give them credit for. After all, big data is only an improvement on the quantitative recording and measurement of society that began at the end of the eighteenth century. What is new, however, is that the boundaries between political–governmental and economic actors are starting to get blurred, which is also due to the fact that modern marketing strategies in diversified consumer markets depend on access to populations, in much the same way as social planning used to.

If there is a call today for a repoliticization of the problem – I have mentioned Evgeny Morozov's appeal – this is indeed consistent and right; for what should a society do other than somehow make collectively binding decisions about its set of problems? And there is in fact considerable need for regulations on a variety of issues. But there is no way one can still get rid of the network and matrix structure of the Internet and its big data possibilities, if all those sensors and measuring points with which society equips itself – and actors do the same, all too ready to use them – go on collecting data over data. Perhaps, then, even legal concepts such as informational self-determination or the preservation of privacy are downright anachronistic figures, because they can hardly formulate defence rights against the state or against third parties as long as whole lifestyles settled there, synchronized with themselves in clouds, expanded the proximity of occasional communications through the net, and long since turned the download Internet into the upload Internet. This should be read neither fatalistically nor in some affirmative way, but rather as a readjustment of what can be called privacy today – and it certainly helps that what I called Privacy 1.0 was structured completely differently from our almost romantic idea of private lifestyles.

By the way, we should not be surprised that intelligence agencies use all the data they can get – what else should they do? It would be absurd to expect that they would not skim off what technology enables them to skim off – and it would be as absurd if there were no strong criticism of this. The irony of the current critique, for instance from the US National Security Agency (NSA), is that it, too, has obviously left behind traces that can be monitored and skimmed off. Edward Snowden – himself from the generation of digital natives, and certainly no coincidence there – passed on to the *Washington Post* and the *Guardian* data that came from the NSA's self-documentation, in other words stored on servers he was able to skim off. All those explosive data were allegedly stored on one stick. One effect of big data is that information becomes small and handy.

9

Debug
Sociology Reborn from the Spirit of Digitalization

A debug, or debugging, is a process for the identification of software errors. One of the techniques of debugging is to install breakpoints into a program in order to be able to check and examine its execution. This book is meant to be such a breakpoint: it has neither looked into the social, political, or cultural consequences of digitalization nor analysed any concrete practices by the sociological method of alienating reality. The book's aim was rather to formulate a sociological theory of digital society that allows us to conceptualize the social place of the digital in a systematic fashion.

The leading question of the book was: *what problem does digitalization solve?* And the question derived from it was: *to what extent was modern society a digital society even before, and in the absence of, digital technologies in the narrow sense?* I built my argument around these two questions. The answer is counterintuitive but basically simple: the reference problem of digitalization is located in the structure of society itself. While premodern societies have constructed incredibly complex forms, their basic structure remains very simple: everything, literally everything conforms to a top-down scheme – social hierarchies, social orders, worldviews, taxonomies, and even the principle of deduction in logic. This is precisely what no longer applies to modernity: the situation becomes more confusing, different forms of order get set up side by side, the principle of differentiation validates parallel structures, and thus the structure of society eludes clear, distinct visibility. This is why I pushed the beginning of explicit digitalization back to a point in time when, amid the emergence of social planning, the operationalization of capitalism, the medical survey of individuals, and the establishment of planning horizons, visibilities had to be comprehensively re-established by statistical, mathematical, and thus digital means.

So then: the main result of my analysis is that we fail to grasp digitalization if we take it to be some kind of colonial power, which encounters a society that wards it off with some energy – pushing against the loss of jobs in repetitive activities, against techniques of control, against the portent of a self-standing technology, and against the imagined loss of autonomy of a quantified self. This book is rather about the realization that, with big data, with pattern recognition technologies, and with the handling of the fundamental invisibility of the world, one rediscovers society in a completely new way – and I have talked about a *third discovery of society*.

This third discovery of society is mainly a discovery of its resistance, its astonishing stability, its basic feature of repetitive confirmation of structures. At first glance this seems counterintuitive, because one associates the digital age rather with the fluidization and disso-lution of traditional structures, with disruptive change, or at least with a considerable pressure to transform. However, the patterns of society (and of other objects on which digital technology works) are precisely the material of digital processing. All the innovations that come into play in product and services markets, through control and steering capabilities, and, not least, in socio-technological and anthropo-technological interfaces use astoundingly expansive computing and processing capacities – and even digital learning technologies, in other words *active* and not just *passive* technologies – to be able to do what they do.

Of course, I radicalized my argument even further: it is not only that the reference problem of digitalization is to be sought in the structure of society. By reconstructing the differentiation of modern society into coded functional systems, I have rather worked out an aesthetic and operational relationship, indeed a homogeneity, between the digital formation of technology and the social formation of functional logics. Just as the almost provocative simplicity of digital technology – I called it the *simplicity* of the medium itself – enables a practically unlimited variety of forms and possibilities to connect, the historically unprecedented variety of forms adopted by society in the modern world is based on an equally provocatively simple basic code of the functional systems. The fact that the economic focuses on numbers–non-numbers, the political on power–non-power, the scientific on matters of truth, the mediatized on information–non-information, the legal on justice–injustice, and the religious on matters of immanence–transcendence makes possible the incredible diversity of forms of modernity. I have described these provocations as *brutal* because they cannot be circumvented at code level; at the level of programs they can.

What may look like mere equivocation is in reality an operational parallel that targets the structural order of self-referential systems. Martin Heidegger's early prediction that in cybernetic modernity everything will ultimately be reduced to information, which in turn refers to information and thus creates a sphere of operational immanence, was meant for data technology and the cybernetic mentality, which for him heralded the end of philosophy. But this is also a characterization of the internal logic of functional systems, which can transcend all possible forms and find almost no hold within themselves, yet remain nevertheless limited to the immanence of their coding.

Digital dynamic and social complexity

Up until now, it has hardly been noticed that the disruptive technology of a digital nature relates mostly to resistance and stability. There are works that explore quite fully the significance of the digital, but make practically no systematic connection between the social structure, which can be understood only digitally, and the technology itself. This, then, is primarily about the experience of surveillance, about self-control versus control by others, about digital forms of self-measurement, and about the topos of self-optimization. Digitalization emerges as a behavioral aspect that ultimately works also through surplus of control. The social radicalness of the digital does not as much as come into view here. This radicalness lies in the fact that the digitality of society is grounded in its own structure and complexity.

In the present book I have not dwelt specifically on this complexity but rather assumed it; but it should be obvious by now that, precisely because of the multiple coding of everything, digital modernity must come to grips with the complexity of the simultaneity of different aspects. After all, digitalization is also an imposition, because it capitalizes on the complexity of social processes. And the dangers of digital strategies for the idea of a deliberative public sphere, for the control of communication processes, for the concentration of power and capital are real. These are elements of that increase in options that has been inherent in modernity since its very inception and that I have explained structurally, through the relatively simple coding of both social and digital functions. It will become clear here which social entities are able to deal with this appropriately. But danger prevention and smart strategies are more likely to increase than to reduce complexity.

In any case, the reverse is true: only if the digital duplication of practices is internally complex enough will it be possible to extract useful information from it. This holds for the problems themselves, but also for the horizons of their solutions. Probably one should stage digitalization as part of the solution. This can also be an opportunity.

Here are two examples to play with:

1. If we think of a problem such as climate change, and hence of an appropriate reaction of society to the carbon dioxide emissions from its metabolism, this is a classic problem of complexity: any reaction and any strategy must know how to handle the simultaneous multiple coding, the multiplication of aspects, and the difference between currently effective and stable structures of practice. The implementation of pollution targets and the conversion to alternative energy and traffic concepts simply follow the brutal rules of a complex, functionally differentiated society; they must be at once practicable politically, economically, legally, scientifically, technologically, mediatically – and also compatible with everyday life. Consequently, the only way to regulate and coordinate processes is through complex forms of reaction. Digitalization will play an essential role here – in energy management, in the control of intelligent energy systems, in new kinds of mobility, but also in the comprehensive surveillance and recording of practices relevant to energy. Given the logistic possibilities of effort avoidance that are already applied to complex logistic processes today, one will also be able to use machine learning and self-learning systems for smart energy and mobility control. Hence it is inevitable that some legal, political, and economic routines will have to be reconsidered. Change in society's metabolism has led to readjustments in earlier times as well – it's enough to think of the consequences of the transition to corporate capitalism and complex administrations, to state monitoring functions, and to democratic publics. Climate change in particular is a problem that has much to do with the interconnectedness of different processes; this problem itself requires an operating temperature capable of complexity, to establish patterns that may lead to practices that could mitigate the carbon dioxide impacts of modern lifestyles. The smart city has on its agenda a reconciliation not only between work and life but also between human and energy metabolism. The question is what resonance such problems have in social communication. If my thesis is correct and digitalization addresses the complexity of society and identifies patterns that elude immediate access, namely in the form of *active* and *passive* technologies, then this must be understood to be an opportunity.

2. Platform capitalism is an ambivalent form. It rearranges the elements of complex value chains – not only organizationally but also economically. We have to abandon the idea that what we have known as corporate capitalism since the nineteenth century represents a form of economy without alternative. That in the end everything must be profitable is written into the coding of the economic system. The problem, then, is not capitalism; the problem is the participation of the various value chains – how they contribute to the total returns and to their distribution. It is likely that more and more companies will become tech companies, even if they are not primarily focused on technological products or services, because the distribution of products, trade, and even development will not be possible without digital contribution. The fact that in most sectors of the platform economy the concentration of capital runs parallel to the concentration of data devalues the physical, material, and activity-intensive parts of the economy more than anyone could have imagined earlier. Just for the sake of entrepreneurial feasibility, new arrangements for remeasuring production shares will have to be made. Here intelligent digital solutions are required not only in the business model itself but also in relation to financing, the distribution of returns, and the arrangement of independent organizational forms. I am not in a position to offer any solutions in this respect, but I just advocate not underestimating the possibilities of controlling processes by digital means, with the aim of more long-term and more stable patterns in the arrangement of different stakeholders.

If you look at it closely, everything has changed, yet everything is still the same. What remains is the problem of complexity, which is further increased by the fact that, due to the technological possibilities, the recombination of different forms and the commensurability of the incommensurable is now exponentially increased, thanks to technological capacities. Perhaps the radicalness of the functional differentiation of society, with its basic codes, and the radicalness of the manifold patterns produced by it come to bear only now.

This is why what the present book proposes is nothing short of a theory of modern society, which cannot help encountering the digitality of the object. This has to do with both the stubbornness and brutal stability of social structures and the operativeness of their practices. In recent years I published quite a few works of social theory; they are inspired by systems theory but go beyond it.[1] This book is on the one hand a follow-up on that, on the other a partial self-correction, because up to this date the basic digital structure has not been seen at all. In this respect, my topic – looking for the reference problem of digitalization – was a methodological decision that paid off. For this topic comes up against the digital society, whose digitalization is a technological phenomenon, but not only that.

A partner in theoretical and empirical kinship to my book could have been *actor–network theory*, along with Bruno Latour's theory of *collectives* and *associations*. The latter had made it its cause to mistrust traditional society's self-describing stories, with their *social* descriptive categories, and to analyse *associations* instead. Accordingly, his research programme proclaims: 'From the study of society to that of associations.'[2] This means to say that one should abandon the consensus-oriented idea of the classical ideal of society and rather keep an empirical eye on which associations of human, non-human, virtual, material, conceptual, and other actors lead to other associations, which generate new forms. This is a productive sociological perspective insofar as it is sensitive to seeing, say, the digital infrastructure not just as an infrastructure, but as associated points of attribution whose assemblage with other actors gives surprising insights.

In the end, however, such a perspective remains strangely toothless, because it relies only on the alienating power of unfamiliar perspectives and is thus more similar to classic sociology and its ambience than the rhetorical demarcation suggests. In an essay on computerized work environments, Latour writes that, after having discovered new associations, we should be mindful not to go right away looking for types of connections, structures, and regularities. All that remains in the end is the interest in the freedom of connectivity. Latour writes: 'The power of networks would be lost if one had to embark in the impossible dream of listing what kind of linkages are allowed and which are forbidden or impossible. A mad socio-logic would succeed the former mad dream of logicians.'[3]

This is an expression of empirical openness – but at the same time capitulation to the very digitality of modern society, whose amazing regularity, *in spite of* always new assemblages and *in spite of* radically new connections of human and non-human actors, is of a digitally coded and brutal stability when it comes to its basic structure. *I offer here, sociologically, the counterintuitive diagnosis that, of all things, it is this fluid-looking digitalization that points to such stabilities.*

An opportunity for sociology

As I argued at the beginning of this book, we have witnessed, with digitalization, a *third discovery of society*, after the invention of the institutional arrangements of modern society in the wake of the French Revolution and after the politicization of the process of shaping society during the episodes of liberalization that took place in the second half of the twentieth century. This third discovery relies much more directly on the structure of society. First, it relies on the experience, which began as early as the nineteenth century, that the structure of society and important operational matters can be made visible only through the digital means of pattern recognition. Second, it relies on the analogy between coding and programming in the functional systems of society and in the data technology itself. On both fronts, this is the structural foundation of hardly controllable options increases, which are rooted in the structure of the thing itself.

It is only at this point that it becomes relevant why quantifications and metric forms of self-control ultimately cannot stop in front of an option and why, again, it is so difficult to get rid of the negatively perceived surplus of control generated by digital technology practices. The critique of neoliberalism in this context, the well-founded fear of surveillance and control, the warnings about the consequences of data practices – all this comes with a whiff of criticism, and hence of political and legal control and regulation. Of crucial importance here could be the diagnosis I am offering: digital technology is so difficult to deal with because it really works.

When it works, technology prevails even against better judgement and better arguments. Obviously there is a great deal of aversion to social areas that are insensitive to consensus and dissent. Currently digital technology is the subject of extremely heated debates of an ethical, legal, moral, and political nature – yet every day proves itself as a *technology*, thereby corrupting the argument. And this is why digitalization is itself a detector that holds up a mirror to society, so that there is no need to imagine it, in traditional fashion, as a space of consensus where one can make collectively binding decisions about everything important. This is an environment-specific dream: the dream of that middle class of intellectuals who talk a lot about practice and technology but in the end cling to a plain social– technological ideal of consensus. These people do not really believe in the resistant character of our topic – perhaps because they form an environment in which acts of resistance flash up in a rather cushioned way.

Nevertheless, there is good reason to believe that the *third discovery of society, namely through digitalization*, opens up a major opportunity for sociology. At the very least, not to perceive the digitality of society as a chance for sociological insight would be an act of spectacular negligence. If I am to cast this in long sentences, then here they are. Let us remember the first two discoveries of modern society – they were really constitutive of a new way of thinking between the euphoria of departure and the recognition of our topic's resistance. Right now others are doing business with this resistance, celebrate successful control, and monitor various processes. Only we can clarify this – if we do so in earnest rather than just indulging in an affected critique of everyday digital manipulation or taking aesthetic pleasure in new associations and assemblies. For it is towards dealing with the inertia, exemplariness, and resistance of society itself that digitalization offers a solution.

And only if sociology takes up this opportunity will there be an appropriate discourse on how the chances, the risks, and the potential for disruption associated with digital technologies are to be assessed. And for the sake of such discourses not just happening as colonization discourses or discourses about disturbance from the outside I present this *theory of digital society* in order not to run such discourses only as discourses of colonization or discourses of external disruption.

Notes

Notes to Introduction

1 For a video recording of the Hegel Lecture, see https://www.fu-berlin.de/en/sites/dhc/videothek/Videothek/948_Hegel_Lecture_mit_Armin_Nassehi/index.html.
2 See e.g. Timo Daum, *Das Kapital sind Wir. Zur Kritik der Digitalen Ökonomie*, Hamburg: Edition Nautilus, 2017; Philipp Staab, *Falsche Versprechen: Wachstum im digitalen Kapitalismus*, Hamburg: Hamburger Edition, 2016; Yvonne Hofstetter, *Das Ende der Demokratie. Wie die künstliche Intelligenz die Politik übernimmt und uns entmündigt*, Munich: Penguin, 2018; Richard David Precht, *Jäger, Hirten, Kritiker: Eine Utopie für die digitale Gesellschaft*, Munich: Goldmann, 2018; Michael Betancourt, *The Critique of Digital Capitalism: An Analysis of the Political Economy of Digital Culture and Technology*, Santa Barbara, CA: Punctum Books, 2015.
3 Sherry Turkle, *Life on the Screen: Identity in the Age of the Internet*, New York: Simon & Schuster, 1997.
4 Deborah Lupton, *Digital Sociology*, New York: Routledge, 2015.
5 Rob Kitchin, *The Data Revolution: Big Data, Open Data, Data Infrastructures and Their Consequences*, London: SAGE, 2014.
6 Shoshana Zuboff, *The Age of Surveillance Capitalism: The Fight for a Human Future at the New Frontier of Power*, New York: PublicAffairs, 2019.
7 Jessie Daniels, Karen Gregory, and Tressie McMillan Cottom (eds), *Digital Sociologies*, Bristol: Policy Press, 2017.
8 Steffen Mau, *The Metric Society: On the Quantification of the Social*, Cambridge: Polity, 2019 (German edn 2017); see also Stefanie Duttweiler et al. (eds), *Leben nach Zahlen: Self-Tracking als Optimierungsprojekt?* Bielefeld: transcript, 2016; Zygmunt Bauman and David Lyon, *Liquid Surveillance: A Conversation*, Cambridge: Polity, 2012.
9 Dirk Helbig, *Towards Digital Enlightenment: Essays on the Dark and Light Sides of the Digital Revolution*, Cham: Springer, 2019.
10 Friedrich Kittler, 'There Is No Software', in Friedrich Kittler and Erik Butler (eds), *The Truth of the Technological World: Essays on the Genealogy of Presence*, Stanford, CA: Stanford University Press, 2014 (German edn 1993), pp. 219–29.
11 Sybille Krämer, *Symbolische Maschinen: Die Idee der Formalisierung im geschichtlichen Abriß*, Darmstadt: Wissenschaftliche Buchgesellschaft, 1988.
12 See Sybille Krämer and Horst Bredekamp (eds), *Bild, Schrift, Zahl* (2nd edn), Munich: Fink, 2009.
13 Felix Stalder, *The Digital Condition*, trans. by Valentine A. Pakis, Cambridge: Polity, 2018 (German edn 2016).

14 See e.g. Edelgard Kutzner and Victoria Schnier, 'Geschlechterverhältnisse in Digitalisierungsprozessen von Arbeit: Konzeptionelle Überlegungen und empirische Fragestellungen', *Arbeit* 26 (2017), pp. 137–57.

15 See e.g. Klaus Dörre, 'Digitalisierung: Neue Prosperität oder Vertiefung gesellschaftlicher Spaltungen?', in Hartmut Hirsch-Kreinsen, Peter Ittermann, and Jonathan Niehaus (eds), *Digitalisierung industrieller Arbeit*, Baden-Baden: Nomos, 2015, pp. 270–85; Paul DiMaggio et al., 'Social Implications of the Internet', *Annual Review of Sociology* 27 (2001), pp. 307–36.

16 See Dominique Cardon, 'Den Algorithmus dekonstruieren: Vier Typen digitaler Informationsberechnung', in Robert Seyfert and Jonathan Roberge (eds), *Algorithmuskulturen: Über die rechnerische Konstruktion der Wirklichkeit*, Bielefeld: transcript, 2017, pp. 131–50; Dominique Cardon, *À quoi rêvent les algorithmes: Nos vies à l'heure des big data*, Paris: Seuil, 2015.

17 On this, see Armin Nassehi, 'Rethinking functionalism: Zur Empiriefähigkeit systemtheoretischer Soziologie', in Herbert Kalthoff (ed.), *Theoretische Empirie: Die Relevanz qualitativer Forschung*, Frankfurt: Suhrkamp, 2008, pp. 79–106.

18 On this, see Armin Nassehi, 'Die erste digitale Generation: Eine kontraintuitive Diagnose', *Kursbuch 178: 1964*, 2014, pp. 31–52.

19 Walter Benjamin, *The Work of Art in the Age of Mechanical Reproduction*, trans. by J. A. Underwood, London: Penguin, 2008.

20 Chris Anderson, 'The End of Theory: The Data Deluge Makes the Scientific Method Obsolete', *Wired*, 23 June 2008; Klaus Mainzer, 'Zur Veränderung des Theoriebegriffs im Zeitalter von Big Data und effizienten Algorithmen', *Berliner Debatte Initial* 27.4 (2016), pp. 22–34.

21 Martina Franzen, 'Die digitale Transformation der Wissenschaft', *Beiträge zur Hochschulforschung* 4.40 (2018), pp. 8–28. http://www.bzh.bayern.de/uploads /media/4_2018_Franzen.pdf.

22 See Nick Srnicek, *Platform Capitalism*, Cambridge: Polity, 2016.

23 For a particularly spectacular example, see Nick Bostrom, *Superintelligence: Paths, Dangers, Strategies*, Oxford: Oxford University Press, 2014.

24 Dirk Helbing, *Towards Digital Enlightenment: Essays on the Dark and Light Sides of the Digital Revolution*, Cham: Springer, 2019.

Notes to Chapter 1

1 Ernst Cassirer, *Substance and Function and Einstein's Theory of Relativity*, trans. by William Curtis Swabey and Marie Collins Swabey, Dover: Dover Publications Inc., 1953, p. 303.

2 Ibid., p. 305.

3 Ibid. p. 318. Incidentally, this epistemological perspective is not only confirmed by current epistemologies in systems theory (see Armin Nassehi, 'Wie wirklich sind Systeme? Zum ontologischen und epistemologischen Status von Luhmanns Theorie sozialer Systeme', in Werner Krawietz and Michael Welker (eds), *Kritik der Theorie sozialer Systeme*, Frankfurt: Suhrkamp, 1992, pp. 43–70); it is also compatible with results in brain research. For example, Wolf Singer says that the brain does not perceive any outside world but only compares states *of its own*, generated by perception (not by what is perceived) to *its own* hypotheses and ultimately looks for confirmation (see Wolf Singer, *Der Beobachter im Gehirn: Essays zur Hirnforschung*, Frankfurt: Suhrkamp, 2002, p. 72). You don't have to agree with Singer's conclusions in cultural studies and humanities to see, at the very least, that nowadays a constructivist epistemology can no longer be played off against naturalistic descriptions.

4 See Dirk Helbing, *The Automation of Society Is Next: How to Survive the Digital Revolution*, Kindle edition, 2015, pp. 22ff. and passim.

5   On this, see *Daniela Döring, Zeugende Zahlen: Mittelmaß und Durchschnittstypen in Proportion, Statistik und Konfektion des 19. Jahrhunderts*, Berlin: Kadmos, 2011.

6   See Armin Nassehi, 'Rethinking functionalism: Zur Empiriefähigkeit system-theoretischer Soziologie', in Herbert Kalthoff (ed.), *Theoretische Empirie: Die Relevanz qualitativer Forschung*, Frankfurt: Suhrkamp, 2008, pp. 79–106.

7   There is an increase in the ratio of determinedness and undeterminedness. See *Gerhard Gamm: Flucht aus der Kategorie: Die Positivierung des Unbestimmten als Ausgang der Moderne*, Frankfurt: Suhrkamp, 1994, p. 236.

8   See Niklas Luhmann, 'Gesellschaftliche Struktur und semantische Tradition', in his *Gesellschaftsstruktur und Semantik: Studien zur Wissenssoziologie der modernen Gesellschaft*, vol. 1, Frankfurt: Suhrkamp, 1980, pp. 9–71.

9   On this, see Stefan Hirschauer, 'Humandifferenzierung: Modi und Grade der Zugehörigkeit', in Stefan Hirschauer (ed.), *Undoing Differences: Praktiken der Humandifferenzierung*, Weilerswist: Velbrück, 2017, pp. 29–54; Armin Nassehi, 'Humandifferenzierung und gesellschaftliche Differenzierung: Eine Verhältnisbestimmung', ibid., pp. 55–78.

10   Michel Foucault: *The Will to Knowledge: The History of Sexuality*, vol. 1, trans. by Robert Hurley, London: Penguin, 1998, p. 139.

11   Dirk Baecker, *Studien zur nächsten Gesellschaft*, Berlin: Suhrkamp, 2007.

12   Dirk Baecker, *4.0 oder Die Lücke, die der Computer lässt*, Leipzig: Merve, 2018, p. 9.

13   Jürgen Habermas, 'The Normative Content of Modernity', in his *The Philosophical Discourse of Modernity: Twelve Lectures*, trans. by Frederick Lawrence, Cambridge: MIT Press, 1987, pp. 336–67.

14   Dirk Baecker, *Studien zur nächsten Gesellschaft*, Berlin: Suhrkamp, 2007, p. 169.

15   On *pars pro toto*, see Stefanie Duttweiler et al. (eds), *Leben nach Zahlen: Self-Tracking als Optimierungsprojekt?* Bielefeld: transcript, 2016; Zygmunt Bauman and David Lyon, *Liquid Surveillance: A Conversation*, Cambridge: Polity 2012; Steffen Mau, *The Metric Society: On the Quantification of the Social*, Cambridge: Polity, 2019.

16   See Auguste Comte, *The Positive Philosophy of Auguste Comte*, vol. 2, trans. by Harriet Martineau, Cambridge: Cambridge University Press, 2009.

17   See Joseph de Maistre, *Against Rousseau: On the State of Nature and On the Sovereignty of the People*, trans. and ed. by Richard A. Lebrun, Montreal: McGill-Queen's University Press, 1996.

18   On this, see Armin Nassehi, *Gab es 1968? Eine Spurensuche*, Hamburg: Kursbuch-Edition, 2018, pp. 56–7; see also Armin Nassehi, 'Permanent Reflection and Inclusion Boosts: The Heritage of the Generation of 1968', *European Sociologist* 42 (2018), special issue '50 Years On, 1968'.

19   See Pierre Bourdieu and Jean-Claude Passeron, *The Inheritors: French Students and Their Relations to Culture*, trans. by Richard Nice, Chicago, IL: University of Chicago Press, 1979; also Pierre Bourdieu and Jean Cluade Passeron: *Reproduction in Education, Society and Culture*, trans. by Richard Nice, London: SAGE, 1990.

20   'Illusion der Chancengleichheit' is the title of the German translation of Bourdieu and Passeron's article 'The Inheritors'.

21   On conceptual history, see Markus Schroer, 'Klassengesellschaft', in Georg Kneer, Armin Nassehi, and Markus Schroer (eds), *Soziologische Gesellschaftsbegriffe 2: Klassische Zeitdiagnosen*, Paderborn: Fink, 2001, pp. 139–78.

22   See Christoph Tripp, *Distributions- und Handelslogistik: Netzwerke und Strategien der Omnichannel-Distribution im Handel*, Wiesbaden: Springer, 2019.

23   Peter Felixberger and Armin Nassehi, *Deutschland: Ein Drehbuch*, Hamburg: Kursbuch-Edition, 2017.

24   See Jacques Derrida, *Writing and Difference*, trans. by Alan Bass, Chicago, IL: University of Chicago Press, 1978.

25 See Gilles Deleuze, *Difference and Repetition*, trans. by Paul Patton, London: Bloomsbury, 2014.

26 See Jean-François Lyotard, *The Differend. Phrases in Dispute*, trans. by Georges Van den Abbeele, Minneapolis: University of Minnesota Press, 1989.

27 On this, see Armin Nassehi, 'Différend, Différance und Distinction, Zur Differenz der Differenzen bei Lyotard, Derrida und in der Formenlogik', in Henk de Berg and Matthias Prangel (eds), *Differenzen: Systemtheorie zwischen Dekonstruktion und Konstruktivismus*, Tübingen: Francke, 1995.

28 Andreas Diekmann, *Empirische Sozialforschung: Grundlagen, Methoden, Anwendungen* (12th edn), Reinbek: Rowohlt, 2018, p. 92.

29 See Stephen M. Stigler, *The History of Statistics: The Measurement of Uncertainty before 1900*, Harvard, CA: Harvard University Press, 2000 [1986], pp. 159–60.

30 Diekmann, *Empirische Sozialforschung*, p. 95.

31 On grounded theory, see especially Aglaja Przyborski and Monika Wohlrab-Sahr, *Qualitative Sozialforschung: Ein Arbeitsbuch* (4th edn), Munich: Oldenbourg, 2014, p. 218.

32 See Armin Nassehi and Irmhild Saake, 'Kontingenz: Methodisch verhindert oder beobachtet? Ein Beitrag zur Methodologie der qualitativen Sozialforschung', *Zeitschrift für Soziologie* 31 (2002), pp. 66–86.

33 On this, see Armin Nassehi, 'Über Beziehungen, Elefanten und Dritte', *Soziologie* 47 (2018), pp. 292–301, here p. 293.

34 Rebecca Jean Emigh, Dylan Riley, and Patricia Ahmed, *Antecedents of Censuses from Medieval to Nation States: How Societies and States Count*, New York: Palgrave Macmillan, 2016, p. 30.

35 See Jürgen Osterhammel, *The Transformation of the World: A Global History of the Nineteenth Century*, trans. by Patrick Camiller, Princeton, NJ: Princeton University Press, 2014, pp. 26–7.

36 On this, see Nassehi, *Gab es 1968?*, pp. 56–7.

37 Rudi Schmidt, 'Der Einfluss der Soziologie auf die Studentenbewegung der 60er Jahre und vice versa', in Hans Georg Soeffner (ed.), *Unsichere Zeiten: Herausforderungen gesellschaftlicher Transformationen. Verhandlungen des 34. Kongresses der DGS in Jena 2008*, vol. 1, Wiesbaden: VS-Verlag, 2010, pp. 661–82.

38 Felix Stalder, *The Digital Condition*, trans. by Valentine A. Pakis, Cambridge: Polity, 2018, pp. 41–2.

39 In Haraway, *Simians, Cyborgs, and Women*, pp. 149–82.

40 Ibid., p. 149.

41 Ibid.. p. 150.

42 On this, see Stefan Hirschauer, 'Das Vergessen des Geschlechts: Zur Praxeologie einer Kategorie sozialer Ordnung', *Kölner Zeitschrift für Soziologie und Sozialpsychologie* 41 (2001), pp. 208–35; this approach is a reaction to the concept suggested by Candace West and Don H. Zimmerman, 'Doing Gender', *Gender and Society* 1 (1987), pp. 125–51. See also Ursula Pasero, 'Gender, Individualität, Diversity', in Ursula Pasero and Christine Weinbach (eds), *Frauen, Männer, Gender Trouble: Systemtheoretische Essays*, Frankfurt: Suhrkamp, 2003, pp. 105–24; Armin Nassehi, 'Geschlecht im System: Die Ontologisierung des Körpers und die Asymmetrie der Geschlechter', ibid., pp. 80–104.

43 Haraway, *Simians, Cyborgs, and Women*, p. 151.

44 Ibid., p. 162.

45 Richard Rorty, *Contingency, Irony, and Solidarity*, New York: Cambridge University Press, 1989, pp. 73–4.

46 On this see Armin Nassehi, 'Der gegenwärtige Kulturkampf: Was heißt es, eine Frau zu sein?', *Frankfurter Allgemeine Zeitung*, 9 April 2019.

47 Haraway, *Simians, Cyborgs, and Women*, pp. 149–82.

Notes to Chapter 2

1 Niklas Luhmann, *Die Wissenschaft der Gesellschaft*, Frankfurt: Suhrkamp, 1990, p. 370.
2 Ibid.
3 See Dominique Cardon, 'Den Algorithmus dekonstruieren: Vier Typen digitaler Informationsberechnung', in Robert Seyfert and Jonathan Roberge (eds), *Algorithmuskulturen: Über die rechnerische Konstruktion der Wirklichkeit*, Bielefeld: transcript, 2017, pp. 131–50. This diagram from Cardon's essay (p. 133) is entitled 'Four types of calculating information'.

	Neben	Oberhalb	Innerhalb	Unterhalb
Beispiele	Publikums-Berechnung, Google Analytics, Werbung	PageRank (Google), Digg, Wikipedia	Facebook Freunde, Twitter Retweets, öffentliche Meinung	Amazon Empfehlungen, personalisierte Werbung
Data	Views	Links	Likes	Verhaltensprofil
Population	Repräsentative Stichproben	Gewichtete (zensuale) Abstimmung	Soziale Netzwerke, erklärte Vorlieben	Vermutetes individuelles Verhalten
Form der Berechnung	Abstimmung	Klassifizierung und Ranking	Benchmarks	Maschinen-Lernen
Prinzip	*Popularität*	*Autorität*	*Reputation*	*Prognose*

4 Edmund Husserl, 'The Crisis of European Sciences and Transcendental Phenomenology. An Introduction to Phenomenological Philosophy', in John Wild and James M. Edie (eds), *Northwestern University Studies in Phenomenology and Existential Philosophy*, trans. by David Carr, Evanston: Northwestern University Press, 1970, p. 34.
5 Ibid., p. 44.
6 Ibid.
7 Ibid., p. 69.
8 David Cope, *Experiments in Musical Intelligence*, Madison, WI: A-R Editions, 1996.
9 *Bach by Design*, Centaur Records, CRC 2184, 1993; *Virtual Bach*, Centaur Records, CRC 2619, 2003.
10 Bruce L. Jacob, 'Algorithmic Composition as a Model of Creativity', *Organised Sound*, 1.3 (1996): 157–65. DOI: 10.1017 / S135577189600022.
11 *Pars pro toto*: for an example of vowels in the context of German language acquisition, see e.g. Anja Hofmann, *Vergleich muttersprachlicher und nicht-muttersprachlicher Vokale mit Deutsch als Zielsprache: Ein statistischer Vergleich in Corpora*, Diss. University of Tübingen, 2011. Remarkable here is the method-ological focus on the statistically detectable patternicity of the different linguistic origins of the test subjects.
12 PEGIDA is an acronym for Patriotische Europäer gegen die Islamisierung des Abendlandes (Patriotic Europeans against the Islamization of the West). It is a right-wing extremist movement founded in Dresden in 2014 that has

particularly criticized the German refugee policy and in some cases questioned the legitimacy of state authorities.

13 Edmund Husserl, *The Phenomenology of Internal Time-Consciousness*, ed. by Martin Heidegger, trans. by James S. Churchill, Bloomington: Indiana University Press, 1964, pp. 43–4.

14 Steffen Mau, too, points out the resemblance of these practices to science. See Steffen Mau, *The Metric Society: On the Quantification of the Social*, trans. by Sharon Howe, Cambridge: Polity, 2019, pp. 12ff.

15 Dirk Baecker, *4.0 oder Die Lücke, die der Computer lässt*, Leipzig: Merve, 2018, p. 16.

16 Klaus Mainzer, 'Zur Veränderung des Theoriebegriffs im Zeitalter von Big Data und effizienten Algorithmen', *Berliner Debatte Initial* 27.4 (2016), pp. 22–34, here p. 31.

17 Ibid., p. 33.

18 See Christian Wadephul, 'Führt Big Data zur abduktiven Wende in den Wissenschaften?', *Berliner Debatte Initial* 27.4 (2016), pp. 35–49, here p. 37.

19 danah boyd and Kate Crawford, 'Six Provocations for Big Data: A Decade', in *Internet Time: Symposium on the Dynamics of the Internet and Society*, 2011, pp. 1–2. https://www.oii.ox.ac.uk/news-events/videos/a-decade-in-internet-time-symposium-on-the-dynamics-of-the-internet-and-society.

20 See Tom Breur, 'Statistical Power Analysis and the Contemporary "Crisis" in Social Sciences', *Journal of Marketing Analysis* 4 (2016), pp. 61–5.

21 Martin Heidegger, 'The Provenance of Art and the Destination of Thought', *Journal of the British Society for Phenomenology* 44.2 (2013), pp. 119–28, here p. 123.

22 Ibid., p. 120.

23 Ibid., p. 123.

24 Ibid.

25 Julian Müller, *Bestimmbare Unbestimmtheiten: Skizze einer indeterministischen Soziologie*, Munich: Fink, 2015, pp. 17–18.

26 Martin Heidegger, 'Positionality', in his *Bremen and Freiburg Lectures: Insights into That Which Is and Basic Principles of Thinking*, trans. by Andrew J. Mitchell, Bloomington: Indiana University Press, 2012, p. 36.

27 Bruno Latour, *We Have Never Been Modern*, Cambridge, MA: Harvard University Press, 1993.

28 'Only a God Can Save Us: *Der Spiegel*'s Interview with Martin Heidegger', *Philosophy Today* 20.4 (1976), pp. 267–84.

29 Jerry Z. Muller, *The Tyranny of Metrics*, Princeton, NJ: Princeton University Press, 2018.

30 Cathy O'Neill, *Weapons of Math Destruction*, New York: Crown Books, 2017.

31 Ernst Cassirer, *Substanzbegriff und Funktionsbegriff: Untersuchungen über die Grundfragen der Erkenntniskritik*, Hamburg: Meiner, 2000, p. 328.

32 Even if one wanted to set art against technology, in Heidegger's style, one would still have to confront it. It would be the other – a motif that runs from Schiller through Schelling to Adorno, as a critique of the rationality and objectivity of modernity. I mention this parallel only in passing, because it is obvious, but I am not going to pursue it, since it is not relevant to my argument.

33 Walter Schulz, *Philosophie in der veränderten Welt*, Pfullingen: Neske, 1972, p. 13.

34 Ibid., pp. 247–8.

35 Claude Shannon and Warren Weaver, *The Mathematical Theory of Communication*, Urbana: University of Illinois Press, 1949. On this, see Armin Nassehi, *Die letzte Stunde der Wahrheit: Kritik der komplexitätsvergessenen Vernunft* (2nd edn), Hamburg: Kursbuch-Edition, 2018, pp. 115–16.

36 See Niklas Luhmann, *Social Systems*, ed. by Timothy Lenoir and Hans Ulrich Gumbrecht, trans. by John Bednarz Jr. and Dirk Baecker, Stanford, CA: Stanford University Press, 1995, pp. 137–8.

37 A good introduction to general and sociological systems theory is to be found in the transcript of an introductory lecture delivered by Niklas Luhmann in the winter semester 1991/2. See Niklas Luhmann, *Introduction to Systems Theory*, ed. by Dirk Baecker, trans. by Peter Gilgen, Cambridge: Polity, 2013.
38 Heidegger, 'Positionality', p. 29.
39 Michel Foucault, *The Order of Things: An Archaeology of the Human Sciences*, London: Routledge, 2005, p. 422.
40 See Niklas Luhmann, 'Die gesellschaftliche Differenzierung und das Individuum', in his *Soziologische Aufklärung*, vol. 6, Opladen: Westdeutscher Verlag, 1995, pp. 125–41.
41 Niklas Luhmann, 'Die Tücke des Subjekts und die Frage nach dem Menschen', in Werner Fuchs and Andreas Göbel (eds), *Der Mensch: Das Medium der Gesellschaft*, Frankfurt: Suhrkamp, 1994, pp. 40–56, here p. 55.
42 On this, see Armin Nassehi, 'Wenn wir wüssten! Kommunikation als Nichtwissensmaschine', in *Kursbuch 180: Nicht wissen*, ed. by Peter Felixberger and Armin Nassehi, Hamburg: Murmann, 2014, pp. 9–25.
43 Martin Heidegger, 'On the Question Concerning the Determination of the Matter for Thinking', trans. by R. Capocianco and Marie Göbel, *Epoché: A Journal for the History of Philosophy* 14.2 (2010), pp. 213–23, here p. 215.
44 Ibid., p. 215.
45 On this, see Armin Nassehi, *Geschlossenheit und Offenheit: Studien zur Theorie der modernen Gesellschaft*, Frankfurt: Suhrkamp, 2003, pp. 27–88; also Armin Nassehi, *Der soziologische Diskurs der Moderne*, Frankfurt: Suhrkamp, 2009, pp. 359–60.
46 Ferdinand de Saussure, *Course in General Linguistics*, trans. by Wade Baskin, New York: Philosophical Library,1959, p. 120.
47 In this way *différe/ance* is made visible and invisible at the same time. To cast it in the form of a paradox, the invisibility of difference is made visible.
48 Jacques Derrida, 'Différance', in his *Margins of Philosophy*, Chicago, IL: University of Chicago Press, 1982, pp. 1–28, here p. 10.
49 Jacques Derrida, *Writing and Difference*, trans. by Alan Bass, Chicago, IL: University of Chicago Press, 1978, p. 281.
50 Fritz Heider, *Ding und Medium* [1926], Berlin: Kadmos, 2005. (See also Dirk Baecker's introduction.)
51 Gregory Bateson, *Steps to an Ecology of Mind*, Toronto: Chandler, 1972, p. 435.
52 Derrida, *Writing and Difference*, p. 281.
53 See Nassehi, *Geschlossenheit und Offenheit*, pp. 34–5.

Notes to Chapter 3

1 This is the subtitle of Armin Nassehi's book *Die letzte Stunde der Wahrheit: Kritik der komplexitätsvergessenen Vernunft* (2nd edn), Hamburg: Kursbuch-Edition, 2018.
2 Armin Nassehi, 'Versuch einer soziologischen Antwort auf die bescheidene Frage, warum es Kunst gibt und nicht vielmehr nicht', in Uta Klein, Katja Mellmann, and Steffanie Metzger (eds), *Heuristiken der Literaturwissenschaft: Disziplinexterne Perspektiven auf Literatur*, Paderborn: Mentis, 2006. For more detail, see Armin Nassehi, *Gesellschaft der Gegenwarten: Studien zur Theorie der modernen Gesellschaft*, vol. 2, Berlin: Suhrkamp, 2011, pp. 310–36.
3 Niklas Luhmann, 'Die Paradoxie der Form', in Dirk Baecker (ed.), *Kalkül der Form*, Frankfurt: Suhrkamp, 1993, pp. 197–215, here p. 199.
4 Ibid.
5 On this, see Markus Nebel, *Formale Grundlagen der Programmierung*, Wiesbaden: Springer, 2012, pp. 117–18.

6 On what follows, see Armin Nassehi, *Geschlossenheit und Offenheit: Studien zur Theorie der modernen Gesellschaft*, Frankfurt: Suhrkamp, 2003, pp. 36–7.

7 Niklas Luhmann, *Social Systems*, ed. by Timothy Lenoir and Hans Ulrich Gumbrecht, trans. by John Bednarz Jr. and Dirk Baecker, Stanford: Stanford University Press, 1995, pp. 195–6.

8 For a more extensive sociological treatment, see Niklas Luhmann, *Theory of Society*, vol. 2, trans. by R. Barrett, Stanford, CA: Stanford University Press, 2012, pp. 65–6.

9 Ibid., pp. 328–9.

10 On this, see Tobias Moorstedt and Obamas Datenakrobaten in Heinrich Geiselberger and Tobias Moorstedt (eds), *Big Data: Das neue Versprechen der Allwissenheit*, Berlin: Suhrkamp, 2013, pp. 35–54.

11 Renee DiResta et al., 'The Tactics & Tropes of the Internet Research Agency', US Senate Documents, University of Nebraska, Lincoln, 2018, p. 99. https://digitalcommons.unl.edu/cgi/viewcontent.cgi?article=1003&context =senatedocs; see also Philip N. Howard et al., 'The IRA, Social Media and Political Polarization in the United States, 2012–2018', Computional Propaganda Project, University of Oxford, 2018. https://digitalcommons.unl .edu/cgi/viewcontent.cgi?article=1004&context=senatedocs.

12 Michael Betancourt, *The Critique of Digital Capitalism: An Analysis of the Political Economy of Digital Culture and Technology*, New York: punctum books, 2016, pp. 28–9.

13 Richard David Precht, *Jäger, Hirten, Kritiker: Eine Utopie für die digitale Gesellschaft*, Munich: Goldmann, 2018.

14 E.g. Eric Schaeffer, *Industry X.0: Realizing Digital Value in Industrial Sectors*, London: Kogan, 2017, who argues along this line.

15 Erik Brynjolfsson and Andrew McAfee, *The Second Machine Age: Work, Progress, and Prosperity in a Time of Brilliant Technologies*, New York: Norton, 2014.

16 Betancourt, *Critique of Digital Capitalism*, p. 33.

17 Alvin Toffler, *The Future Shock*, New York: Random House, 1970.

18 On this, see Dirk Baecker, 'Metadaten: Eine Annäherung an Big Data', in Heinrich Geiselberger and Tobias Moorstedt (eds), *Big Data: Das neue Versprechen der Allwissenheit*, Berlin: Suhrkamp 2013, pp. 156–86, here pp. 160–1.

19 Chris Anderson, 'The End of Theory: The Data Deluge Makes the Scientific Method Obsolete', *Wired*, 23 June 2008.

20 On this, see Ryan Shaw, 'Big Data and Reality', *Big Data & Society*, 2.2 (2015). DOI: 10.1177/2053951715608877.

21 Anderson, 'The End of Theory'.

22 Jean Francois Bonnefon, Azim Shariff, and Iyad Rahwan, 'Autonomous Vehicles Need Experimental Ethics: Are We Ready for Utilitarian Cars?' *arXiv*, 12 October 2015.

23 Betancourt, *Critique of Digital Capitalism*, pp. 52.

24 Dirk Helbing, *Towards Digital Enlightenment. Essays on the Dark and Light Sides of the Digital Revolution*, Cham: Springer, 2019, pp. 99–100.

25 Florian Süssenguth, 'Die Organisation des digitalen Wandels: Zur Funktion von Digitalisierungssemantiken in Wirtschaft, Medien und Politik', in Florian Süssenguth (ed.), *Die Gesellschaft der Daten: Über die digitale Transformation der sozialen Ordnung*, Bielefeld: transcript, 2015, pp. 93–121, here pp. 115–16.

26 Luhmann, *Theory of Society*, p. 78.

27 Jacques Derrida, *Margins of Philosophy*, trans. by Alan Bass, Chicago, IL: University of Chicago Press, 1978, p. 24.

28 See Bernhard Ganter, *Diskrete Mathematik: Geordnete Mengen*, Berlin: Springer Spektrum, 2013.

29 Aristotle, *Physics*, Book IV, 220a, as translated by Philipp H. Wicksteed and Francis M. Cornford, Cambridge, MA: Harvard University Press, 1957.

30 Fritz Heider, 'On Perception, Event Structure, and Psychological Environment', *Psychological Issues* 1.3 (1959). See also Julian Müller, 'Systemtheorie als Medientheorie', in Oliver Jahraus et al. (eds), *Luhmann-Handbuch: Leben, Werk, Wirkung*, Stuttgart: Metzler, 2012, pp. 57–61, here p. 61.

31 See Elena Esposito, 'Was man von den unsichtbaren Medien sehen kann', *Soziale Systeme* 12 (2006), pp. 54–78.

32 Baeker puts forward a similar argument, which similarly refers to the distinction medium–object or medium–form: see Dirk Baecker, *4.0 oder die Lücke, die der Rechner lässt*, Leipzig: Merve, 2018, pp. 21–2.

33 See Stefanie Duttweiler et al. (eds), *Leben nach Zahlen. Self-Tracking als Optimierungsprojekt?*, Bielefeld: transcript, 2016; Deborah Lupton, *The Quantified Self*, Cambridge: Polity, 2016.

34 Steffen Mau, *The Metric Society: On the Quantification of the Social*, trans. by Sharon Howe, Cambridge: Polity, 2019, pp. 21–2.

35 Bruno Latour, 'Achtung: Ihre Phantasie hinterlässt digitale Spuren!', in Heinrich Geiselberger and Tobias Moorstedt (eds), *Big Data: Das neue Versprechen der Allwissenheit*, Berlin: Suhrkamp, 2013, pp. 119–23.

36 Brynolfsson and McAfee speak of a 'digitization of about everything'. Erik Brynjolfsson and Andrew McAfee, *The Second Machine Age: Work, Progress, and Prosperity in a Time of Brilliant Technologies*, New York: Norton, 2014, Kindle edition, 829–30.

37 Peter Struijs, Barteld Braaksma, and Piet J. H. Daas, 'Official Statistics and Big Data', *Big Data & Society*, 2014. DOI: 10 1177 /2053951714538417.

38 See William E. Scheuermann, 'Digital Disobedience and the Law', *New Political Science*, 38 (2916), pp. 299–314; Karl-Heinz Ladeur, 'Die Gesellschaft der Netzwerke und ihre Wissensordnung: Big Data, Datenschutz und die ‹relationale Persönlichkeit', in Florian Süssenguth (ed.), *Die Gesellschaft der Daten: Über die digitale Transformation der sozialen Ordnung*, Bielefeld: transcript, 2015, pp. 225–52.

Notes to Chapter 4

1 The floating point operations per second (FLOPS) unit is a measurement unit for the speed of computers that does not simply give the clock speed, like the Mega-Hertz unit, but the frequency of possible floating-point operations to be processed per second. Floating-point operations are additions and multiplications. PFLOPS are PetaFlops, that is, 10^{15} FLOPS. Frequency is not the crucial factor here, because in supercomputers such as the Summit a large number of servers are connected to one another.

2 On this, see 'Move Over, China: US Is again Home to World's Speediest Supercomputer', *New York Times*, 8 June 2018. https://www.nytimes.com/2018 /06/08/technology/supercomputer-china-us.html.

3 See Rob Kitchin, *The Data Revolution: Big Data, Open Data, Data Infrastructures and Their Consequences*, London: SAGE, 2014, pp. 4–5.

4 On this, see Stanislas Dehaene, *Reading in the Brain: The Science and Evolution of a Human Invention*, New York: Viking, 2009.

5 Already Norbert Wiener describes this as a particular feature of the programming of machines: 'a small error or even a small chance of error may have disproportionally large and serious consequences' (Norbert Wiener, *God and Golem, Inc.: A Comment on Certain Points where Cybernetics Impinges on Religion*, Cambridge, MA: MIT Press, 1964, p. 79).

6 Friedrich Kittler, 'There Is No Software', in Friedrich Kittler and E. Butler

(eds), *The Truth of the Technological World: Essays on the Genealogy of Presence*, Stanford, CA: Stanford University Press, 2014, pp. 219–29, here p. 221.

7 Werner Rammert, 'Where the Action Is: Distributed Agency between Humans, Machines, and Programs', in U. Seifert, J. Hyun Kim, and A. Moore (eds), *Paradoxes of Interactivity*, Bielefeld: transcript, 2008, pp. 62–91.

8 Erich von Holst and Horst Mittelstaedt, 'The Principle of Reafference: Interactions between the Central Nervous System and the Peripheral Organs', in P. C. Dodwell (ed.), *Perceptual Processing: Stimulus Equivalence and Pattern Recognition*, New York: Appleton-Century-Crofts, 1971, pp. 41–72.

9 Ernst Pöppel, *Der Rahmen: Ein Blick des Gehirns auf unser Ich*, Munich: Hanser, 2006, p. 463.

10 Igor Douven, 'Abduction', in *The Stanford Encyclopedia of Philosophy* (summer 2017 edn), ed. by Edward N. Zalta. https://plato.stanford.edu/archives/sum2017 /entries/abduction.

11 Jürgen Adamy, *Fuzzy-Logik, neuronale Netze und evolutionäre Algorithmen* (4th edn), Herzogenrath: Shaker, 2015.

12 Such as Kerstin Sahlin and Linda Wedlin, 'Circulating Ideas: Imitation, Translation, and Editing', in Royston Greenwood et al. (eds), *The SAGE Handbook of Organizational Institutionalism*, Thousand Oaks, CA: SAGE, 2008, pp. 218–42; Wendy Hui Kyong Chun, 'On "Sourcery" or Code as Fetish', *Configurations*, 16.3 (2008), pp. 299–324; Ted Striphas, 'Algorithmic Culture', *European Journal of Cultural Studies* 18 (2015), pp. 395–412; Malte Ziewitz, 'Governing Algorithms: Myth, Mess, and Methods', *Science, Technology & Human Values* 4 (2016), pp. 3–16; Evelyn Ruppert, John Law, and Mike Savage, 'Reassembling Social Science Methods: The Challenge of Digital Devices', *Theory, Culture & Society* 30 (2013), pp. 22–46. A good overview is provided by Jonathan Berge and Robert Seyfert, 'Was sind Algorithmuskulturen?', in Jonathan Berge and Robert Seyfert (eds), *Algorithmuskulturen: Über die rechnerische Konstruktion der Wirklichkeit*, Bielefeld: transcript, 2017, pp. 7–40.

13 Rob Kitchin, 'Thinking Critically about and Researching Algorithms', in *The Programmable City Working Paper*, Maynooth, Republic of Ireland: Maynooth University, 2014. http://papers.ssrn.com/sol3/papers.cfm?abstract_id=2515786.

14 Yuval Noah Harari, *Homo deus: A Brief History of Tomorrow*, London: Vintage, 2017.

15 Martin Heidegger, 'The Provenance of Art and the Destination of Thought', *Journal of the British Society for Phenomenology* 44.2 (2013), pp. 119–28, here p. 123.

16 See Niklas Luhmann, *Theory of Society*, vol. 2, trans. by R. Barrett, Stanford, CA: Stanford University Press, pp. 87–8. On the entire sociological complex of this sometimes very controversial debate, see Armin Nassehi, 'Die Theorie funktionaler Differenzierung im Horizont ihrer Kritik', *Zeitschrift für Soziologie* 33 (2004), pp. 98–118; Armin Nassehi, 'Moderne Gesellschaft', in Georg Kneer, Armin Nassehi, and Markus Schroer (eds), *Soziologische Gesellschaftsbegriffe*, vol. 2: *Klassische Zeitdiagnosen*, Munich: Fink (UTB), 2001, pp. 208–45; Armin Nassehi, 'Funktionale Differenzierung revisited: Vom Setzkasten zur Echtzeitmaschine', in Eva Barlösius, Hans-Peter Müller, and Steffen Sigmund (eds), *Gesellschaftsbilder im Umbruch*, Opladen: Leske und Budrich, 2001, pp. 155–78.

17 See Ranulph Glanville, *Objekte*, Berlin: Merve, 1988; Gregory Bateson, *Steps to an Ecology of Mind*, Toronto: Chandler, 1972; W. Ross Ashby, *An Introduction to Cybernetics*, London: Chapman & Hall, 1971; Heinz von Foerster, *Sicht und Einsicht: Versuche zu einer operativen Erkenntnistheorie*, Wiesbaden: Springer, 1985.

18 See Joachim Knape, *Was ist Rhetorik?* Stuttgart: Reclam, 2000.

19 See Matthias Remenyi, 'Gottes Gegenwart denken: Eine fundamentaltheologische Programmskizze: Antrittsvorlesung an der Universität Würzburg am 16. Mai 2018'. https://www.theologie-und-kirche.de/Remenyi Antrittsvorlesung.pdf.

20 See Walter Schulz, *Philosophie in der veränderten Welt*, Pfullingen: Klostermann, 1972.
21 On this idea of the annihilation of contingency as an achievement of order, see Armin Nassehi and Irmhild Saake, 'Kontingenz: Methodisch verhindert oder beobachtet? Ein Beitrag zur Methodologie der qualitativen Sozialforschung', *Zeitschrift für Soziologie* 31 (2002), pp. 66–86.
22 Niklas Luhmann, *Theory of Society*, vol. 1, trans. by R. Barret, Stanford: Stanford University Press, 2012, p. 215.
23 See Armin Nassehi, *Die letzte Stunde der Wahrheit: Kritik der komplexitätsvergessenen Vernunft* (2nd edn), Hamburg: Kursbuch, 2018, pp. 92 and 107.
24 See Niklas Luhmann, 'Haltlose Komplexität', in his *Soziologische Aufklärung*, vol. 5, Opladen: Westdeutscher Verlag, 1990, pp. 58–74.
25 Harari, *Homo deus*.
26 Dirk Helbing (ed.), *Towards Digital Enlightenment: Essays on the Dark and Light Sides of the Digital Revolution*, Cham: Springer, 2019.
27 Rob Kitchin, *The Data Revolution: Big Data, Open Data, Data Infrastructures and Their Consequences*, London: SAGE, 2014.
28 Deborah Lupton, *The Quantified Self*, Cambridge: Polity, 2016; Deborah Lupton, *Digital Sociology*, Milton Park: Routledge, 2015.
29 Zygmunt Bauman and David Lyon, *Liquid Surveillance: A Conversation*, Cambridge: Polity, 2013.
30 Manuela Lenzen, *Künstliche Intelligenz: Was sie kann und was uns erwartet*, Munich: C. H. Beck, 2018.
31 Steffen Mau, *The Metric Society: On the Quantification of the Social*, trans. by Sharon Howe, Cambridge: Polity, 2019, p. 11.
32 Dirk Baecker, *Studien zur nächsten Gesellschaft*, Berlin: Suhrkamp, 2007, p. 169.
33 Armin Nassehi, 'Das Problem der Optionssteigerung: Überlegungen zur Risikokultur der Moderne', *Berliner Journal für Soziologie* 7 (1997), pp. 21–36; Armin Nassehi, 'Optionssteigerung und Risikokultur', in Gerhard von Graevenitz, Alois Hahn, Axel Honneth, and David Wellbery (eds), *Konzepte der Moderne*, Munich: Fink, 1999, pp. 82–101; and more recently Armin Nassehi, *Die letzte Stunde der Wahrheit: Kritik der komplexitätsvergessenen Vernunft* (2nd edn), Hamburg: Kursbuch-Edition, 2018, p. 89.
34 Niklas Luhmann, *Risk: A Sociological Theory*, trans. by R. Barret, New Brunswick, NJ: Aldine Transaction, 2008, pp. 78–9.
35 Armin Nassehi, 'Der Ausnahmezustand als Normalfall: Modernität als Krise', in his *Kursbuch 170: Krisen lieben*, Hamburg: Murmann Verlag, 2012, pp. 34–49.

Notes to Excursus

1 For an overview, see Lutz Zündorf, *Das Weltsystem des Erdöls: Entstehungszusammenhang, Funktionsweise, Wandlungstendenzen*, Wiesbaden: VS-Verlag, 2008.
2 Michael Betancourt, *The Critique of Digital Capitalism: An Analysis of the Political Economy of Digital Culture and Technology*, New York: punctum books, 2015, p. 196.
3 Jeremy Rifkin, *The Zero Marginal Cost Society: The Internet of Things, the Collaborative Commons, and the Eclipse of Capitalism*, New York: St Martins Press, 2014.
4 Nick Srnicek, *Platform Capitalism*, Cambridge: Polity, 2017.
5 On this, see Gemeinsame Stellungnahme der Nationalen Akademie der Wissenschaften Leopoldina und Deutsche Akademie der Technikwissenschaften und der Union der deutschen Akademien der Wissenschaften, *Rohstoffe für die Energiewende: Wege zu einer sicheren und nachhaltigen Versorgung*, Berlin,

2017 (cover and presentation at https://www.leopoldina.org/publikationen
/detailansicht/publication/rohstoffe-fuer-die-energiewende-wege-zu-einer
-sicheren-und-nachhaltigen-versorgung-2017).

6 R. Hintemann and K. Fichter, 'Energy Demand of Workplace Computer
Solutions: A Comprehensive Assessment Including both End-User Devices and
the Power Consumption They Induce in Data Centers', in *EnviroInfo & ICT4S:
Conference Proceedings*, Part 1, Copenhagen, 2015, pp. 165–71.

7 Friedemann Mattern: 'Wieviel Strom braucht das Internet?', Zukunftsblog
Energie, ETH Zürich, 3 March 2015.

8 For a summary, see Ralph Hintemann, 'Rechenzentren: Energiefresser oder
Effizienzwunder?', *Informatik-aktuell*, 26 January 2016.

9 Mattern, 'Wieviel Strom braucht das Internet?'.

10 Ralf Hintemann and Simon Hinterholzer, *Smarte Rahmenbedingungen für
Energie- und Ressourceneinsparungen bei vernetzten Haushaltsprodukten*, Berlin:
Borderstep Institut, 2018. https://www.bund.net/fileadmin/user_upload_bund
/publikationen/energiewende/energiewende_studie_vernetzte_produkte.pdf.

11 In its answer to a minor interpellation by the parliamentary group of the Green
Party in the German Bundestag, the federal government assumed in 2017 that the
total consumption of electricity in Germany up until 2025 would rise to 46 TWh.
In view of the Borderstep Institut study, this is not a dramatically low prediction.

12 For an expert opinion on behalf of the German Federal Ministry of Economics,
see Bundesministerium für Wirtschaft und Energie, *Digitalisierung der
Energiewende*, Berlin, 2019. https://www.bmwk.de/Redaktion/DE/Publikationen
/Studien/digitalisierung-der-energiewende-thema-1.pdf?__blob=publicationFile
&v=4

13 Hanns Günther Hilpert and Antje Elisabeth Kröger: *Chinesisches Monopol bei
Seltenen Erden: Risiko für die Hochtechnologie, DIW Wochenbericht*, 19 (2011).
https://www.diw.de/documents/publikationen/73/diw_01.c.372387.de/11-19-1.pdf.

14 See Luitgard Marschall and Heike Holdinghausen: *Seltene Erden: Umkämpfte
Rohstoffe des Hightech-Zeitalters*, Munich: Oekom, 2017.

15 Hanns Günther Hilpert and Antje Elisabeth Kröger, 'Chinesisches Monopol
bei Seltenen Erden: Risiko für die Hochtechnologie', DIW Wochenbericht 19
/2011. https://www.diw.de/documents/publikationen/73/diw_01.c.372387.de/11
-19-1.pdf.

16 E.g. the Fraunhofer Lighthouse Project 'Critical Rare Earths'. Head of project:
Ralf B. Wehrspohn, Fraunhofer-Institut für Mikrostruktur von Werkstoffen und
Systemen IMWS, Halle/Saale. https://www.fraunhofer.de/en/research/lighthouse
-projects-fraunhofer-initiatives/fraunhofer-lighthouse-projects/fraunhofer-rare
-earths.html.

Notes to Chapter 5

1 Ernst Cassirer, 'Form and Technology', in A. S. Hoel and I. Folkvord (eds),
Ernst Cassirer on Form and Technology, London: Palgrave Macmillan, 2012.

2 Werner Rammert, 'New Rules of Sociological Method: Rethinking Technology
Studies', *British Journal of Sociology* 48.2 (1997), pp. 171–91, here p. 176.

3 So too Karen Barad, 'Agential Realism: How Material–Discursive Practices Matter',
in her *Meeting the Universe Halfway: Quantum Physics and the Entanglement of
Matter and Meaning*, Durham, CA: Duke University Press, 2007, pp. 132–85.

4 See also Annemarie Mol and John Law, *Complexities: Social Studies of
Knowledge Practices*, Durham, NC: Duke University Press, 2002.

5 Bruno Latour, *Reassembling the Social: An Introduction to Actor–Network-
Theory*, Oxford: Oxford University Press, 2005, p. 46.

6 Armin Nassehi, 'The Person as an Effect of Communication', in Sabine Maasen

(ed.), *On Willing Selves: Neoliberal Politics and the Challenge of Neuroscience*, Hampshire: Palgrave, 2007, pp. 100–20.

7 Rammert, 'New Rules of Sociological Method', p. 177.
8 See Betsy Anne Williams, Catherine F. Brooks, and Yotam Shmargad, 'How Algorithms Discriminate Based on Data They Lack: Challenges, Solutions, and Policy Implications', *Journal of Information Policy* 8 (2018), pp. 78–115.
9 See Zeynep Tufekci, 'The Year We Get Creeped Out by Algorithms', in NiemanLab, *Predictions for Journalism 2015*. https://www.niemanlab.org/2014 /12/the-year-we-get-creeped-out-by-algorithms.
10 See Niklas Luhmann, *Social Systems*, trans. by J. Bednarz Jr and D. Baecker, Stanford, CA: Stanford University Press, 1995, pp. 193–4.
11 See Niklas Luhmann, *Theory of Society*, vol. 1, trans. by R. Barret, Stanford: Stanford University Press, 2012, pp. 320–1.
12 Ibid., p. 313.
13 Ibid., p. 317.
14 Ibid., p. 318.
15 Ibid., p. 317.
16 Sherry Turkle, *Life on the Screen: Identity in the Age of the Internet*, New York: Simon & Schuster Paperbacks, 1995, p. 44.
17 Rammert, 'New Rules of Sociological Method', p. 176.
18 See Thomas Rohkrämer, *Eine andere Moderne? Zivilisationskritik, Natur und Technik in Deutschland, 1880–1933*, Paderborn: Schöningh, 1999.
19 Manfred Spitzer, *Cyberkrank! Wie das digitalisierte Leben unsere Gesundheit ruiniert*, Munich: Droemer, 2015; Manfred Spitzer, *Die Smartphone-Epidemie: Gefahren für Gesundheit, Bildung und Gesellschaft*, Stuttgart: Klett-Cotta, 2018.
20 Markus Albers, *Digitale Erschöpfung: Wie wir die Kontrolle über unser Leben wiedergewinnen*, Munich: Hanser, 2017.
21 Nick Bostrom, 'Ethical Issues in Advanced Artificial Intelligence', Nick Bostrom's Homepage, n.d. https://nickbostrom.com/ethics/ai.
22 Friedrich Georg Jünger, *The Failure of Technology: Perfection without Purpose*, trans. by F. D. Wieck, Hinsdale, IL: Regnery, 1949.
23 Niklas Luhmann, *Theory of Society*, vol. 2, trans. by R. Barret, Stanford, CA: Stanford University Press, 2013, p. 347.
24 Luhmann, *Theory of Society*, vol. 1, p. 319.
25 Norbert Wiener, *God and Golem, Inc.: A Comment on Certain Points Where Cybernetics Impinges on Religion*, Cambridge, MA: MIT Press, 1964, p. 32.
26 Alan M. Turing, 'Computing Machinery and Intelligence', *Mind* 59.236 (1950), pp. 433–60.
27 Lauren Goode, 'How Google's EERIE Robot Phone Calls Hint at AI's Future', *Wired*, 8 May 2018.
28 John Searle, 'Minds, Brains, and Programs', *Behavioral and Brain Sciences* 3 (1980), pp. 417–57.
29 See Andreas K. Engel, 'Bewusstsein: Vom Käfer in der Schachtel, den noch keiner gesehen hat', in Michael Madeja and Joachim Müller-Jung (eds), *Hirnforschung: Was kann sie wirklich?*, Munich: C. H. Beck, 2016, pp. 79–87.
30 Lorina Naci, Rodri Cusack, Mimma Anello, and Adrian M. Owen, 'A Common Neural Code for Similar Conscious Experiences in Different Individuals', *Proceedings of the American Academy of Science* 111.39 (2014), pp. 14277–82.
31 Overviews of the relation of brain and consciousness that even laypeople can understand are to be found in Ernst Pöppel, *Der Rahmen: Ein Blick des Gehirns auf unser Ich*, Munich: Hanser, 2006 and Michael S. Gazzaniga, *Who's in Charge? Free Will and the Science of the Brain: The Gifford Lectures 2009*, New York: HarperCollins, 2011.
32 See in detail Armin Nassehi, 'Mentalizing Theories oder Theories of Mentalizing?

Ein soziologischer Beitrag zur *Theory of Mind*, in Hans Förstl (ed.), *Theory of Mind* (2nd edn), Berlin: Springer, 2012, pp. 39–52.

33 See Armin Nassehi, *Soziologie: Zehn einführende Vorlesungen* (2nd edn), Wiesbaden: VS Verlag, 2011, p. 35.

34 See Christer Clerwall, 'Enter the Robot Journalist', *Journalism Practice* 8 (2014), pp. 519–31.

35 For an example from dermatological oncology, see Holger Haenßle et al., 'Man against Machine: Diagnostic Performance of a Deep Learning Convolutional Neural Network for Dermoscopic Melanoma Recognition in Comparison to 58 Dermatologists', *Annals of Oncology* (2018). https://doi.org/10.1093/annonc /mdy166.

36 See Jörg Carlsson, Norbert W. Paul, Matthias Dann, Jörg Neuzner, and Dietrich Pfeiffer, 'The Deactivation of Implantable Cardioverter-Defibrillators Medical, Ethical, Practical, and Legal Considerations', *Deutsches Ärzteblatt International* 109.33–34 (2012), pp. 535–41.

37 See the project Moral Machine at https://www.moralmachine.net; on the ethical side of the debate, see Julian Nida-Rümelin and Alexander Hevelke, 'Responsibility of Crashes of Autonomous Vehicles: An Ethical Analysis', *Science and Engineering* 21 (2015), pp. 619–30.

38 Very instructive in this respect is Corinna Budras, 'Wenn der Computer wie ein Mensch klingt: KI am Telefon', *FAZ-online*, 15 April 2019. https://www.faz .net/aktuell/wirtschaft/kuenstliche-intelligenz/kuenstliche-intelligenz-wenn-der -roboterwie-ein-mensch-klingt-16140063.html.

39 'Do We Have to Be Afraid of Google, Mr. Pichai?' Interview with Sundar Pichai by Patrick Bernau and Corinna Budras, *FAZ.net Diginomics*, 27 January 2019. https://www.faz.net/aktuell/wirtschaft/diginomics/interview-with-google-ceosundar-pichai-do-we-have-to-be-afraid-of-google-16010193.html?printPage dArticle=true#pageIndex_0.

40 See Charles Perrow, *Normal Accidents: Living with High-Risk Technologies*, Princeton, NJ: Princeton University Press, 1999.

Notes to Chapter 6

1 One example is the Fraunhofer Industry 4.0 project EVOLOPRO, which models the biological evolutionary mechanisms for processes of production and development. https://www.produktion.fraunhofer.de/de/forschung-im-verbund /formate/leitprojekte/evolopro.html.

2 See Luciana Parisi, 'Das Lernen lernen oder die algorithmische Entdeckung von Informationen', in Christoph Engemann and Andreas Sudmann (eds), *Machine Learning: Medien, Infrastrukturen und Technologien der Künstlichen Intelligenz*, Bielefeld: transcript, 2018 (henceforth Engemann and Sudmann, *Machine Learning*), pp. 93–113, here p. 95.

3 Yann LeCun, Yoshua Bengio, and Geoffrey Hinton, 'Deep Learning', *Nature* 521 (2015), pp. 436–44, here p. 436.

4 A good and readable outline of such methods, not encumbered by mathematical and epistemological detail, can be found in Thomas Ramge, *Mensch und Maschine: Wie künstliche Intelligenz und Roboter unser Leben verändern*, Stuttgart: Reclam, 2018.

5 LeCun et al., 'Deep Learning', p. 436.

6 Ibid., p. 437; see also Wolfgang Ziegler, *Neuronale Netze*, entwickler.press, 2015 (e-book).

7 George Berkeley, *A Treatise Concerning the Principles of Human Knowledge*, ed. by Jonathan Dancy, Oxford: Oxford University Press, 1998, p. 104.

8 Ibid.

9 LeCun et al., 'Deep Learning', p. 438.
10 Ibid., p. 441.
11 Bernhard J. Dotzler, '"Down-to-Earth Resolutions": Erinnerungen an die KI als eine "häretische Theorie"', in Engemann and Sudmann, *Machine Learning*, pp. 39–54, here p. 47.
12 Ibid.
13 LeCun et al., 'Deep Learning', p. 442.
14 Parisi, 'Das Lernen lernen', p. 99.
15 Charles Sanders Peirce, *Collected Papers*, ed. by Charles Hartshorne and Paul Weiss, Cambridge, MA: Harvard University Press, 1931–5, vol. 5, p. 171.
16 Ibid., vol. 2, p. 636.
17 Ibid., vol. 5, p. 171.
18 Thus quoted in Dotzler, '"Down-to-Earth Resolutions": Erinnerungen', p. 41.
19 Parisi, 'Das Lernen lernen', p. 109.
20 See Detlef H. Rost, *Handbuch Intelligenz*, Beltz: Weinheim, 2013.
21 See Michael S. Gazzaniga, *Who's in Charge? Free Will and the Science of the Brain: The Gifford Lectures 2009*, New York: HarperCollins, 2011; Wolf Singer, *Der Beobachter im Gehirn: Essays zur Hirnforschung*, Frankfurt: Suhrkamp, 2002; Wolf Singer, *Ein neues Menschenbild? Gespräche über Hirnforschung*, Frankfurt: Suhrkamp, 2003.
22 Nick Bostrom, *Superintelligence: Paths, Dangers, Strategies*, Oxford: Oxford University Press, 2014, p. 54.
23 Armin Nassehi, *Die letzte Stunde der Wahrheit: Kritik der komplexitätsvergessenen Vernunft* (2nd edn), Hamburg: Kursbuch-Edition, 2018, pp. 65–6.
24 David Grace and Honggang Zhang, *Cognitive Communications: Distributed Artificial Intelligence (DAI), Regulatory Policy and Economics, Implementation*, Hoboken, NJ: John Wiley & Sons Inc., 2012. This semantic field also covers collective intelligence or swarm intelligence, although the uses of these terms do not overlap. Distributed intelligence emphasizes the aspect of differentiation, whereas collective or swarm intelligence address the unity of differentiation. A good overview of conceptual understandings is given by Angelika Karger, 'Wissensmanagement und "Swarm Intelligence": Wissenschaftstheoretische, semiotische und kognitionsphilosophische Analysen und Perspektiven', in Jürgen Mittelstraß (ed.), *Die Zukunft des Wissens*, Constance: Universitäts-Verlag Konstanz, 1999, pp. 1288–96.
25 See Christian Wadephul, 'Führt Big Data zur abduktiven Wende in den Wissenschaften?', *Berliner Debatte Initial* 27.4 (2016), pp. 35–49.
26 See Sebastian Harrach, *Neugierige Strukturvorschläge im maschinellen Lernen*, Bielefeld: transcript, 2014, pp. 304–5.
27 I follow here detailed oral information from the brain researcher and medical psychologist Ernst Pöppel of the Ludwig Maximilian University in Munich. This information reminds us a little that the Aristotelian table of categories and, even more so, its application in Kant's transcendental philosophy always proceed from prior or more primitive categorial understandings, which serve to organize the multiplicity of perceptual data or must be assumed through logical necessity – for example causality or interactions, the identity of an object or the boundaries between individual things. It is obvious that this can never be a closed structure, like a deduction from something already known. Rather it is an adaption process that does not simply perceive but actively opens up a form.
28 Ranulph Glanville, 'The Question of Cybernetics', *Cybernetcis and Systems: An International Journal* 18.2 (1987), pp. 99–112, here p. 108.
29 Martin Heidegger, 'The Provenance of Art and the Destination of Thought', *Journal of the British Society for Phenomenology* 44(2), pp. 119–28, here p. 123.
30 Ibid.
31 Bostrom, *Superintelligence*, p. 92.

32 Ibid., p. 93.
33 See Bruno Latour, *Reassembling the Social: An Introduction to Actor–Network-Theory*, Oxford: Oxford University Press, 2005, pp. 63–4.
34 On the overall complex, see Irmhild Saake, 'Erleben/Handeln', in Oliver Jahraus et al. (eds), *Luhmann Handbuch: Leben, Werk, Wirkung*, Stuttgart: Metzler, 2012, pp. 77–9.
35 Niklas Luhmann, *Theory of Society*, vol. 1, trans. by Rhodes Barrett, Stanford, CA: Stanford University Press, 2012, p. 200.
36 See Rob Kitchin, 'Big Data, New Epistemologies and Paradigm Shifts', *Big Data & Society*, April–June 2014, pp. 1–12; Klaus Mainzer, 'Zur Veränderung des Theoriebegriffs im Zeitalter von Big Data und effizienten Algorithmen', *Berliner Debatte Initial* 27.4 (2016), pp. 22–34.
37 See Albert Menne, *Einführung in die formale Logik: Eine Orientierung über die Lehre von der Folgerichtigkeit, ihre Geschichte, Strukturen und Anwendungen*, Darmstadt: Wissenschaftliche Buchgesellschaft, 1985.
38 Kurt Gödel, *On Formally Undecidable Propositions of Principia Mathematica and Related Systems*, trans. by Bernard Meltzer, Edinburgh: Oliver & Boyd, 1962, pp. 65–6.
39 Julian Nida-Rümelin and Nathalie Weidenfeld, *Digital Humanism: For a Humane Transformation of Democracy, Economy and Culture in the Digital Age*, Cham: Springer, 2022, p. 59.
40 See Armin Nassehi, 'Paradoxie', in Oliver Jahraus et al. (eds), *Luhmann Handbuch: Leben, Werk, Wirkung*, Stuttgart: Metzler, 2012, pp. 110–11.
41 Niklas Luhmann, 'Stenographie', in Niklas Luhmann et al. (eds), *Beobachter: Konvergenz der Erkenntnistheorien?*, Munich: Fink, 1990, pp. 119–37, here p. 122.
42 Ibid. p. 130.
43 Armin Nassehi, *Die Zeit der Gesellschaft: Auf dem Weg zu einer soziologischen Theorie der Zeit*, 2nd edn, Wiesbaden: Springer, 2008, pp. 182–210, esp. p. 187.
44 Parisi, 'Das Lernen lernen', p. 106.
45 Ibid., p. 99.
46 Dotzler, '"Down-to-Earth Resolutions": Erinnerungen', p. 52.
47 This is Talcott Parsons's description of the latency function of culture: Talcott Parsons, *The System of Modern Societies*, Englewood Cliffs, NJ: Prentice-Hall, 1971, pp. 4–5.
48 See Latour, *Reassembling the Social*; also Armin Nassehi, 'De rebus rerum: Bruno Latours Neuordnung des Sozialen', *Soziologische Revue* 31 (2008), pp. 350–6.
49 Norbert Wiener, *God and Golem, Inc.: A Comment on Certain Points where Cybernetics Impinges on Religion*, Cambridge, MA: MIT Press, 1964, p. 72.
50 Lauren Goode, 'How Google's EERIE Robot Phone Calls Hint at AI's Future', *Wired*, 8 May 2018.
51 On the difference between body and *corpus*, see Helmut Plessner, *Philosophische Anthropologie*, Frankfurt: S. Fischer, 1970, p. 43.
52 Gazzaniga, *Who's in Charge?*, p. 68.
53 See Erik Brynjolfsson and Andrew McAfee, *The Second Machine Age: Work, Progress, and Prosperity in a Time of Brilliant Technologies*, New York: Norton, 2014.

Notes to Chapter 7

1 Parts of this chapter are based on thoughts that I have already developed in Armin Nassehi, 'Wir werden es gewusst haben: Das Internet als Massenmedium', *Kursbuch* 195 (2018), pp. 53–69.
2 'Google Plus Will Be Shut Down after User Information Was Exposed', *New*

York Times, 8 October 2018. https://www.nytimes.com/2018/10/08/technology
/google-plus-security-disclosure.html.

3   Nick Srnicek, *Platform Capitalism*. Cambridge: Polity, 2017, p. 107.
4   Ibid. p. 119.
5   Shoshana Zuboff, *The Age of Surveillance Capitalism: The Fight for a Human
    Future at the New Frontier of Power*, London: Profile Books, 2019, p. 203.
6   Ibid., p. 204.
7   See Armin Nassehi, *Die Zeit der Gesellschaft: Auf dem Weg zu einer soziolo-
    gischen Theorie der Zeit*, vol. 2, Wiesbaden, 2008, pp. 299–300.
8   Bruno Latour, *We Have Never Been Modern*, Cambridge, MA: Harvard
    University Press, 1993.
9   Niklas Luhmann, *The Reality of the Mass Media*, Cambridge: Polity, 2000, p. 1.
10 Peter Berger and Thomas Luckmann, *The Social Construction of Reality: A
    Treatise in the Sociology of Knowledge*, New York: Penguin, 1966, pp. 149–50.
11 Paul DiMaggio et al., 'Social Implications of the Internet', *Annual Review of
    Sociology* 27 (2001), pp. 307–36.
12 Howard Rheingold, *The Virtual Community: Homesteading on the Electronic
    Frontier*, Cambridge, MA: MIT Press, 2000 [1993].
13 Albert O. Hirschman, *Exit, Voice and Loyalty: Responses to Decline in Firms,
    Organizations and States*, Cambridge, MA: Harvard University Press, 1970.
14 This is how the feuilleton editor of *Frankfurter Allgemeine Zeitung* charac-
    terized the function of the feuilleton; see 'Jürgen Kaube im Gespräch mit Peter
    Felixberger und Armin Nassehi', *Kursbuch* 195 (2018), pp. 78–97.
15 See in detail Armin Nassehi, *Die letzte Stunde der Wahrheit: Kritik der komplex-
    itätsvergessenen Vernunft* (2nd edn), Hamburg: Kursbuch-Edition, 2018.
16 Claude Lévi-Strauss, *Wild Thought*, trans. by J. Mehlman and J. Leavitt,
    Chicago, IL: University of Chicago Press, 2021 [Fr. edn. 1962].
17 This term was already suggested in Armin Nassehi, 'Unsere Gesellschaft läuft
    sich an ihren Debatten heiß', *Welt am Sonntag*, 3 February 2019.
18 See Soroush Vosoughi, 'Deb Roy and Sinan Aral: The Spread of True and False
    News Online', *Science* 359 (2018), pp. 1146–51.
19 Charles Perrow, *Normal Accidents: Living with High-Risk Technologies*,
    Princeton, NJ: Princeton University Press, 1999.

Notes to Chapter 8

1   See Ronald Petrlic and Christoph Sorge, *Datenschutz: Einführung in technischen
    Datenschutz, Datenschutzrecht und angewandte Kryptographie*, Wiesbaden:
    Springer Vieweg, 2017, pp. 139–40.
2   See Charlie Campbell, 'How China Is Using "Social Credit Scores" to Reward
    and Punish Its Citizens'. https://time.com/collection/davos-2019/5502592/china
    -social-credit-score.
3   See Dirk Baecker, *Studien zur nächsten Gesellschaft*, Frankfurt: Suhrkamp, 2007,
    p. 140.
4   See Armin Nassehi, *Der soziologische Diskurs der Moderne*, Frankfurt:
    Suhrkamp, 2009, pp. 133–4. The *locus classicus* for the foundation of action
    theory in a theory of praxis is Theodore Schatzki, *The Site of the Social: A
    Philosophical Account of the Constitution of Social Life and Change*, University
    Park: Pennsylvania State University Press, 2002.
5   See George Herbert Mead, *Mind, Self, and Society: From the Standpoint of a
    Social Behaviorist*, ed. by Charles W. Morris, Chicago, IL: University of Chicago
    Press, 1972, p. 18.
6   It is worth having a look at the origins of the concept of invocation or appeal.
    The concept comes from the French Marxist Louis Althusser and his theory of

ideology, according to which every subject is constituted as a product of, and hence is subjected to, ideological state apparatuses. Although the term refers to the social genesis of individuality, it must always take it to be illegitimate, thus also negating the business basis of any social science perspective. The widespread use of the term is pure non-academic posturing, but appears in all possible variants of a critique of 'neoliberalism'. Resorting to the term 'invocation' suggests the prior illegitimacy of any kind of state prescription on individual choices. See Louis Althusser, 'Ideology and Ideological State Apparatuses: Notes towards an Investigation', in his *Lenin and Philosophy and Other Essays*, trans. by Ben Brewster, New York: Monthly Review Press, 1971, pp. 127–86.

7 Jörg Becker even speaks of a kind of invocation whose observance, he says, is 'voluntary' – which, of course, is a conceptual curiosity; see Jörg Becker, *Die Digitalisierung von Medien und Kultur*, Wiesbaden: Springer, 2012, p. 79.

8 See e.g. Evgeny Morozov, 'Wir brauchen einen neuen Glauben an die Politik!', *Frankfurter Allgemeine Zeitung*, 14 January 2014, in answer to Sascha Lobo's complaint that the Internet is now broken.

9 The forthcoming considerations are partly based on Armin Nassehi, 'Die Zurichtung des Privaten: Gibt es analoge Privatheit in einer digitalen Welt?', in *Kursbuch 177: Privat 2.0*, Hamburg: Murmann, 2014, pp. 27–46.

10 Howard Rheingold, *The Virtual Community: Homesteading at the Electronic Frontier*, Cambridge, MA: MIT Press, 2000 [1993].

11 Howard Rheingold, *Smart Mobs: The Next Social Revolution*, Jackson, MS: Basic Books, 2003.

12 See Rahel Jaeggi, *Critique of Forms of Life*, trans. by Ciaran Cronin, Harvard, MA: Harvard University Press, 2018.

13 Michel Foucault, *The Will to Knowledge: The History of Sexuality*, vol. 1, trans. by Robert Hurley, London: Penguin, 1998, p. 47.

14 Ibid., p. 56.

15 Ibid., p. 62.

16 Ibid., p. 140.

17 Ibid., p. 147.

18 Paula-Irene Villa, *Sexy Bodies: Eine soziologische Reise durch den Geschlechtskörper* (4th edn), Wiesbaden: VS Verlag, 2011.

19 Shoshana Zuboff, *The Age of Surveillance Capitalism: The Fight for a Human Future at the New Frontier of Power*, London: Profile Books, 2019, p. 8.

20 See Daniela Döring, *Zeugende Zahlen: Mittelmaß und Durchschnittstypen in Proportion, Statistik und Konfektion des 19. Jahrhunderts*, Berlin: Kadmos, 2011.

21 See Armin Nassehi, 'Asymmetrien als Problem und als Lösung', in Bijan Fateh-Moghadam, Stephan Sellmaier, and Wilhelm Vossenkuhl (eds), *Grenzen des Paternalismus*, Stuttgart: Kohlhammer, 2009.

22 Very informative in this respect is the website of the Kreditech company (www.kreditech.com) in Hamburg.

23 Gesa Lindemann calls it 'the matrix of digital space time'; see Gesa Lindemann, 'In der Matrix der digitalen Raumzeit', in *Kursbuch 177: Privat 2.0*, Hamburg: Murmann, 2014, pp. 27–46.

24 Bruno Latour, *Reassembling the Social: An Introduction to Actor-Network-Theory*, Oxford: Oxford University Press, 2005, p. 217.

Notes to Chapter 9

1 Armin Nassehi, *Geschlossenheit und Offenheit: Studien zur Theorie der modernen Gesellschaft*, Frankfurt: Suhrkamp, 2003; Armin Nassehi, *Die Zeit der Gesellschaft: Auf dem Weg zu einer soziologischen Theorie der Zeit* (2nd edn),

Wiesbaden: VS Verlag, 2008; Armin Nassehi, *Der soziologische Diskurs der Moderne* (2nd edn), Frankfurt: Suhrkamp, 2009; Armin Nassehi, *Gesellschaft der Gegenwarten: Studien zur Theorie der modernen Gesellschaft*, vol. 2, Berlin: Suhrkamp, 2011; Armin Nassehi, *Die letzte Stunde der Wahrheit: Kritik der komplexitätsvergessenen Vernunft* (2nd edn), Hamburg: Kursbuch-Edition, 2018.

2 Bruno Latour, 'The Powers of Association', *Sociological Review* 32.1 (1984), pp. 264–80, here p. 276. See also Bruno Latour, *Reassembling the Social: An Introduction to Actor–Network Theory*, Oxford: Oxford University Press, 2005, esp. pp. 1–17 and 159–64.

3 Bruno Latour, 'Social Theory and the Study of Computerized Work Sites', in W. J. Orlikowski, G. Walsham, M. R. Jones, and J. I. DeGross (eds), *Information Technology and Changes in Organizational Work: Proceedings of the IFIP WG8.2 Working Conference on Information Technology and Changes in Organizational Work, December 1995*, Boston, MA: Springer, 1996, pp. 295–307, here p. 304.

Index